THEOLOGY AND MEANING

THEOLOGY AND MEANING

A CRITIQUE OF
METATHEOLOGICAL SCEPTICISM

RAEBURNE S. HEIMBECK

STANFORD UNIVERSITY PRESS
STANFORD, CALIFORNIA

1969

Stanford University Press
Stanford, California
© 1965, 1969 by Raeburne Seeley Heimbeck

L.C. 68–13146

PRINTED IN GREAT BRITAIN

To George E. Hughes

PREFACE

This book takes a long, hard look at the philosophical charge that 'God'-talk is nonsense. The charge is a serious one. It is also ambiguous, since there are several species of nonsense. Here are some: 'Twas brillig, and the slithy toves did gire and gimble' is *unintelligible* (incoherent, incomprehensible, cognitively meaningless). 'The state of California is about to crack away from the continent and drop into the sea' is *implausible* (incredible, unwarranted, unconvincing, non-cogent, counter-intuitive). 'Exactly fourteen angels can dance at once on the head of a pin' is *irrelevant* (uninteresting, boring, trivial, pointless, unexistential). I happen to be interested in the arguments of those philosophers who intend the charge in the first sense listed above. It has been somewhat fashionable recently in philosophical circles to challenge the intelligibility of various sorts of commonly used idiom. With respect to the idiom of religion, I have often wondered if some sceptical philosophers did not confuse implausibility with unintelligibility, if the former was not their real vexation and the latter merely a cloak. Be that as it may, in what follows I shall argue as vigorously as I can for the intelligibility of religious discourse. The other two sorts of nonsense will not enter into the picture here, although threats against religion in their name come from other quarters today.

This book is a treatise in philosophical logic pure and simple. That alone accounts for a number of its characteristics which might (but not by deliberate calculation) irk the reader. Its style is plain, striving toward precison without elegance. It is closely argued, attentive to detail, given to excursions into philosophically interesting byways. Furthermore, it is filled with difficult distinctions, between (to mention some of the important ones) sentence and statement, actual statement and putative (apparent) statement, genuine statement and spurious statement, conventional *M*eaning (*U*se) and contextual *m*eaning (*u*se), criteria and evidence, truth-conditions and checking procedures, entailment/incompatibility and verification/falsification, cognitively meaningful and checkable, checkable in principle and checkable in practice, conclusivley checkable and inconclusively checkable, directly checkable and indirectly checkable, presupposition and entailment, identification in thought and identification in experience. (Such distinctions are the stock in trade of all philosophical work.) These features result as much from the nature of the author, unfortunately, as from the nature of the subject matter. If the book has one virtue, it is that the overarching argument is uncomplex and (I'd like to think) even comprehensible. I try also to avoid implausibility and irrelevancy. In a word, I try not to talk nonsense about the nonsense charge!

But what about irrelevancy? Does the study really address an issue of substance, or is it after all only an intellectual exercise? I should have thought that any problem with power to unsettle a man's basic commitments was substantial enough. The problems taken up in this book, when fully understood, have that kind of power. Besides, the logical analyst needn't stand aloof from the concerns of the real world (as some picture him), simply taking concepts apart within the four walls of his own mind all the day. Philosophical work of the type here practised can produce a new vision of the way things are in the world. It can—to point a line from a philosopher who deeply stimulates me (John Wisdom)—help us to see the familiar anew. This raises the prospect, however remote, that the pages following might generate some theological as well as metatheological insight.

My motive for writing, if I may be allowed to discuss it, is quite personal: At one time I myself was embrangled in the doubts I here try to dispel. Working them through was a kind of therapy. What stands here written was in the making a rather painful philosophical journey for the author, albeit one also productive of growth. That was a period of six to ten years ago. While revising the manuscript for publication at this time, other intellectual difficulties of a personal nature have been encountered. This study takes as grist for the mill of philosophical analysis a theological perspective with which I at one time felt but no longer feel quite comfortable. I believe this fact in no wise disqualifies what I have written. It is not that I myself disbelieve what I have said about that theological perspective (that it is by all odds intelligible to the human mind). It is that traversing these thought-paths again after a lapse of several years has had a disquieting effect upon me and added to the spiritual ferment I share with so many today who take certain philosophical and theological problems to heart. I mention these matters because I myself am often curious about the by-play between an author and his book, but seldom has that curiosity been assuaged to any extent.

I wish to acknowledge with gratitude those who have read the manuscript in part or whole, given me the benefit of their cheerful criticism, and saved me from many an inadvertency of thought or speech: Professors Daniel C. Bennett, John D. Goheen, George I. Mavrodes, John L. Mothershead, Brooks Otis, and Richard Wasserstrom. I am indebted to the United States Educational Foundation in New Zealand for a Fulbright Grant enabling me to carry out the initial research behind the book. While in New Zealand, it was my great privilege to study under Professor George E. Hughes, to whom the book is warmly dedicated. I own no greater influence upon the formation of my philosophical habits and convictions. I have been fortunate in my mentors and critics. And if I have not always heeded their advice, at least I have never hesitated to ponder it. This should absolve them of any mistakes which persist.

CONTENTS

CHAPTER I

METATHEOLOGY

―――――

1. PHILOSOPHICAL THEOLOGY IN THE AGE OF ANALYSIS

The revolution in Anglo-Saxon philosophy during the past half-century[1] has had profound repercussions upon recent philosophical theology, the questions it asks and the methods it employs. The magnitude of the influence I speak of can be seen in the contrast between, say, F. R. Tennant's *Philosophical Theology*,[2] a monumental treatise done in the traditional mode and untouched by the new influences, and *New Essays in Philosophical Theology*,[3] a collection of some of the better early articles in the new philosophical theology as transformed by the spirit and practice of logical analysis.

Tennant's scope is semi-encyclopaedic and his programme exceedingly ambitious. He asks and attempts to answer most of the 'big questions'—the soul and its faculties, the world and its laws, evil, and finally God. His ultimate objective is to assemble a philosophical scaffolding for natural theology; to sustain a ramified teleological argument on evidences drawn from psychology, epistemology, natural science, and metaphysics; to synthesize a theistic interpretation of the world.

The contributors to the *New Essays* volume, on the other hand, ignore synthesis and concentrate on analysis, concerned not with proving the existence of God but with understanding the meaning of theological words, phrases, and sentences. They analyse piecemeal some of the central concepts of theology, such as creation and miracles; they scrutinize the logical puzzles

---

[1] I refer to the contemporary philosophical movement described in such works as A. J. Ayer, *et al.*, *The Revolution in Philosophy* (London, 1956); J. O. Urmson, *Philosophical Analysis: Its Development Between the Two World Wars* (Oxford, 1956); and G. J. Warnock, *English Philosophy Since 1900* (London, 1958).

[2] 2 vols., Cambridge, 1928 and 1930.

[3] Edited by Antony Flew and Alasdair MacIntyre, New York, 1955. [Hereafter cited as *New Essays.*]

implicit in the notions of divine omnipotence and human freedom when taken together, and in the idea of the perfect good; they explore with the falsifiability criterion the nature of religious language and put special religious ways of knowing to the tests of logical rigour. The marked contrast between these two works serves as one index to the distinction between two diverse ways in philosophical theology.[1]

Another approach to defining the difference between the old philosophical theology and the new is to note how they line up on the things/words distinction and on the object-language/metalanguage distinction. The traditional philosophical theology talks about God; the new talks about the word 'God' and about 'God'-talk. The traditional employs an object-language for talking about God, whereas the new employs a metalanguage for talking about the language of theology and religion. Furthermore, the questions which the traditional philosophical theology asks are for the most part first-order questions, such as 'Can the existence of God be verified empirically?'. The questions which the new philosophical theology puts, on the other hand, are in the main second-order questions, such as 'Can the sentence "God exists" be used to make a statement which is verifiable empirically?'.[2]

Someone struck by apparent similarities between the members of certain first-order/second-order question pairs (such as the pair of questions mentioned immediately above) might interject that metatheological second-order questions simply ask the

[1] For a supplementary characterization of these two ways, see H. A. Hodges, 'What Is to Become of Philosophical Theology?', in H. D. Lewis, ed., *Contemporary British Philosophy*, Third Series (London and New York, 1956), pp. 212-217.

[2] The foregoing account stands in need of three qualifications. First of all, the account employs the words 'old' and 'new' in making the distinction. These words suggest that the distinction is mainly historical, whereas in fact it is mainly methodological and only secondarily historical. Secondly, the contrast has only limited validity as a historical contrast. Theology has always been concerned with conceptual questions. And though in discussing them she has usually employed the material rather than the formal mode, the discussion has occasionally been couched in metalinguistic terms. Witness, for example, the treatment of the divine names by Dionysius and Areopagite and the Scholastic doctrine of analogical predication. Nor should we overlook that the modern metatheologian does not always employ the formal mode for his conceptual analysis. Thirdly, not every question couched in the metalanguage is a question about meanings. The presence of quotation marks within the sentence, in other words, is not an infallible sign that the point of the sentence is conceptual.

same questions as their first-order counterparts, only in a different mode. This person might suggest the only real difference between the old philosophical theology and the new is a preference on the part of the latter for the formal mode in raising and answering questions.

It is true, for some first-order questions the corresponding second-order questions ask the very same question only in a different mode. But since the metatheologian is interested in few (if any) of these second-order questions, their existence does not trivialize the new philosophical theology. The majority of metatheological second-order questions have no first-order equivalents. Specifically these second-order questions have an importance warranting them the serious attention of philosophers and theologians alike.

To illustrate, the first-order question, 'Is the existence of God verifiable?' and the second-order question 'Is the statement which the sentence "God exists" is used to make verifiable?' both ask the very same question. It is a question about verifiability, the verifiability of the existence of God or (what amounts to the same) the statement that God exists. But neither of these questions is to be confused with the second-order question about meaning which resembles them, the question 'Is the sentence "God exists" used to make a statement which is verifiable?'. The latter question is logically prior to the other two and must be answered before either of the other two can be answered or even arises.

Consider the following demonstration: If it were true that the latter question really asked the same question that the other two ask, then an affirmative answer to the latter would entail an affirmative answer to both of the others and a negative answer to the latter would entail a negative answer to the others—the minimal conditions for upholding the equivalence of the questions. An affirmative answer to the question 'Is the sentence "God exists" used to make a statement which is verifiable?' does in fact entail an affirmative answer to the questions 'Is the existence of God verifiable?' and 'Is the statement which the sentence "God exists" is used to make vertifiable?'. But since the question 'Is the sentence "God exists" used to make a statement which is verifiable?' does not prejudge the meaning of the sentence 'God exists' (the point of that question being precisely to pose a request for information about its meaning) and does not presuppose that this sentence is used to make a statement of any sort, a negative answer to that question does not entail negative answers to the other two; on the contrary, a negative answer to that question renders the other two pointless. For negative answers to the two questions which are equivalent still presuppose a commitment to the position that the sentence 'God exists' is used to make a statement of some sort; a negative answer to the remaining question, on the other hand, expressly denies such a commitment.

To require that attention first be given to the logically prior metatheological second-order questions is not to disparage theological first-order questions out of hand. It is only to lay down an injunction to which the theologian ought thankfully submit, namely that he get clear on the meaning and metatheological implications of his first-order questions before attempting to answer them.

Clarity, coherence, and intelligibility of meaning are fundaments not ornaments of any rationally sound discipline of inquiry, theology included. The meaning of common religious belief as well as of abstract theology is notoriously elusive. It is not only that simple believer and professional theologian alike often find it unusually difficult to state translucently an analysis of what their religious discourse means, while knowing full well at the level of practice (intuitively) what it means. At times they themselves appear not to know what it means; they appear as puzzled by their own speech as the outsider. Such is the semantic perplexity of theology, spelling out precisely the purpose of the new philosophical theology. Not to prove God or any theological perspective on life but to get the meaning of 'God'-talk—the conceptualization of religious discourse—firmly and clearly fixed in mind, this is the compelling motive behind the new philosophical theology.

In the light of the differences mentioned so far—in method, subject matter, mode of expression, order of question asked and guiding purpose—I shall make it a practice to distinguish the new philosophical theology (from the traditional) as *metatheology*, in order to underscore its conceptual thrust and its preoccupation with the problem of meaning clarification in theology. 'Metatheology'[1] will be my name for the type of investigation conducted in this study—the logical analysis of the nature of religious language. Metatheology is philosophical theology in the age of analysis.

2. A BRIEF HISTORY OF MODERN METATHEOLOGY

Philosophical theology, together with philosophy of law, political philosophy, and aesthetics, was one of the last areas of philosophy to be brought within the scope and under the discipline of the recent philosophical revolution. The early practitioners of the new philosophical methods—such people as G. E. Moore, Bertrand Russell, the early Wittgenstein, and the members of the Vienna Circle—devoted themselves instead to ethics, logic, philosophy of science and of mathematics, epistemology, and philosophy of language.

The breakthrough came with A. J. Ayer's famous critique of theology,[2] and in the interim since then the development of metatheological thinking and discussion has paralleled somewhat closely the changes and shifts of emphasis in analytic philosophy. The three major milestones in the new literature of metatheology illustrate this point rather nicely. The first of these, Ayer's *Language, Truth and Logic*, has been called a manifesto of Logical Positivism, whose doctrines pervaded the philosophical scene in Britain during the thirties and early forties and long after that in the United States. The next milestone, an intriguing attempt to come to grips with the kind of sceptical threat introduced by Ayer, was John Wisdom's article entitled, 'Gods',[3] a representative example of Cambridge

---

[1] The term 'metatheology' was first suggested to me by Professor George E. Hughes of the Victoria University of Wellington, New Zealand, to whom my indebtedness throughout this study is too extensive to be recognized by footnote at every point I draw from him. I have since found the term in print also. See I. M. Crombie, 'The Possibility of Theological Statements', in Basil Mitchell, ed., *Faith and Logic: Oxford Essays in Philosophical Theology* (London, 1957), p. 77; and Peter Munz, *Problems of Religious Knowledge* (London, 1959), p. 12.

[2] *Language, Truth and Logic*, Second Edition (London, 1946), pp. 114–120. The First Edition is dated 1936.

[3] *Proceedings of the Aristotelian Society*, N.S. XLV (1944–45): 185–206. Reprinted in Antony Flew, ed., *Logic and Language*, First Series (Oxford, 1951) [hereafter cited as *LL-I*]; and in John Wisdom, *Philosophy and Psycho-Analysis* (Oxford, 1953).

therapeutic analysis deriving from the later Wittgenstein.[1] Finally, reflecting to a degree the emphases of what is variously known as Oxford Philosophy or Ordinary Language Philosophy, also deriving from the later Wittgenstein, we have *New Essays in Philosophical Theology*, edited by Flew and MacIntyre. About ten years separates each of these three milestones.

Up until 1955 when the Flew-MacIntyre volume was published, the modern metatheological discussion was only in its incipient stage really, lending a measure of truth to Gilbert Ryle's statement, 'In our half century philosophy and theology have not been on speaking terms'.[2] Before 1950, there was very little activity in the field. Between 1950 and 1955, the discussion began to gain momentum. And since 1955, the quantity of metatheological literature has multiplied many times over. Modern metatheology has come into its own since 1955 and is today still vigorous.

From the very start, British Commonwealth philosophers have taken the initiative, so much so that until the late 1950's, modern metatheology could almost be characterized as a British movement. The lag on the part of American philosophers can be

[1] The question of Wittgenstein's own metatheological views is an interesting one. There is nothing overtly metatheological in his *Tractatus Logico-Philosophicus*, tr. first by C. K. Ogden (London, 1922) and later by D. F. Pears and B. F. McGuinness (London, 1961). For an attempt, however, to make the early Wittgenstein's notions of 'the mystical' and of the limits of language (*Tractatus*, sec. 6.432 through sec. 7), together with Rudolf Otto's idea of the numinous, into a metatheological account, see Thomas McPherson, 'Religion as the Inexpressible', *New Essays*, pp. 131–143.

As for the later Wittgenstein, G. E. Moore gives us a terse paragraph on some logical remarks of Wittgenstein's about the word 'God' in 'Wittgenstein's Lectures in 1930–33', *Philosophical Papers* (New York, 1962), p. 306. For reconstruction from a student's notes of his lectures on religious belief dating about the summer of 1938, see Cyril Barrett, ed., *L. Wittgenstein: Lectures & Conversations on Aesthetics, Psychology and Religious Belief* (Oxford, 1966), pp. 53–72. And on p. 116e of *Philosophical Investigations*, tr. G. E. M. Anscombe, Second Edition (Oxford, 1958), we find the parenthetical remark, 'Theology as grammar', following the statement, 'Grammar tells what kind of object anything is'.

Brief comments on Wittgenstein's pro-attitudes toward religion and on the compatibility of his later philosophizing with theistic belief may be found in Maxwell J. Charlesworth, *Philosophy and Linguistic Analysis* (Pittsburgh, 1959), pp. 100–101; and in Norman Malcolm, *Ludwig Wittgenstein: A Memoir* (London, 1958), pp. 70–72.

For a detailed study of the metatheological implications of Wittgenstein's later work, see Dallas M. High, *Language, Persons, and Belief: Studies in Wittgenstein's 'Philosophical Investigations' and Religious Uses of Language* (London, 1967).

[2] Quoted in Mitchell, *op. cit.*, p. 2.

explained partly by the prolongation of the Logical Positivist phase of the analytic movement in the United States. Many of the Vienna Circle members took positions on faculties of philosophy in America when the holocaust descended upon Europe in the late thirties, and their influence upon recent American philosophy has been enormous, an influence which has been impervious to, if not at times inimical toward, philosophy of religion. Up to 1960, one could mention very few items published in America that could be counted in with the new literature in metatheology.[1]

The dawn of modern metatheology in the 1930s has by no means eclipsed the old philosophical theology. The traditional methods, though often in modification now, still have their practitioners, and one could point to scores of volumes in the traditional mode published since the inception of the new movement. Nor have the more traditionally minded philosophers of religion been silent in criticizing the new movement in defence of their own ways and preferences, in the process of which they themselves have contributed to the metatheological discussion.[2]

3. METATHEOLOGICAL SCEPTICISM

No body of universally accepted conclusions has emerged from the metatheological discussion of the past three decades. What has emerged is this: general agreement that the central issue is the question of the cognitive significance of 'God'-sentences (sentences containing the word 'God'), but on the level of conclusions about this question a radical split between the cognitivists and the non-cognitivists or metatheological sceptics

[1] For bibliographies of books and articles published on both sides of the Atlantic during and prior to 1960, see Ruel Tyson, 'Philosophical Analysis and Religious Language: A Selected Bibliography', *The Christian Scholar*, XLIII (1960): 245–250; and Frederick Ferré, *Language, Logic and God* (New York, 1961), pp. 167–173.

[2] For four critical appraisals of *New Essays* done by more traditionally minded (but analytically aware) philosophers, see Raphael Demos, 'The Meaningfulness of Religious Language', *Philosophy and Phenomenological Research*, XVIII (1957): 96–106; A. Boyce Gibson, 'Modern Philosophers Consider Religion', *Australasian Journal of Philosophy*, XXXV (1957): 170–185; H. D. Lewis, 'Contemporary Empiricism and the Philosophy of Religion', *Philosophy*, XXXII (1957): 193–205; and John A. Passmore, 'Christianity and Positivism', *Australasian Journal of Philosophy*, XXXV (1957): 125–136.

as I prefer to call them.[1] What these two positions amount to and what is at stake in the issue separating them can be made clear by examining the position of the challenger—metatheological scepticism. What is metatheological scepticism? A scrutiny of Ayer's famed critique of theology will provide an initial answer.

[1] It may prove helpful to have before us at this juncture an overview of what has been written on the issue, aside from the extensive periodical literature which will be cited throughout the study when relevant.

These are some of the books containing important contributions on the cognitivist side of the debate: Kent Bendall and Frederick Ferré, *Exploring the Logic of Faith: A Dialogue on the Relation of Modern Philosophy to Christian Faith* (New York, 1962); Joseph M. Bochenski, *The Logic of Religion* (New York, 1965); William A. Christian, *Meaning and Truth in Religion* (Princeton, 1964); Frederick Copleston, *Contemporary Philosophy: Studies of Logical Positivism and Existentialism* (London, 1956); Frank B. Dilley, *Metaphysics and Religious Language* (New York and London, 1964); Frederick Ferré, *Basic Modern Philosophy of Religion* (New York, 1967) and *Language, Logic and God;* John Hick, *Faith and Knowledge: A Modern Introduction to the Problem of Religious Knowledge* (Ithaca, New York, 1957) and *Philosophy of Religion* (Englewood Cliffs, New Jersey, 1963); William Hordern, *Speaking of God: The Nature and Purpose of Theological Language* (New York and London, 1964); John A. Hutchinson, *Language and Faith: Studies in Sign, Symbol, and Meaning* (Philadelphia, 1963); H. D. Lewis, *Our Experience of God* (London and New York, 1959); E. L. Mascall. *Words and Images: A Study in Theological Discourse* (New York, 1957); Thomas McPherson, *The Philosophy of Religion* (London, 1965); Basil Mitchell, ed., *Faith and Logic: Oxford Essays in Philosophical Theology;* H. J. Paton, *The Modern Predicament: A Study in the Philosophy of Religion* (London, 1955); D. Z. Phillips, *The Concept of Prayer* (London, 1965); Ian T. Ramsey, *Christian Discourse: Some Logical Explorations* (London, 1965) and *Religious Language: An Empirical Placing of Theological Phrases* (London, 1957); Ninian Smart, *Reasons and Faiths: An Investigation of Religious Discourse, Christian and Non-Christian* (London, 1958); John Wilson, *Language and Christian Belief* (London, 1958) and *Philosophy and Religion: The Logic of Religious Belief* (London, 1961); John Wisdom, *Paradox and Discovery* (Oxford, 1965); and Willem F. Zuurdeeg, *An Analytical Philosophy of Religion* (New York, 1958).

And on the non-cognitive side: A. J. Ayer, *Language, Truth and Logic*, Second Edition (New York, 1946); William T. Blackstone, *The Problem of Religious Knowledge: The Impact of Philosophical Analysis on the Question of Religious Knowledge* (Englewood Cliffs, New Jersey, 1963); R. B. Braithwaite, *An Empiricist's View of the Nature of Religious Belief* (Cambridge, 1955); F. Gerald Downing, *Has Christianity A Revelation?* (London, 1964); Antony Flew, *God and Philosophy* (London, 1966); Ronald W. Hepburn, *Christianity and Paradox: Critical Studies in Twentieth-Century Theology* (London, 1958); C. B. Martin, *Religious Belief* (Ithaca, New York, 1959); T. R. Miles, *Religion and the Scientific Outlook* (London, 1959); Peter Munz, *Problems of Religious Knowledge* (London, 1959); Paul F. Schmidt, *Religious Knowledge* (Glencoe, Illinois, 1961); and Paul M. van Buren, *The Secular Meaning of the Gospel: Based on an Analysis of Its Language* (London, 1963).

The following anthologies contain contributions from both camps: Flew and MacIntyre, eds., *New Essays in Philosophical Theology;* John Hick, ed., *The Exis-*

It would be a mistake to think that Ayer denied the truth of some or all theological affirmations, as though he were an ordinary theological sceptic. He cut far deeper than that. For Ayer, such affirmations are not in simple fact false; they *could* not be false (logical 'could'). But that does not mean that they are thereby true, for they *could* not be true either (logical 'could' again). By means of the verification principle for testing cognitive significance, Ayer challenged the very *possibility* of either the truth or the falsity of *all* theological affirmations about a transcendent God. Believing them to be unverifiable in principle, he pronounced the sentences purporting to state them categorically and unreservedly meaningless.[1]

Such a viewpoint is metatheological, because it pronounces on the meaning of a class of theological sentences; it is sceptical, because it denies that these sentences are used to make actual propositions of fact with reference to God. Metatheological

---

tence of God (New York and London, 1964) and *Faith and the Philosophers* (London, 1964); Sidney Hook, ed., *Religious Experience and Truth: A Symposium* (New York, 1961); and Alasdair MacIntyre, ed., *Metaphysical Beliefs: Three Essays* (London, 1957).

It must be firmly held in mind throughout this study that the issue between the cognitivist and non-cognitivist positions is being treated here as a purely logical and not as a religious issue. Strange as it may at first appear, metatheological scepticism is combinable with a variety of religious attitudes, practices, and even beliefs. The aforementioned works by Braithwaite, Downing, Hepburn, Miles, Munz, Schmidt and van Buren witness to this. Furthermore, some of the foremost theologians of the day hold views of God, knowledge of God, and speech about God approaching the metatheological sceptic's position, though I think falling short of its full force in most cases. See, for example, Rudolf Bultmann, 'Welchen Sinn hat es, von Gott zu reden?', *Theologische Blätter*, IV (1925): 129–135, tr. by Franklin H. Littell as 'What Sense Is There to Speak of God?' *The Christian Scholar*, XLIII (1960): 213–222. This inner sympathy between metatheological scepticism and much of modern theology either of the existentialist or of the secularist sort is significant and will occasion further comment later on. One virtue of Paul van Buren's *The Secular Meaning of the Gospel* is that it establishes this linkage explicitly. Van Buren, writing as a theologian, is an exponent both of what is called 'secular Christianity' and of metatheological scepticism in its full measure. For him, the two viewpoints are integral to one another.

[1] 'No sentence which purports to describe the nature of a transcendent god can possess any literal significance.' 'The religious utterances of the theist are not genuine propositions at all.' 'The point which we wish to establish is that there cannot be any transcendent truths of religion. For the sentences which the theist uses to express such "truths" are not literally significant.' 'The theist, like the moralist, may believe that his experiences are cognitive experiences, but, unless he can formulate his "knowledge" in propositions that are empirically verifiable, we may be sure that he is deceiving himself.' A. J. Ayer, *Language, Truth and Logic*, pp. 114–120 *passim*.

scepticism, therefore, is the view that denies the cognitive significance of 'God'-sentences as traditionally understood; it denies that sentences containing the word 'God' or its cognates (when these words are given their typically religious uses) have factual or informative import relative to transcendence; and it denies that they can be used to make knowledge-claims about God.[1]

Whereas Ayer flatly condemned 'God'-sentences as totally meaningless, later metatheological sceptics have been more cautious and charitable. Operating under the aegis of the maxim that an expression which has a *use* in the language has a *meaning*, they have either ascribed various non-cognitive meanings to 'God'-sentences,[2] or sought a cognitive meaning for such sentences in the sphere of reductionist interpretations which, in most cases, take 'God'-sentences to be asserting something about the meaning of human existence without making reference to divine transcendence at all.[3]

But what is distinctive of all metatheological sceptics—the identifying characteristic of the position they hold—is their explicit denial to 'God'-sentences of any cognitive meaning that implies reference to some sort of transcendent reality called 'God'.[4]

[1] My use of 'scepticism' to name a position which takes a definite stand and makes a negative affirmation (denial) without reservation or uncertainty is supported by *Webster's Third New International Dictionary of the English Language Unabridged* (Springfield, Mass., 1961), p. 2132; and by the following, where I learned it: A. J. Ayer, 'Philosophical Scepticism', in H. D. Lewis, ed., *Contemporary British Philosophy*, Third Series, pp. 47–62; A. J. Ayer, *The Problem of Knowledge* (Harmondsworth, Middlesex, 1956), Chapter 2 especially; and John Wisdom, *Other Minds* (Oxford, 1952), and *Philosophy and Psycho-Analysis*.

[2] For an attempt to assimilate religious language to a 'pro-attitude' account of moral discourse, see R. B. Braithwaite, *op. cit.*, p. 19: 'My contention then is that the primary use of religious assertions is to announce allegiance to a set of moral principles'. Hepburn, *op. cit.*, and Schmidt *op. cit.*, develop positions similar to Braithwaite's. For the first suggestion of an emotive theory of religious language, see C. K. Ogden and I. A. Richards, *The Meaning of Meaning: A Study of the Influence of Language Upon Thought and of the Science of Symbolism*, Eighth Edition (New York, n.d. [first published in 1923]), p. 158. This whole matter of the alternative non-cognitive accounts of the meaning of 'God'-sentences and the inadequacy of these accounts will be taken up in Chapter VII.

[3] For examples of such a move, see Miles, *op. cit.*, Munz, *op. cit.*, and van Buren, *op. cit.*

[4] What it is for a sentence to have cognitive meaning, to state a fact, to convey information, to make a knowledge-claim—these are extremely important and difficult questions. For the present, it must be assumed that the reader has some grasp of what it is for a sentence to be so used. The detailed explanations will come later, beginning with the next section of the present chapter.

The crucial difference between ordinary theological scepticism and metatheological scepticism is illuminated by Ayer's perception that his criticism of 'God'-sentences, if valid, undercuts atheism and agnosticism as well as theism.[1] Atheism and agnosticism are both forms of theological scepticism; the first denies the existence of God outright, and the second deems it necessary to suspend judgement on the question of God's existence. But both positions are committed to the cognitive significance of the claim that God exists; both are disqualified if that claim can be shown to be cognitively meaningless. So, the traditional positions of theological scepticism are placed under the same 'linguistic veto'[2] with theism, if the case for metatheological scepticism stands.

The nature of metatheological scepticism can be further explicated by extending the contrast between it and ordinary theological scepticism. Theological scepticism involves doubt about or denial of the truth of particular claims made by theists. The theological sceptic justifies his stand on the grounds that there is no evidence, insufficient evidence, or counter evidence for the claims made by the theist. But, by allowing that something could conceivably count either for or against such claims, the theological sceptic upholds the cognitive significance of the claims themselves.

The metatheological sceptic, on the other hand, denies that 'the evidence' offered either for or against any theological claim is really evidence; in his view, nothing could conceivably count either for or against such claims. This charge is supported either by reference to some predetermined logical standard (such as the verification principle) or by generalization from the examination of many particular cases. The doubt of the theological sceptic, therefore, is directed against the truth or our knowledge of the truth of God-claims, whereas the doubt of the metatheological sceptic is registered against the cognitive meaningfulness of 'God'-sentences. The theological sceptic says that certain claims are false or undecidable though cognitively significant; the metatheological sceptic maintains that certain 'claims' are not really (cognitive) claims and hence neither false nor true.

[1] *Op. cit.*, pp. 115–116.
[2] A provocative term used by Paton, *op. cit.*, Chap. II.

Our comprehension of metatheological scepticism can be advanced further by noting that between it and theological scepticism on the one hand and between the two members of certain other scepticism/meta-scepticism pairs on the other hand there are some striking parallels. In the following set of contrasts, I mean to draw the reader's attention to the similarities between metatheological scepticism and four traditional epistemological problems, in order to illuminate the former: the problem of our knowledge of the past, the problem of our knowledge of other minds, the problem of our knowledge of the external world, and the problem of our knowledge of the future (the problem of induction). The nature of the doubt involved in all five of these meta-scepticisms can be brought out by contrasting them with their corresponding non-meta scepticisms.

Suppose someone were to say: 'We don't really know whether it was in 800 or in 801 that Charlemagne was crowned Holy Roman Emperor by Pope Leo III. The primary authorities are divided, and the evidence on either side is quite tenuous.' Such a doubt is altogether in keeping with the spirit of historical research. Judgement should be reserved when the evidence is in such a state. But what is being questioned in the doubt is not the intelligibility of the historical claim, 'Charlemagne was crowned in 800', but its truth.

Now suppose that someone else rejoined: 'Not only do we not know when Charlemagne was crowned, we don't even know if there was such a person as Charlemagne. No matter how much "evidence" we may have in support of any historical claim, it would never be enough to justify our saying that we *knew* such-and-such about the past. Besides, it is highly questionable, if not an outright mistake, for us to count the type of thing we do count as evidence for any claim about the past. All our "evidences" are present perceptions; the past is past, and it is logically impossible for the past to be present all over again. How can we justify an argument from present perceptions to past events? We can (logical "can") never really know anything about the past, and therefore historical claims are meaningless on the authority of the verifiability criterion.'

Here we have expressions of historical scepticism and of meta-historical scepticism. The one casts doubt upon our knowledge of particular situations in the past on the ground of historical principles for appraising evidence; the other casts doubt over all historical principles and over the intelligibility of all historical claims by proposing that the 'evidence' for them is not really evidence.

Consider another pair of doubts with similarities to the first pair. Someone might reflect: 'We don't know if Khrushchev was really enraged over the spy plane affair. He appeared to be enraged, but he may have been feigning rage in order to create a diplomatic incident. There is some reason to believe that he subverted the May 1960 Summit Conference because of turmoil in the internal politics of Russia at that time.' In this case, doubt about Khrushchev's actual state of mind at the Summit is an outgrowth of the ambiguity of the evidence. But the intelligibility of statements in general about other people's minds is not being challenged, nor is it questioned that bodily behaviour can count for such claims or that other circumstances, regardless of bodily behaviour, can count against them.

Contrast: 'Even if there were no ambiguity in the evidence, even if we had a great deal more evidence than we do have (and it were all positive), we still would not be justified in saying that we knew that Krushchev was enraged at the Summit. We never really know what goes on in the minds of others, or even that they have minds. All we know are their bodily states, and from these we are not justified in making any pronouncements about their mental states. All psychological statements about anyone but oneself are uncheckable and therefore absolutely unintelligible.' The metapsychological sceptic refuses to recognize the evidence as evidence.

To these two pairs of doubts we could add two more: doubt as to the veridicality of a given perception of the external world because of the likelihood of illusion on that occasion, in contrast to doubt as to the cognitive meaningfulness of all statements about external objects because of either the infinite corrigibility of such statements or the gap between them and the sense-data statements upon which (the sceptic claims) they are based; and doubt as to the validity of a particular inductive argument, in contrast to doubt as to the intelligibility of all statements which base future predictions on past experiences. All four of these pairs are parallel to one another and to the theological/metatheological pair. It might comfort the theologian to point out that if the ascendance of metatheological scepticism would threaten the entire theological enterprise, the historian, the scientist, and the psychologist stand to lose every bit as much at the hands of their meta-sceptical detractors.

These five varieties of meta-scepticism are drawn from common sources. Sometimes the meta-sceptic plays upon the infinite corrigibility (i.e., the impossibility of all the evidence being in at any given time) of statements about the past, about other minds, about the future, about the external world, or about God. But more frequently he seeks to make a devastating logical criticism out of the fact of the gap in type between any one of these species of statement and the species of statement that serves as evidence for it. He presses the point, for instance, that statements about mental states and statements about bodily states are different in type: The former cannot be reduced to the latter, and the latter do not entail the former. From the fact of this gap, he argues that the 'evidence' is not really evidence, because no known and accepted system of logic (he has entailment in mind as the standard) can carry us across the gap. In combination with the theory which says that every sentence which fails to make a verifiable statement lacks cognitive meaning, the corrigibility doubt and the type-gap doubt play decisive roles in metatheological scepticism (as we shall see in Chapters V and VI), as well as in the other sorts of meta-scepticism.[1]

One more feature of metatheological scepticism needs to be pointed out in the light of the comparisons with these other

---

[1] According to John Wisdom, *Other Minds*, pp. 1–5, the meta-sceptic has in addition to the corrigibility and type-gap doubts a third gambit—the conflict doubt. Though this does not emerge in the above examples, the meta-sceptic often capitalizes upon a conflict in the criteria for applying a word to a particular case. Is a leopard without spots a leopard, a zebra without stripes a zebra? Or, to borrow another example of Wisdom's, 'Can a man keep a promise by mistake?' Suppose I have promised to meet a friend in the lobby of the library at a specified time. I forget the appointment but happen by chance to be in the lobby of the library at the designated time inspecting a book display. There I encounter my friend. Have I kept my promise, or have I not? Some of the criteria for applying 'keeping a promise' to this situation are present: I was there at the appointed time. But some are not: I was not there as the result of the express intention of meeting my friend. What shall we say? Is this a case of promise keeping? We are inclined to say both 'yes' and 'no'. We are in conflict. The conflict doubt too has considerable relevance for metatheological scepticism, as we shall see in Chapter VII where discussion of whether or not 'God'-sentences satisfy the criteria of cognitive significance is culminated.

varieties of meta-scepticism. Examining the other meta-scepticisms helps one to comprehend the sources of metatheological doubt as a variety of meta-doubt in its own right. But, to make matters more nettling, the metatheologian often finds the meta-doubt about God compounded with the other meta-doubts. 'God is angered by human sin but pleased with men of pure hearts' is a sentence purporting to make an other minds statement as well as a God-statement.[1] In it the other minds doubt is

[1] Up to this point, the term ' "God"-sentence' (abbreviated in subsequent chapters as ' "G"-sentence') has been used, but not the term 'God-statement' (abbreviated as 'G-statement'). This is an appropriate place, therefore, to introduce the reader to the usage which will govern these two terms throughout this study, since in that usage the two are not identical.

A 'G'-sentence is any sentence containing the word 'God' (usually as subject), and indicative 'G'-sentences are almost without exception the focal point of concern. The expression ' "G"-sentence' is non-committal with reference to the central question of this study, because it does not imply that such sentences are used to perform any specific linguistic function. The expression leaves open the question of the cognitive significance of any sentence to which it refers, in other words. A G-statement, on the other hand, is any statement about God, any statement entailing a statement about God, or any statement presupposing a commitment to the existence of God. As such, the expression 'G-statement' is not non-committal with reference to the central question, for it suggests that at least some 'G'-sentences are used in a specific way, namely to make statements about God.

The question of whether or not any 'G'-sentences can be used to make actual statements about God is precisely the question at issue in this entire study, and it must not be prejudged. On the other hand, there is at least one good reason for introducing the use of the expression 'G-statement' into the discussion: Much of the discussion will revolve around verifiability and falsifiability, and it seems much more natural to speak of G-statements than of 'G'-sentences in this connection; it would sound odd to speak of verifying or falsifying sentences, since sentences are grammatical things.

Maximum caution might suggest employing a term such as '(putative) G-statement' to signify an expression which *purports* to be a statement about God. This term would be non-committal with respect to the actual linguistic function of 'G'-sentences, though it would suggest that many people have *regarded* at least some 'G'-sentences as functioning to make statements. By using the expression '(putative) G-statement' the question of the actual use of 'G'-sentences would not be begged.

But '(putative) G-statement' is an unnecessarily cumbersome expression. So, for convenience sake and with all of the proper reservations in mind, 'G-statement' will be used throughout the subsequent chapters where '(putative) G-statement' might more cautiously have been used. This explanation should protect such usage against the criticism that the central issue has been prejudged by the terminology employed.

It should be added that throughout this study I shall adhere to Strawson's practice of distinguishing between 'sentence' and 'statement', of viewing sentences as combinations of words some of which (combinations) are meaningful and some meaningless, of construing a statement as a use made of a cognitively significant sentence (non-cognitively significant sentences have uses other than the statement-

compounded with the God-doubt. Similarly, 'God raised up Jesus of Nazareth from the dead' is a sentence traditionally understood as making a statement about the past as well as a God-statement. In it the problem of our knowledge of the past is compounded with the problem of our knowledge of God.

All in all, a good many God-statements are compounded with one or another, or more than one, of these other types of statement. But this does not mean that we cannot for the purpose of analysis isolate the God-doubt from the other doubts compounded in God-statements. Nor does it mean that God-statements are any worse off than the rest. 'Khrushchev was angry at the Summit' is a statement about the past as well as an other minds statement. God-statements are logically tricky, but not necessarily more intractable than other types of statement mentioned.

4. 'COGNITIVELY SIGNIFICANT'

It has been maintained that the debate between the cognitivists and the non-cognitivists has enjoyed pride of place in the literature of metatheology. Are 'God'-sentences cognitively significant, or are they not? This, it would seem, is the main issue. Metatheological scepticism denies that 'God'-sentences are cognitively significant.[1] In the previous section, we saw *why*

---

making use) and of reserving the application of 'entails', 'is incompatible with', 'true', 'false', 'verifiable', and 'falsifiable', to statements rather than to sentences. See P. F. Strawson, *Introduction to Logical Theory* (London, 1952) pp. 3–4, 174–176, 211–214; and 'On Referring', in Antony Flew, ed., *Essays in Conceptual Analysis* (London, 1956), pp. 27–33. Whatever objections might be brought against those philosophical theses of Strawson's in which he employs 'sentence' and 'statement' in the foregoing manner need not cast a shadow across his sentence-statement distinction. In this study the adoption of that distinction expedites clarity without prejudicing the outcome of the investigation.

[1] This is to put the matter summarily, without making explicit mention of the qualification already recognized, namely, that some metatheological sceptics (Miles, Munz, and van Buren, for example) allow cognitive significance to 'God'-sentences where a reductionist interpretation of some sort is in play and no reference to the divine reality is thought to be involved. Therefore, throughout the remainder of the study, the claim that the metatheological sceptic denies cognitive significance to 'God'-sentences must be understood as the claim that he denies 'God'-sentences can be used to make God-statements in the sense just explained. Such an understanding will hold up for all instances of the position that has been described as metatheological scepticism. What is finally at issue is whether or not 'God'-sentences can be used to make God-statements, which presuppose commitment to the reality of God.

the metatheological sceptic makes this denial (the three sources of the meta-doubt). But *what* is it to deny cognitive significance to 'God'-sentences? What is being denied? What is it for a sentence to be, or fail to be, cognitively significant?

Though an understanding of its meaning might without excessive risk be taken for granted in philosophical discussion, the term 'cognitively significant' most probably will not be understood by the layman and therefore requires explication.[1] The fact that the concepts here employed as explicata are themselves philosophical battlegrounds need cause no alarm. This is hardly avoidable in philosophy and will scandalize only the person who perseveres in the misguided hope that there is for every philosophically troublesome notion an ultimate philosophical analysis into unproblematic terms, an analysis which will permanently terminate all further puzzlement. So, if the explicating concepts used here convey in their ordinary senses more to the reader than 'cognitively significant' conveys, they will have served their present purpose.

Etymologically, 'cognition' and 'knowledge' are very closely related. We might expect, therefore, an understanding of the verb 'to know' to shed light upon the meaning of 'cognitively significant'. And so it does, for one way of explaining cognitive significance is to say that a sentence is cognitively significant if and only if it can be used to make a knowledge-claim or (for that matter) the denial of a knowledge-claim. A knowledge-claim is that which the sentence frame 'I know that . . .' is ordinarily used to make. A sentence is cognitively significant, then, if and only if the reading of that sentence into the frame 'I know

[1] The word 'cognitive' has been chosen as the key term in the central question because of its extensive employment in philosophical discussions of meaning. Herbert Feigl divides meanings into cognitive and non-cognitive in his article 'Logical Empiricism', in H. Feigl and W. Sellars, eds., *Readings in Philosophical Analysis* (New York, 1949), p. 7; Philip B. Rice classifies ethical theories as either cognitive or non-cognitive in his book *On the Knowledge of Good and Evil* (New York, 1955); the word 'cognitive' has found its way into American metatheological controversy in an exchange between R. Demos and C. J. Ducasse, 'Symposium: Are Religious Dogmas Cognitive and Meaningful?', in Morton White, ed., *Academic Freedom, Logic, and Religion* (Philadelphia, 1953), II, 71–97, and in the remarks precipitated by that symposium, for which see Virgil C. Aldrich, *et al.*, 'The Sense of Dogmatic Religious Expression', *Journal of Philosophy*, LI (1954): 145–172. See also, among other more recent works, Bendall and Ferré, *op. cit.*, an extended metatheological discussion in which the term 'cognitive' is operative throughout.

that . . .' makes sense.[1] The sentence, S, is cognitively significant if and only if 'I know that S' (or even 'I do not know that S') makes sense. Suppose S stands for the sentence 'There is life on Venus'. Then S is cognitively significant if and only if it makes sense to assert 'I know that there is life on Venus' (which need not be true in order for the point to hold) or 'I do not know that there is life on Venus'.

So, the argument here goes that if a person comprehends what it means to say 'I know that . . .' and can apply the rules which determine which sentences fit meaningfully into that sentence frame and which do not, he understands in a practical way (intuitively) what cognitive meaningfulness is and is capable of deciding in general which sentences are cognitively meaningful and which are not. 'What a beautiful sunset!' does not make sense in the sentence frame 'I know that . . .'; it is not cognitively significant. 'There is life on Venus' does make sense in that frame; it is cognitively significant. To deny with the metatheological sceptic that 'God'-sentences are cognitively meaningful, therefore, is to deny that it makes sense to assert such things as 'I know that S' where S is a 'God'-sentence.[2]

Another approach to the meaning of 'cognitively significant' employs the concepts 'true' and false' as explicata. A sentence is cognitively significant if and only if it can be used to make a statement which is either true or false. To put the argument

---

[1] Interestingly enough, whatever can be said in this regard of the sentence frames 'I know that . . .' and 'I do not know that . . .' holds also for 'I doubt that . . .' and 'I do not doubt that . . .'. Testing the meaningfulness of a sentence, S, in the frames 'I doubt that S' and 'I do not doubt that S' is, consequently, another way of testing the *cognitive* significance of S.

[2] The effectiveness of this analysis does presuppose that the reader has a better conceptual grasp of 'know' than of 'cognitively significant'. A detailed descriptive analysis of the actual uses of 'know' would be helpful but would take us too far afield. Instead, the reader is referred to J. L. Austin, 'Other Minds', in Antony Flew, ed., *Logic and Langauge*, Second Series (Oxford, 1953) [hereafter cited as *LL*-II], pp. 123–158; and to A. J. Ayer, *The Problem of Knowledge*, Chaps. 1 and 2. Ayer summarizes his position as follows: 'I conclude then that the necessary and sufficient conditions for knowing that something is the case are first that what one is said to know be true, secondly that one be sure of it, and thirdly that one should have the right to be sure.' (p. 35). There are divergences between Austin's and Ayer's accounts. The important point here is that both accounts break decisively with the account which equates knowledge with logical certainty, an account which inevitably terminates in philosophical scepticism—'We never really know anything at all.' On the sceptic's use of 'know', see Wisdom, *Other Minds*, pp. 114–130, 157–158, 167–191, 206–211, 238–239.

into a form parallel to the one involving 'know' as the explicans, a sentence, S, is cognitively significant if and only if it makes sense to assert 'It is true that S' or 'It is false that S'. And these two assertions make sense if and only if it is possible to specify under what conditions S would make a true statement and under what conditions a false statement. To deny with the metatheological sceptic that 'God'-sentences are cognitively significant, then, is to deny that it is possible to specify under what conditions S would make a true statement and under what conditions a false statement when S is a 'God'-sentence. It is to deny that it makes sense to assert 'It is true that S' or 'It is false that S' when S is a 'God'-sentence.[1]

Yet another attempt to get at the meaning of 'cognitively significant' trades on the concepts 'analyticity' and 'fact'.[2] Under this explication, a sentence is cognitively significant if and only if it can be used to make either an analytic assertion or a factual assertion (i.e., one that conveys information). Since we are not

[1] Here again, the arguments would be strengthened if we had the time to probe the concepts 'true' and 'false'. Along this line, the reader is referred to George Pitcher, ed., *Truth* (Englewood Cliffs, New Jersey, 1964).

[2] The distinction frequently drawn in recent philosophy between analytic statements and factual statements is highly misleading, if the answer to the question 'What is it for a statement to be a factual statement?' must take into consideration (as I believe it must) the uses made in common parlance of all the idioms containing the word 'fact'. For what is the inquiry about if not about the meaning of 'fact'?

The way the distinction is drawn in philosophy is misleading for two reasons. First of all, the philosophical distinction dichotomizes that which in ordinary language is a species-genus relationship. For in common speech, analytic statements are just one type of factual statement, since it makes sense to say 'It is a fact that S' where S is a sentence (such as 'All bachelors are unmarried males') which states an analytic fact. Secondly, if the point of the philosophical distinction is to underscore the differences between analytic factual claims and empirical factual claims, then the distinction is patently impregnated with a philosophical theory and one with which we need not agree. For in ordinary speech analytic factual claims and empirical factual claims do not exhaust the category 'factual claims'. If it makes sense to assert (as it surely does in ordinary discourse) such things as 'The U.S., as a matter of fact, has a moral obligation to aid the underdeveloped countries', ' "Paris" is in fact a shorter word than "London",' and 'In point of fact, the square root of two is an irrational number', then there are such things as factual claims about morals, factual claims about words, factual claims about numbers, etc., as well as factual claims about the meanings of words and about the empirical world.

For some commentary on the philosophical analysis of 'fact', see A. C. Ewing, 'Pseudo-Solutions', *Proceedings of the Aristotelian Society*, N. S. LVII (1956–57): 31–52; Peter Herbst, 'The Nature of Facts', in Antony Flew, ed., *Essays in Conceptual Analysis*, pp. 134–156; F. Waismann, 'Verifiability', in *LL*-I, pp. 136–141; and Ludwig Wittgenstein, *The Blue and Brown Books* (Oxford, 1958), pp. 31–32.

C

concerned in this study with whatever 'God'-sentences may be used to make analytic assertions, we shall concentrate on the possibility of using 'fact' as an explicans for 'cognitively significant'. In line with the two preceding explications, a 'God'-sentence, S, is cognitively significant if and only if it makes sense to assert 'It is a fact that S' or 'It is not a fact that S', and that same sentence is not cognitively significant if the assertion of those frames fails to make sense when they contain S.

In summary, then, a sentence is cognitively significant if and only if it can be used to make a knowledge-claim or express a doubt, or make a statement which is either true of false, or convey factual information or misinformation. No attempt has been made to mask the difficulty of giving a satisfactory philosophical analysis of 'know', 'true', 'false', and 'fact'. These words have been used in the explication of 'cognitively significant' because of the high degree of probability that their meanings (in ordinary language) would be familiar to the reader whose active vocabulary does not contain 'cognitively significant'. If the reader understands 'know', 'true', 'false', and 'fact', then 'cognitively significant' together with the thrust and import of the metatheological sceptic's denial can be grasped.

In view of this analysis of 'cognitively significant', the metatheological sceptic's denial that 'God'-sentences are cognitively significant in the requisite God-statement making use appears blatantly paradoxical. For there is ample precedent in conventional or ordinary use of language for inserting 'God-sentences into cognitive frames. In common speech, it is perfectly legitimate and seems to make good sense to say such things as 'We know God loves each one of his creatures', 'We do not know when God will judge the quick and the dead', 'It is true that God is no respecter of persons', 'It is false that God has abandoned his people Israel', 'It is a fact that God sent his son to redeem the world', and 'It is contrary to fact that God justifies a man on the basis of works rather than faith'. Any argument against the cognitive significance of religious discourse, therefore, must from the standpoint of ordinary language be judged invalid.

Such an argument, nevertheless, may be highly illuminating and serve to point up features of this species of discourse which are masked when it is closely associated in our thinking with

other species of cognitive discourse such as empirical propositions. The contribution the sceptic with his paradoxes has to
make to our understanding of religious language must not be
minimized. For one of the most strategic functions of philosophy
(and hence of metatheology) is to provide new angles of vision,
to break through blinding conventions, to cause us to make new
and illuminating groupings of the elements of our experience,
and to force us to view the world (through grammatical innova-
tions) in fresh ways.[1] I do not argue for the abandoning of
conventions and old groupings in thought, but only for the
breaking of the blinding spell they sometimes have over us. We
often need the old groupings (though not their spell) when the
reasons behind them are good, lest we fall under some new spell
just as blinding. (The sceptic has his own brand of magic, it
must be remembered.)

At any rate, ordinary language so-called is never in and of
itself the ultimate court of appeals in philosophical disputation.[2]
What really counts are the *reasons* behind ordinary use.
Ordinary language is to be preferred to the sometimes drastic
(but often illuminating) verbal proposals of the meta-sceptic
only if there is clear reason for adhering to the rules as they now
stand rather than changing them along the lines of the meta-
sceptic's recommendations. Religious discourse is cognitively
significant, if at all, not merely because under the rules presently
in force it makes sense to say something like 'It is true that S'
or 'It is contrary to fact that S' were S is a 'God'-sentence; it is
cognitively meaningful only if there are better reasons for
preserving those rules than for changing them.

These points indicate an amicable disposition toward the

---

[1] This point is underscored by Friedrich Waismann, 'How I See Philosophy',
in H. D. Lewis, ed., *Contemporary British Philosophy*, Third Series, pp. 447-490;
G. J. Warnock, who speaks of 'the inventive aspect of philosophical imagination'
in his chapter in *The Revolution in Philosophy*, pp. 120-123; and John Wisdom
throughout *Paradox and Discovery* and in *Philosophy and Psycho-Analysis*, pp. 40-41,
176-178, 226-228, 263-264, 266, 272-273.

[2] The analysis of the ordinary use is the place to start, the begin-all though not
the end-all in philosophical work, to paraphrase a famous comment of J. L. Austin's
cited by Morris Weitz, 'Oxford Philosophy', *Philosophical Review*, LXII (1953):
188. For cogent objections to the use of ordinary language as the ultimate court
of appeals in philosophy, see Charlesworth, *op. cit.*, 177-182; David Pole, *The
Later Philosophy of Wittgenstein: A Short Introduction with an Epilogue on John
Wisdom* (London, 1958), pp. 38-39, 57, 84; and Wisdom, *Philosophy and Psycho-
Analysis*, p. 41.

metatheological sceptic. We may be critical of his position, but we can be instructed by it as well.

5. PROSPECTUS

The study that follows is metatheological. It is an investigation of the meaning of religious language, an investigation informed by the concerns of modern analytic philosophy. At the very heart of the investigation stands the issue of cognitive significance, spelled out in the controversy between the metatheological cognitivist and the metatheological sceptic.

In order to preserve some of the dialectical flavour of this controversy as it has unfolded in the literature, the investigation assumes the form of an extended critique of the position of the challenger—metatheological scepticism. 'Are "God"-sentences ever cognitively significant in the requisite God-statement making use?' is posed as the pilot question, and the central argument backing up the metatheological sceptic's negative answer is examined at length, the results of the examination of it being applied toward constructive conclusions. That argument, in brief, involves first the claim that checkability (verifiability and/or falsifiability) on empirical grounds alone is a necessary condition for cognitive significance of the sort we are interested in and secondly the claim that 'God'-sentences do not make God-statements which are either verifiable of falsifiable on empirical grounds alone.

Against this argument, I shall advance the cognitivist rejoinder, contending that checkability on empirical grounds alone is a sufficient but not a necessary condition for cognitive significance, that 'God'-sentences satisfy those conditions which are truly necessary, and that at least some of them even satisfy the criterion of verifiability and falsifiability on empirical grounds alone. The thrust of the whole study, therefore, is to show the metatheological sceptic that even on his own terms at least some 'God'-sentences ought to be acknowledged as cognitively significant in the God-statement making use we are testing for.

In working out this programme the following strategy will be employed: Since the metatheological sceptic's case is predicated upon the checkability theory of meaning, an appraisal of that theory (Chapter II) is fundamental to any further progress. In the course of looking at the various versions of the theory which links checking procedures with cognitive meaning and/or meaningfulness, we shall discover that having checking procedures (verification and falsification procedures) is a sufficient but not a necessary condition of cognitive significance, and that having semantical entailments and incompatibles (which also display the meaning of cognitively meaningful sentences) is both a necessary and a sufficient criterion of cognitive significance. The crux of the problem inherent in the checkability theory of meaning will be shown to be the confusion between verification and entailment, between falsification and incompatibility, in short, between evidence and criteria of meaning.

With the result of our analysis of the checkability theory of meaning as our standard for judgement, we shall move on to examine the argumentation of two of the challengers, Antony Flew (in Chapter III) and R. B. Braithwaite (in Chapter IV), who treat respectively the falsifiability and verifiability problems in theology. Both conflate evidence and criteria of meaning, a mistake which leads naturally to another, i.e., requiring empirical checkability for cognitive meaningfulness. Both are convinced likewise that 'God'-sentences cannot meet the requirement. The shortcomings of their arguments are pointed out, but their challenge taken up: to show that at least some 'God'-sentences are used to make God-statements in principle conclusively falsifiable (Chapter V) and conclusively verifiable (Chapter VI) on empirical grounds alone.

The proofs of these two claims turn on the soundness of a method of inference analogous to *modus tollens* (in the case of falsifiability) and on the adequacy of my analysis of theological sign reasoning (in the case of verifiability) involving the notion 'God-configuration'. The basic falsifiability argument (I offer two, the lesser of which will be explained in Chapter V) goes like this: If a 'God'-sentence is used to make a God-statement which entails another statement conclusively falsifiable on empirical grounds alone, then the entailing God-statement (by analogy with *modus tollens*) is also conclusively falsifiable on empirical grounds alone and the 'God'-sentence thereby cognitively significant. The verifiability argument takes the following form: If a 'God'-sentence is used to make a God-statement which is infered from empirical data that manifest a pattern correlating with the model God-configuration, then those data constitute a sign cluster signifying the truth of the God-statement (i.e., verifying the God-statement conclusively on empirical grounds alone), thereby showing the corresponding 'God'-sentence to be cognitively significant.

These arguments are applied to a special class of 'God'-sentences exclusively, i.e., to those 'God'-sentences which serve to record what some theologians call the mighty acts of God in history, 'God'-sentences such as 'God raised Jesus of Nazareth from the dead'. But it is further asserted that, since 'God'-sentences used in making God-statements which are not empirically checkable are checked by reference to God-statements which are empirically checkable, those 'God'-sentences are also cognitively significant.

We shall then be in a position to give an answer to the pilot question (Chapter VII): 'Are "God"-sentences cognitively significant in the God-statement making use?' The cognitive affinities of 'God'-sentences argue that they are in the requisite way cognitively significant: the checkability of the God-statements they are used to make, the fact that those God-statements have entailments and incompatibles, and the fact that 'God'-sentences make sense in cognitive frames such as 'I know that . . .' and 'It is false that . . .', etc. The non-cognitive functions of 'God'-sentences, ironically enough, also argue for rather than against the cognitive significance of those sentences, for the non-cognitive meanings of indicative 'God'-sentences are always contextual and depend totally upon their conventional meanings being cognitive.

At this juncture, it should become obvious that the pilot question 'Are "God"-sentences cognitively significant in the God-statement making use?' is not only a request for information about 'God'-sentences but also (and perhaps even more) a demand for a linguisitic decision either to enforce the old rules governing the application of 'cognitively significant' (in which case 'God'-sentences would have to be included) or to change those rules (in which case compelling reasons would have to be given for the change). In the absence of any compelling reasons for a change, the cognitivist position on 'God'-sentences can finally be affirmed with authority.

Now that the central thrust of this study has been explained and the arguments outlined, the limitations within which the study will be carried out need to be set down.

In the first place, religious language is an immense and variegated field. The language of the Hebraic-Christian tradition alone, therefore, will be under scrutiny here, with no intent of extending remarks and conclusions to Islam, Buddhism, Hinduism, etc. It would be presumptuous to suppose that the logic of religious language was for each religion exactly the same. One investigation into the comparative logic of religious language tends to corroborate this view.[1] Besides, practically all of the literature in the modern metatheological discussion has the Hebraic-Christian tradition as its theological frame of reference.

Secondly, there are sizable areas within the field of Hebraic-Christian religious language itself which I have no intention of subjecting to analysis because of the immensity of the task. The language of liturgy, prayer, hymns and psalms, and myth, though of tremendous importance in the life of the believer and of the church, will be excluded. The concentration will be on the type of formulation found in the didactic passages of the Bible, in the great creeds and confessions of the church, and in the works of outstanding Christian theologians.[2]

---

[1] Ninian Smart in his excellent book, *Reasons and Faiths: An investigation of Religious Discourse, Christian and Non-Christian*, argues that, while there are important similarities among the logics of the languages of the world's great religions due to the fact that there are four logically separable strands within the worldwide religious frame of language, still there are important differences in which of the four strands any one religion employs and the way it weaves them together. Christianity and Hinduism, for example, have logically rich religious languages, because they both employ all four of the strands: the numinous, the mystical, the incarnational, and the ethical. Hinayana Buddhism, on the other hand, employs only the mystical strand. Other works venturing into comparative metatheology include Bochenski, *op. cit.*; Christian, *op cit.*; and Munz, *op. cit.*

[2] The religious as well as the logical propriety of such theological discourse has been called into question. R. F. Holland, 'Religious Discourse and Theological Discourse', *Australasian Journal of Philosophy*, XXXIV (1956): 147-163, distinguishes between 'talk *to* God' and 'talk *about* God' and gives reasons for doing away with the latter in deference to the former. The latter, according to Holland, is inessential to religious life, practice, and belief, so it does not require or warrant defence.

Much that Holland says makes sense, but I am convinced that he has not

But, in the third place, the scope is still too broad. For within the type of formulation mentioned above, we shall not be concerned with those which speak of man (anthropology), the church (ecclesiology), salvation (soteriology), last things (eschatology), or any of the other sub-areas of Christian theology except in so far as they overlap with that sub-area known as theology proper or the doctrine of God. The specific focus, then, is on 'God'-sentences, those sentences which are used (putatively—so the believer thinks they are used) to make assertions about God's existence, his nature, his attributes, his acts, his counsels and decrees, and the like.[1]

Religious language being as logically heterogeneous as it is, it would be contrary to reason to suppose that the whole of it is cognitively significant. I have reduced the scope of my subject matter to that sub-area of Hebraic-Christian religious language which surely *would* be cognitively significant if any of it is and which surely *must* be cognitively significant if the cognitivist is to make good his case. Since 'God'-sentences are foundational to the whole theological structure, if they are not cognitively significant it hardly matters if other religious utterances are.[2]

---

adequately seen how talk *about* God is intrinsic to and pre-supposed in all talk *to* God. Consider what is presupposed in the invocative phrase 'Almighty and most merciful Father . . .', for instance. Holland's interpretation of such statements as Augustine's famous 'Thou hast made us for Thyself' as being about the believer or, perhaps better, about the believer's relationship to God, *but not about God*, seems to me implausible. Similarly his suggested translation of 'God exists' into 'I believe in God'.

For criticisms of Holland's thesis, see J. M. Cameron, 'R. F. Holland on "Religious Discourse and Theological Discourse",' *Australasian Journal of Philosophy*, XXXIV (1956): 203-207; and A. Boyce Gibson, 'Modern Philosophers Consider Religion', *op. cit.*, pp. 175-177. Holland replies to Gibson, 'Modern Philosophers Consider Religion: A Reply', *Australasian Journal of Philosophy*, XXXVI (1958): 208-209.

[1] For a brief but insightful discussion of religious language with special emphasis upon its logical variety and upon the centrality of 'God'-sentences in its complex fabric, see Bernard Williams, 'Tertullian's Paradox', in *New Essays*, pp. 192-200.

[2] The non-religious uses of 'God'-sentences are to be discounted in this analysis. When Mr Khrushchev, for instance, an avowed atheist, raised his fist at the May 1960 Summit Conference and said, 'God is my witness', he was using 'God' in a non-religious sense quite obviously, perhaps we could say an inverted-commas sense. See R. M. Hare, *The Language of Morals* (Oxford, 1952), pp. 124-125, for his remarks on the inverted-commas use of 'good'. Other examples of inverted-commas uses of 'God' would be the commonplaces 'God helps those who

Fourthly, it is to be admitted with regret that the philosophical purposes of this study have prevented me from entering into
dialogue with contemporary theologians as fully as I would have
liked. Interest in the meaning of religious language is one that is
shared between philosophers and theologians at the present
time, albeit from somewhat differing angles of vision. Much has
recently been written from the theological standpoint under the
name 'hermeneutic', a term brought back into theological
currency with new connotations by such men as Rudolf Bultmann and Gerhard Ebeling.[1] The cross-fertilization of the
thought of the hermeneutical theologians with that of the
analytic philosophers of religion is a priority project but one
which cannot be taken up in any kind of systematic fashion
here.

One last limitation, in league with the point immediately
preceding, must be acknowledged, underscored, and justified—a
limitation which will be glaringly obvious and perhaps also
disconcerting to anyone knowledgeable in the field of contemporary theology. Theology, like jurisprudence and literary
criticism, is itself in large part a hermeneutical or interpretative
enterprise focused upon what already stands written, in this case
the Bible and its tradition. Differing systems of theological
thought enshrine competing hermeneutical principles and
theories and consequently render different interpretations of one
and the same set of Hebraic-Christian 'God'-sentences. This has
ramifications for metatheology: Every metatheological investigation presupposes, consciously or unconsciously, some system
or systems of theological understanding as the starting-point for
analysis. Every metatheological inquiry, that is to say, accepts
prima facie and addresses itself to one or more of several
hermeneutical understandings of the meaning of 'God'-sentences,
proceeding from there to test for conceptual clarity and

---

help themselves' and 'God is on the side of the big battalions' when used in contexts
which obviously bear no theological import. Common profanity constitutes another
variety of non-religious use of 'God'.
   [1] See especially Rudolf Bultmann, 'The Problem of Hermeneutics', *Essays
Philosophical and Theological*, tr. by James C. G. Greig (London, 1955), pp. 234-261;
Gerhard Ebeling, *Word and Faith*, tr. by James W. Leitch (Philadelphia, 1963);
and James M. Robinson and John B. Cobb, Jr., eds., *The New Hermeneutic* (New
York, 1964).

coherence, cognitivity, checkability, and its other concerns. Its findings, however, are always relative to and limited to the hermeneutical understanding(s) with which it started.

This important point has gone almost without notice in the metatheological discussions of the past several decades among British and American analytic philosophers. One might mistakenly infer from those discussions that there is abroad today but a single hermeneutical interpretation of Hebraic-Christian 'God'-sentences, whereas in actuality the field contains many intriguing new options provided by existentialist theology (Bultmann, Tillich), process theology (Whitehead, Hartshorne, Teilhard de Chardin), and the like, however much they may seem like heresy to the orthodox believer or like evasion to the analytic philosopher. Hence, it is not surprising that a modern theologian should fault a metatheological endeavour productive of negative results with theological ignorance for having presupposed an 'erroneous' hermeneutic as starting-point.[1] Modern metatheology has not been as theologically astute as it perhaps might have been (and *vice versa*).

The metatheological study that follows is in all candour selective theologically. (Some members of the theological *avant-garde* might insist that it is also obsolescent, though this is debatable.) It approaches its task in the full knowledge that its results are incomplete (having attempted to solve the cognitivity problem for only one of several systems of theological interpretation), but in the conviction that a reasonably thorough job demands strict self-limitation in scope and in the hope that

[1] In his article, 'God and Philosophy: A Discussion with Antony Flew', *Journal of Religion*, XLVIII (1968): 161-181, Schubert M. Ogden argues that Flew is right in dismissing much of classical theism as meaningless but mistaken in taking classical theism as a valid expression of authentic Christian faith. In order to displace classical theism and re-establish contact with the original and hence normative meaning of Christian faith, Ogden advocates a hermeneutical programme based on Bultmann's existentialist interpretation, Whitehead's process philosophy, and Hartshorne's neoclassical theism. I would hold that Ogden has conceded prematurely to Flew's metatheological condemnation of classical theism. There seems to be a tendency on the part of representatives of the newer theologies to regard metatheological scepticism as an ally in the struggle against classical theism. The metatheological sceptic from his side may not be as sanguine about such an alliance. Flew, for one, finds Ogden's Whitehead-Hartshorne-Bultmann reconstruction as unintelligible as classical theism. See his article, 'Reflections on "The Reality of God"', *Journal of Religion*, XLVIII (1968): 150-161.

patterns and standards herein developed might assist an extension of the enterprise to other systems of theological interpretation.

The theological system presupposed in the present metatheological exploration is not so much a monolithic structure as a cluster of converging systems with many variations but a common core of agreement. From the standpoint of contemporary theology, it is often referred to broadly and summarily as 'classical Christian theism', a kind of consensus theology which endured over the centuries unchallenged until the time of Schleiermacher (early nineteenth century). It conceives of God as a supernatural being, immaterial and hence invisible and intangible, infinite and immutable, essentially personal, transcendent yet immanent and evident in both nature and history. More importantly for our purposes, it centres squarely in a traditional and unreconstructed understanding of what in theological parlance is known as 'salvation history' or 'the mighty acts of God in history', i.e., supposed historical happenings in which God is believed to have been active with redemptive purpose. Presupposition in this study of such a system of theological understanding comes most strikingly to the fore in the repeated claim that 'God raised Jesus of Nazareth from the dead at t_2' is to be construed as making a statement which entails that Jesus of Nazareth was dead at t_1 but alive again in an empirically determinable sense at t_3. Salvation history—the drama of God's creation, redemption, and final judgement of mankind—is the hub of classical Christian theism.

An exponent of one of today's new frontier theologies might well find my selection of hermeneutical starting-point anachronistic and my metatheological conclusions for that reason irrelevant. Bypassed is Charles Hartshorne's neoclassical theism with its refurbished ontological argument and its finite, mutable though perfect God. Bypassed also is Paul Tillich's 'God beyond the God of theism', conceived of as the ground of all being, supra-personal and disobjectified. Bypassed also is the existentialist interpretation of Rudolf Bultmann which, in the conviction that every statement about God is really a statement about the meaning of human existence from the divine perspective, subsumes salvation history under the category of myth the hidden meaning of which is supposed to be disclosed through a hermeneutical process known as demythologization.[1]

The newer theologies pose some exciting possibilities for reflection. I pass over them out of no conviction that they are either theologically or metatheologically inferior to classical theism. I have learned, not without resistance, to esteem them theologically, even to prefer them to classical Christian theism. But it is no part of my project to judge among theologies; my project is to test for the cognitive significance of 'God'-sentences as construed by one theological perspective—classical Christian theism. I intend in this study to make no brief for this theology *qua* theology, only to vouch for its cognitive meaningfulness, its intelligibility.

Why then the choice of classical Christian theism as the theological premise for this metatheological analysis? There are several reasons. In the first place, classical Christian theism to the best of my knowledge continues to be that theology which informs the understanding of faith held by the numerical majority (though not the *avant-garde*) of common believers and professional theologians alike. This situation may change, in our own times even; some claim already to be able to see the signs of such change. But until such time, the metatheological analysis of classical Christian theism is rightfully, it seems to me, the most pressing business in this area of philosophical work. Secondly, virtually the whole metatheological debate of recent decades between the cognitivists and non-cognitivists has been predicated upon the theological presupposition of classical Christian theism. Since it is my purpose to make the most direct contact possible with that discussion, I would miss my mark by shifting hermeneutical ground. Thirdly, some modern theologians seem almost pleased to think that classical Christian theism suffers from just the sort of conceptual difficulties the metatheological sceptic charges it with. I am of the opinion that such views reflect logical and semantical confusions. Whatever theological objections classical Christian theism might be subject to, it is not in the last analysis, I shall attempt to prove, vulnerable to metatheological scepticism. Having resolved to

[1] For a clear statement of one version of the existentialist interpretation of salvation history, see Schubert M. Ogden, "What Sense Does It Make to Say, "God Acts in History"?', *The Reality of God and Other Essays* (New York, 1966), pp. 164-187.

limit my scope, in my main remarks at least, to a single system of theological understanding, it occurred to me there might be some merit in selecting what many regard as the most problematic case. If these reasons do not suffice, the only other consolation I can offer my reader is the promise to comment on the newer theologies along the way, when the opportunity affords itself.

CHAPTER II

CHECKABILITY

The metatheological sceptic propounds a negative answer to the pilot question 'Are "G"-sentences as understood by classical Christian theism cognitively significant in the requisite God-statement making use?'. In constructing his case, the most powerful and persistent charge he brings against his opponent (the metatheological cognitivist) is the charge that G-statements are not checkable (i.e., not verifiable or falsifiable) and hence not actually statements. Such a charge indicates a solid commitment on the part of the metatheological sceptic to some version of the checkability theory of cognitive meaning and/or meaningfulness.[1] For implicit or explicit in his argument from the uncheckability of G-statements to the cognitive meaninglessness of 'G'-sentences is the assumption of an important connection between cognitive meaning and/or meaningfulness and checkability.

Although this prime argument in the case for metatheological scepticism turns ultimately upon the truth or falsity of the claim that G-statements are uncheckable rather than upon the merits or demerits of the checkability theory of meaning, the assumption of an important connection between checkability and cognitive meaning and/or meaningfulness must not be allowed to slip by unchallenged and unexamined. The assumption gives rise to three questions: (1) Is there really a connection between the two? (2) If so, what is its exact nature? And (3) can such a connection, supposing there is one, sustain the metatheological sceptic's prime argument? Searching for satisfactory answers to these questions will not only take us to the very heart of the checkability theory of meaning but will also provide the foundations for the metatheological cognitivist's counter-argument. His strategy will be to argue that under the only defensible version of the checkability theory his claim is upheld, not the

[1] This theory will be referred to simply as 'the checkability theory of meaning'.

sceptic's. His strategy, in other words, will be to permit the sceptic to choose the battlefield (checkability) and then to try to beat the sceptic on his own ground.

Is there really a connection between checkability and cognitive meaning and/or meaningfulness, and if so, what is its exact nature? These first two questions point up the need to state and examine minutely the several versions of the checkability theory (as will be done in the second section of this chapter). But since the key to this inquiry is to be found in the important but frequently neglected distinction between criteria and evidence, in the following section that distinction will be established and its terms defined, some findings about entailment and incompatibility applied to it, and two qualifications acknowledged.

1. CRITERIA AND EVIDENCE

The criteria-evidence distinction has achieved a certain amount of currency in contemporary analytic philosophy. Yet its use in this study requires careful introduction because of the extensive dependence of subsequent argumentation upon it and in order to prevent confusion with other distinctions for which it might be mistaken.[1]

[1] I am indebted to Professor George E. Hughes for both the distinction and the terminology in which it is expressed. I would guess that his source in turn was Wittgenstein, whose terminology is only slightly different ('symptom' for 'evidence') and, I think, less flexible. See *The Blue and Brown Books*, pp. 24-25; and *Philosophical Investigations*, pp. 112e-113e.

The distinction as it is drawn by Hughes and Wittgenstein must not be confused with the 'meaning-criteria' distinction in Hare, *The Language of Morals*, pp. 94-110; or with the 'force-criteria' distinction in Stephen E. Toulmin, *The Uses of Argument* (Cambridge, 1958), pp. 30-35. Hare's distinction corresponds rather closely (though he might dispute it) to the distinction I shall draw in Chapter VII between contextual *meaning* or *use* (the special purposes for which individual speakers use language on particular occasions) and conventional *Meaning* or *Use* (the rules, linguistic group habits, or institutions which determine the general understanding of language), a distinction suggested to me by Professor Daniel C. Bennett of Brandeis University. Hare's use of 'criteria' coincides with its use by Hughes and Wittgenstein, however. Toulmin's distinction is ambiguously drawn and seems at first to approximate Hare's but later to gravitate toward Wittgenstein's.

The criteria-evidence distinction also must not be confused with the analytic-synthetic distinction, which refers to two different types of cognitive sentence. The criteria-evidence distinction, on the other hand, refers to two different aspects of every cognitive sentence whether it be analytic or synthetic. For with both analytic and synthetic statements, it is one thing for them to be true (or false) and another thing for us to know that they are true or false.

Throughout this study, the term 'criteria' will be used in a specialized sense to mean the conditions defining or determining the meaning of a cognitive sentence. 'Criteria' will be used interchangeably with 'truth-conditions', setting up an identification between the conditions defining or determining the meaning of a cognitive sentence and the conditions under which the statement made by a cognitive sentence would be true. Consequently, knowing the truth-conditions for a statement is the same thing as knowing the criteria for the meaning of the sentence used in making that statement, and giving its truth-conditions is the same things as giving the criteria for the meaning of that sentence.[1]

The term 'evidence', on the other hand, will be used in its regular sense to mean the conditions under which we would know or have reason to believe that a statement is true or false. 'Evidence' will be used interchangeably with 'checking conditions' (referring either to verification-conditions or to falsification-conditions).

If we admit, therefore, that it is one thing for something *to be the case* (or not to be the case) and another thing for us *to know or have reason for believing* that it is the case (or not the case), and if we admit that it is one thing for a statement *to be true* (or false) and quite another thing for us *to know or have reaon for believing* that it is true (or false), then we have *ipso facto* acknowledged the validity of the distinction between criteria and evidence. For the gist of that distinction, to repeat, is simply the difference between the conditions which would have to be fulfilled for a statement to be true (or false) and the conditions which would have to be fulfilled for us to know or have reason for believing it to be true (or false).

To elucidate the distinction, consider the sentence 'Mrs Jones is pregnant', an example in which the difference between criteria and evidence should be clear and indisputable. If Mrs Jones has an embryo or foetus in her womb, then the statement

---

[1] For support on this point, see Strawson, *Introduction to Logical Theory*, pp. 211-214. One qualification must be added to the point: Since knowing the conditions which would make a statement *false* often helps in a negative way to know the meaning, there are such things as negative criteria. Therefore, either 'truth-conditions should be understood broadly as including falsity-conditions, or 'criteria' should be taken as interchangeable with 'either truth-conditions or falsity-conditions'.

made by the sentence 'Mrs Jones is pregnant' is true. For having an embryo or foetus in her womb is the *criterion* (the truth-condition) of her being pregnant, and 'Mrs Jones has an embryo or foetus in her womb' states the criterion (the truth-condition) for 'Mrs Jones is pregnant'. If, on the other hand, we get positive results from Mrs Jones's rabbit and/or frog test(s), or if an X-ray photograph of her abdomen reveals the presence of an embryo or foetus adhering to the wall of her uterus, then we know or have very good reason for believing that the statement made by the sentence 'Mrs Jones is pregnant' is true. For positive results of Mrs Jones's rabbit and/or frog test(s) and such an X-ray photograph are *evidence* (verification-conditions) for her being pregnant, and 'The results of Mrs Jones's rabbit and/or frog test(s) are positive' and 'An X-ray photograph of Mrs Jones's abdomen reveals the presence of an embryo or foetus adhering to the wall of her uterus' state the conclusive evidence (verification-conditions) for the statement made by 'Mrs Jones is pregnant'. To perceive the difference between 'Mrs Jones has an embryo or foetus in her womb' and 'The results of Mrs Jones's rabbit and/or frog test(s) are positive, and an X-ray photograph of Mrs Jones's abdomen reveals the presence of an embryo or foetus adhering to the wall of her uterus' in relation to 'Mrs Jones is pregnant', therefore, is to perceive the difference between criterion and evidence.

There are several good reasons for inserting at this juncture an excursus on the notions of entailment and incompatibility. First of all, they are key concepts for this entire study, and so their meanings in the context of the study should be introduced with the necessary explanations at the earliest opportunity. Secondly, an elaboration of the special functional relationship between entailment and incompatibility on the one hand and criteria on the other should shed further light upon the concept of criteria itself. Thirdly, perceiving within the framework of the criteria-evidence distinction the close connection between entailment and incompatibility on the one side and criteria on the other should help us to see through the verification-entailment and falsification-incompatibility conflations when we encounter them (Chapters III and IV) in the writings of two prominent metatheological sceptics. And lastly, from the

D

criteria/entailment-and-incompatibility connection there is an important corollary to be drawn, which contributes to our understanding of the necessary and sufficient conditions for establishing cognitive significance. The discussion that follows, therefore, is an organic part of the exposition of the criteria-evidence distinction.

'Entailment', 'incompatibility', and their cognates have a range of uses. In everyday, non-philosophical speech, we say such things as 'Biology 100 entails two laboratory sessions per week' (where 'entails' means 'involves one in certain consequences') and 'John and Mary discovered before marriage that they had incompatible interests, goals and personalities' or 'The colours in her costume were incompatible' (where 'incompatible' means 'inharmonious'). Since the present study is philosophical in nature, however, we shall be concerned with the philosophical rather than the everyday meanings of these words. In philosophical parlance, 'entailment', 'incompatibility', and their cognates have specialized meanings which trade on but are not altogether consonant with their meanings in ordinary speech. It must first be made plain, therefore, which of the specialized meanings of these words are in force throughout this study, and then we can relate these meanings to the criteria-evidence distinction.

When the logical relations within purely formal systems or calculi are the locus of discussion, then the notions of entailment and incompatibility are syntactical and name relations that obtain between purely syntactical forms called sentences or formulae.[1] In this context, it is said that 'A or B' entails 'B or A', that 'A and B' entails 'A' and 'B', that 'All S is P' entails 'Some S is P', that 'A' is incompatible with 'not-A', that 'If A then B' is incompatible with 'A and not-B', and that 'All S is P' is incompatible with 'No S is P' (where in each case 'A' and

[1] A formula is any expression containing individual, predicate, or sentential variables, e.g. 'x is tall' (where 'x' is an individual variable which can be replaced by a proper name, definite description, etc.) 'John Smith is P' (where 'P' is a predicate variable which can be replaced by the name of a property or relation), and 'A or B' (where 'A' and 'B' are sentential variables which can be replaced by sentences). A sentence is any expression obtained by replacing all the individual, predicate, and sentential variables in a formula with the names of individuals or properties or with sentences. When a formula has all of its variables replaced, it is said to be 'interpreted'. A sentence in formal logic, therefore, is a formula interpreted.

'B' are sentential variables and 'S' and 'P' predicate variables).
For in formal logic, the syntactical forms (plus, of course, the
special meanings given to the logical constants such as 'or',
'and', 'not', 'if', 'all', and 'some') alone and without any
consideration of the *meanings* of the words, phrases, and
sentences which can replace individual, predicate, and sentential
variables determine whether or not the logical relations of
entailment and incompatibility hold between sentences or
formulae.

But our concern in this study is not with the formal transformations that can be worked upon uninterpreted formulae or
upon formulae interpreted into sentences, nor is it with the
formal incompatibility relations that might obtain between such
formulae uninterpreted or interpreted. Our concern is with the
meanings of words, phrases, and sentences, more specifically
with the meaning of the word 'God' and of phrases and particularly sentences containing the word 'God'. Clearly, therefore, the
syntactical notions of entailment and incompatibility are not the
ones in force throughout this study, for those notions have
nothing to do with the meaning of 'G'-sentences.

When, on the other hand, the logical relations within non-
formal arguments are the locus of discussion, then the notions
of entailment and incompatibility are semantical and name
relations that obtain between statements (statement-making
being the primary use to which cognitively significant sentences
are put) rather than between sentences or formulae when
'sentence' and 'formula' are understood to name syntactical
forms. Outside of formal logic, in the domain of live argumentation, syntactical forms and the formal relations between them
count for very little, and it is possible to give an account of the
meaning of a sentence of the form 'A and not-A' (where 'A' is a
sentential variable) in which that sentence does not make a
self-contradictory statement.[1]

Under the semantical account of incompatibility, any two
statements, p and q, are incompatible if and only if they cannot
both be true together expressly because the meanings of the
sentences used in making them reject one another.[2] And under

[1] *Ibid.*, p. 3: 'If someone asks you whether you were pleased by something, you
may reply: "Well, I was and I wasn't", and you will communicate perfectly well.'
[2] There are two kinds of incompatibles (or inconsistencies)—contraries and

the semantical account of entailment, p entails q if and only if the truth of p necessitates the truth of q expressly because the meaning of the sentence used to make p includes the meaning of the sentence used to make q, and not by virtue of the syntactical forms of the sentences used in making p and q.[1] This notion of entailment is sometimes referred to in logic textbooks as 'necessary implication' or 'intensional implication' and is claimed to be the construction we usually put on 'entails' when it functions as a logical relator.[2] The semantical notions of entailment and incompatibility are the ones in force throughout this study, therefore, for they by nature have a great deal to do

---

contradictories. Two statements, p and q, are contraries if and only if they can be false together but not true together; they are contradictories if and only if they can be neither true together nor false together, i.e., if one must be true and the other false, So incompatibility is here defined in terms of the least common denominator between contraries and contradictories: p and q are incompatible if and only if the truth of one entails the falsity of the other, i.e. if they cannot both be true.

[1] Ralph M. Eaton, *General Logic: An Introductory Survey* (New York, 1931), pp. 231-234.

[2] Three parenthetical remarks about the semantical notion of entailment are in order.

First, the paradoxes of material implication (i.e., the theorems stating that 'If p then q' is true either if p is false or if q is true) do not hold for the notion of semantical entailment, even as they do not arise for the informal arguments of everyday speech. See *ibid.*, pp. 231, 233; Strawson, *Introduction to Logical Theory*, pp. 217-223; and G. E. Moore, *Philosophical Studies* (London, 1922), p. 295.

Secondly, the semantical notion of entailment has affinities with the semantical notion of analyticity. The statement 'p entails q' is not itself analytic; but if it is true, then 'If p then q' is analytic. For example, if 'Tabby is a black cat' entails 'Tabby is a cat', then 'If Tabby is a black cat, then Tabby is a cat' is analytic, or ' "Tabby is a black cat" entails "Tabby is a cat" ' if and only if ' "If Tabby is a black cat then Tabby is a cat" is analytic'. See Eaton, *op. cit.*, p. 232; and Moore, *op. cit.* pp. 291, 302.

And lastly, I am fully aware that the topics of meaning and the inclusion or exclusion of meanings, of analyticity and of intensional implication are all very much insettled in contemporary philosophy; it is impossible to find semantical concepts that are not. See, for example, Morton White, 'The Analytic and the Synthetic: An Untenable Dualism', in Leonard Linsky, ed., *Semantics and the Philosophy of Language* (Urbana, 1952), pp. 272-286. This does not argue for their abolition, however. I realize that, once having attempted to explicate the semantical notion of entailment in terms of these other semantical notions, I leave myself open to the demand that these explicata in turn be explicated. My only defence at this point is to stress that some terms must be accepted as primitive or be given rough and intuitive (in contrast to philosophically precise) definitions in every discussion. Otherwise no philosophical investigation could even begin to get up momentum. It is hoped that these other semantical notions, though problematic themselves, will be better understood (intuitively) than entailment and hence serviceable as explicata.

with the meanings of sentences and hence with the meanings of 'G'-sentences.

The relevance of entailment and incompatibility to considerations of meaning becomes even more pronounced when we examine the functions of and backing for entailment-rules and incompatibility-rules. The terms 'entails' and 'is incompatible with' function in our context of interest basically as logical relators: He who asserts 'p entails q' asserts that q follows necessarily from p, and he who asserts 'p is incompatible with q' asserts that not-q follows necessarily from p or that not-p follows necessarily from q. But since the assertion of entailment and incompatibility relations is predicated strictly upon the meanings of the sentences used in making the statements related by 'entails' and 'is incompatible with',[1] the expressions 'p entails q' and 'q is incompatible with p' can take on another function. Since they reflect the linguistic rules that determine and underlie them, they themselves can function as criteria for the meaning of the sentence employed in making p.

Because the essence of entailment is to exhibit the determination of one meaning by another,[2] q (if 'p entails q' is true) lays down, gives, or exhibits at least part of the meaning of the sentence used in making p. And since explaining (or knowing) the meaning of a statement-making sentence is saying (or knowing) under what conditions someone who used it would be making a true statement, one way of giving a partial account of these conditions is to mention some of the entailments of the statement the sentence is used to make.[3] An entailment-rule, therefore, of the form 'p entails q' can function as a rule for the meaning of the sentence employed in making p, a rule in which q exhibits at least part of the meaning of the sentence 'p'. And incompatibility-rules also can function to demarcate the meaning of 'p', but they do so negatively by laying down what meanings are rejected by 'p'.

How are entailment-rules and incompatibility-rules of this sort backed? How do we know when the statements made by 'p entails q' and 'q is incompatible with p' are true? How do we

---

[1] Linguistic rules about the meanings of sentences underlie and determine all entailment-rules and incompatibility-rules, according to Strawson, *op. cit.*, pp. 9-12.

[2] Eaton, *op. cit.*, pp. 233-234.

[3] Strawson, *op. cit.*, p. 211.

know when q is included in the meaning of 'p' and when it is rejected? Since entailment-rules and incompatibility-rules, after a fashion, are to the meanings of sentences what definitions are to the meanings of words and expressions, the answers to these questions will depend upon whether reportive rules or stipulative rules are in play (compare this with the difference between reportive and stipulative definitions).

It is one thing to give a report on an entailment-rule or incompatibility-rule already in use, another thing to stipulate such rules for novel and special uses.   Reportive entailment- and incompatibility-rules are backed empirically. We know when 'p entails q' and 'q is incompatible with p' functioning as reportive rules are true by establishing empirically that the meanings of the sentences used in making p and q (the sentences 'p' and 'q') have the status of conventions in the linguistic habits and practices of the language group, i.e., by establishing empirically that for the vast majority of the people who use the sentences 'p' and 'q' the statement q is either included in the meaning of the sentence used to make the statement p (entailment-rule) or rejected by the meaning of that sentence (incompatibility-rule).

Stipulative entailment- and incompatibility-rules, on the other hand, are neither true nor false, and so the question of their truth or falsity does not arise. But such rules can be either practical or impractical, and so the reasons for stipulating such rules will be either good reasons or bad reasons. Consequently, even stipulative entailment- and incompatibility-rules can be backed in the sense that their utility can be defended. In this case the backing will take either the form of pointing up the inadequacies (ambiguity, vagueness, etc.) of the entailment- and incompatibility-rules already in force for p or of indicating the needs of the immediate context for special rules. The important point here is that with both the reportive and the stipulative we have established and defensible procedures for backing entailment- and incompatibility-rules of the semantical type.

The foregoing excursus on entailment and incompatibility may now be applied to the criteria-evidence distinction. There are three points to be brought out here, two of them relating entailment and incompatibility to criteria and the third relating them to evidence.

In the first place, under certain conditions we can use entailment-rules (such as 'p entails q') to discover or infer criteria, i.e., truth-conditions. In order to explain this point already alluded to, it must first be said that entailment-rules, such as 'p entails q', take one of two 'directions' (in a manner of speaking), and it is impossible to know which without knowing just what statements 'p' and 'q' name. For want of better terms, perhaps we could call the two directions 'the analytic direction' and 'the synthetic direction'.

An entailment-rule takes the analytic direction when p and q are related as analyzandum to analyzans, i.e., when q states the essentials comprised in what p states. ' "Mrs Jones is pregnant" entails "Mrs Jones has an embryo or foetus in her womb" ' and ' "This liquid is an acid" entails "This liquid can turn blue litmus paper red, is capable of neutralizing alkalis, etc." ' would be examples of entailment-rules with the analytic direction. An entailment-rule takes the synthetic direction, on the other hand, when p and q are related as detail to summary, i.e., when q sums up the detail(s) stated in p or redescribes the detail(s) summarily without asserting anything new beyond what is asserted in p. As examples of entailment-rules with the synthetic direction, we could cite the two examples used to illustrate the analytic direction, only with the member statements reversed: ' "Mrs Jones has an embryo or foetus in her womb" entails "Mrs Jones is pregnant" ' and ' "This liquid can turn blue litmus paper red, is capable of neutralizing alkalis, etc." entails "This liquid is an acid" '. (I do not mean to suggest that *all* entailment-rules are reversible the way these two are).

With this explanation of the difference between entailment-rules with the analytic direction and those with the synthetic direction in mind, we may proceed to finish the point about entailment-rules being used to discover or infer criteria. Whenever the entailments of a statement take the analytic direction, those entailments analyse, state, or display at least part of the meaning of the sentence used in making the entailing statement. That is, whenever 'p entails q' takes the analytic direction, q states, analyses, or displays at least part of the meaning of 'p' (the sentence used in stating p). It has been said that the criteria for a cognitively significant sentence are identical to the truth-conditions for the statement that sentence is used to make and that knowing (or giving) the truth-conditions for that statement is the same thing as knowing (or giving) the meaning of the sentence used in making it. And so knowing (or giving) the criteria for a cognitively significant sentence is the same thing as knowing (or giving) its meaning. We may conclude that, since the entailments of p and the criteria of 'p' both function to state or display the meaning of 'p', we can infer from the entailments of p what the criteria of 'p' are, and, *vice versa*, we can infer from the criteria of 'p' what the entailments of p are. This works, I repeat, only when the entailment takes the analytic direction.

The second point is a corollary of the first and may be stated tersely. Due to the particularly close connection between entailments and criteria, our understanding of the conditions for establishing cognitive significance is enhanced. If there are criteria of cognitive significance for a sentence, (it goes without saying) that sentence is cognitively significant. But giving the criteria for 'p' and giving the entailments (analytic direction) of p amount to the same thing. So, it follows that if a sentence is used in such a way that its use has entailments (or incompatibles), then that sentence is cognitively significant. The converse also holds, obviously. A necessary and sufficient condition for the cognitive significance of 'p', therefore, is that p have entailments and incompatibles.

This holds for 'G'-sentences too, of course. A 'G'-sentence is cognitively significant if and only if in use it has entailments and incompatibles. We shall see in subsequent chapters that 'G'-sentences fulfil this necessary and sufficient condition for cognitive significance. Whereas the central inquiry of this entire study could therefore well terminate with the demonstration that 'G'-sentences in use have entailments and incompatibles, it would be even more effective to meet the metatheological sceptic's challenge on his own ground if possible. Since that is by all means possible, the inquiry will not be broken off at this early point. Instead, in the following chapters the argument that 'G'-sentences are cognitively significant because in use they have entailments and incompatibles will occupy a position secondary to the argument that they are cognitively significant because they are used to make G-statements which are checkable.

The third point relates entailment and incompatibility to

evidence rather than criteria. 'Evidence' has been explained in terms of checking conditions (verification-conditions and falsification-conditions), i.e., those conditions under which we would know or have reason to believe that such-and-such a statement is true or false. For the sake of clarification before proceeding with the point, we must distinguish briefly between checking *conditions* (verification-*conditions* as well as falsification-*conditions*) on the one hand, and checking *procedures* (verification *procedures* as well as falsification *procedures*) on the other.

Checking procedures are the prescriptions for the tests through which evidence is obtained, whereas evidence is the result obtained by following out the test prescription. The two are obviously related: To list evidence statements is to suggest what tests were applied in obtaining the evidence, and this knowledge of the tests can then be generalized into statements of the checking procedures. On the other hand, to list the checking procedures is to suggest what evidence statements would have to be found true or false in checking a claim. Exponents of the checkability theory of meaning have usually couched their theses in terms of checking procedures (e.g., 'The meaning of a sentence is the *method of checking* the statement it is used to make') rather than in terms of checking-conditions (evidence). There is no harm, however, in mixing the language of evidence ('is evidence for or against', 'counts for or against', 'tends to verify or to falsify') with the language of checking procedures ('method of checking', 'test prescriptions') almost indiscriminately, as will be the practice throughout the remainder of this study. For the two are functionally related. Now back to the point.

Entailment and incompatibility are related to evidence, because it is possible under certain conditions to use an entailment-rule to back the assertion that p is evidence for q and to use an incompatibility-rule to back the assertion that p is evidence against q.[1] This fact in no way blurs the criteria-

[1] Wittgenstein evidently missed this point. He seemed to conceive of the 'is evidence for' relation strictly as an empirical correlation, such that 'p is evidence for q' would in every case be a hypothesis established or backed by experience alone. In *The Blue and Brown Books*, p. 25, he says: 'I call "symptom" a phenomenon of which *experience* has taught us that it *coincided*, in some way or other, with

evidence distinction, for it does not suggest that 'entails' and 'is incompatible with' respectively have the same meaning as or even overlap in meaning with 'is evidence for' and 'is evidence against'. Nor does it authorize the entailment-verification and incompatibility-falsification conflations that we shall encounter in the writings of certain metatheological sceptics.

There are two conditions under which it is possible to use an entailment-rule to back the assertion that p is evidence for q or to use an incompatibility-rule to back the assertion that p is evidence against q: (1) The argument 'p is evidence for q' must be an argument from the criteria for applying a designation to the application of that designation, or the argument 'p is evidence against q' must be an argument from the absence of criteria for applying a designation to the denial of the application of that designation, and (2) the entailment-rule 'p entails q' or the incompatibility-rule 'p is incompatible with q' must take the synthetic direction.

For example, we can imagine a man arguing: 'The fact that this liquid can turn blue litmus paper red, is capable of neutralizing alkalis, etc., proves that (is conclusive evidence for) this liquid is an acid.' If challenged on the matter, he might back up his claim by saying: 'The reason why I am entitled to that inference is that "This liquid can turn blue litmus paper red, is capable of neutralizing alkalis, etc." entails "This liquid is an

---

the phenomenon which is our defining criterion. Then to say "A man has angina if this bacillus is found in him" is a tautology or it is a loose way of stating the definition of "angina". But to say, "A man has angina whenever he has an inflamed throat' is to make a *hypothesis*.' (Italics mine).

This stand of Wittgenstein's plays right into the hands of a dogmatic empiricism and is deficient on two counts. In the first place, it does not take account of what will be referred to as 'the argument from the criteria for applying a designation to the application of that designation', i.e., the argument-type under consideration in the text above. If I am right in my account, those arguments are backed by entailment- or incompatibility-rules, not by empirical correlations. In the second place, there is a class of trans-type arguments which (as I shall argue in Chapter VI) is backed not by a straighforward empirical correlation but by a correlation between a model and the pattern (if any) in the data from which the conclusion is derived. This class of arguments includes the argument from bodily behaviour to state of mind, from sense experience to external world, and from historical event (or whatever) to God—all those arguments, in other words, in which it is theoretically impossible to get a 'side-on view', a simultaneous perception of the evidence along side of the thing evidenced (which is the basis of an empirical correlation).

acid".' This argument is an argument from criteria of application of designation to application of designation, i.e., in calling the liquid an acid no new detail is asserted about it, but rather the details already mentioned are redescribed in a summary designation. We can also imagine someone arguing 'The fact that this liquid cannot turn blue litmus paper red, is incapable of neutralizing alkalis, etc., proves that it is not an acid (is conclusive evidence against it being an acid)' and backing it up with ' "This liquid cannot turn blue litmus paper red, is incapable of neutralizing alkalis, etc." is incompatible with "This liquid is an acid" '.

There is a parallelism between the argument from criteria of application of summary designation to application of summary designation and the synthetic direction of the entailment-rule that backs it up, a parallelism which explains why and how the entailment-rule can serve to back up that type of argument. (The same point can be made, of course, for the argument from the denial of criteria of application to the rejection of the summary designation and the synthetic direction of the incompatibility-rule that backs it up, but we need make the point only once and it will suffice for both cases.) The reason why the argument works only when it is from criteria to designation (rather than from designation to criteria) and the reason why the entailment-rule which backs the argument must have the synthetic direction (rather than the analytic direction) is obvious as soon as we try to reverse the process and find that the result makes no sense. Try to imagine someone arguing: 'The fact that this liquid is an acid *is conclusive evidence or proves that* it can turn blue litmus paper red, can neutralize alkalis, etc.' The point is not that we never have occasion to make inferences from summary designation to criteria; on the contrary, we do. One can imagine a student in the chemistry laboratory reasoning as follows (but backing it up with a *analytic*-direction entailment-rule): 'The laboratory instructor told us that this liquid is an acid, in which case it would be able to turn blue litmus paper red, etc.' The point is that it does not make sense to mark such inferences with terms like 'proves' or 'is conclusive evidence for'. The point is about the grammar of 'proves' and 'is conclusive evidence for', about the propriety of their use.

One last matter. We may safely concede that entailment-rules can function to back a certain class of assertions that p is evidence for q without endangering the distinctions between entailment and verification and between criteria and evidence because of the difference in meaning between 'p is evidence for q' and 'p entails q'. The latter, when 'entails' functions strictly as a logical relator, asserts only what follows from p because of the meaning of 'p' and does not make or suggest the presupposition that p is true. The former, on the other hand, bears the suggestion—if not the outright implication—that p is true. It is the function of 'p is evidence for q', therefore, not to state what would follow from p if p were true, but to state what does in fact follow from p because p is true. The two sentences 'p entails q' and 'p is evidence for q' function respectively to trace out the ramifications of p and to establish the truth of q; they clearly differ in meaning, even though the entailment-rule that the former states (under certain conditions listed above) can serve to back or ground an argument of the form given by the latter.

Now that the criteria-evidence distinction has been explained and certain findings about entailment and incompatibility applied to it, there are two qualifications on the distinction that must be acknowledged before moving on to a critique of the checkability theory of meaning. Even with distinctions that are very clear in concept, difficulties sometimes arise when the distinction is applied to actual cases. This is certainly true of the criteria-evidence distinction.

To begin with, there are whole classes of statements over which competent judges disagree as to what are to be considered criteria and what is to count as evidence. Second- and third-person psychological statements such as 'Jones is in pain' provide an excellent example of this sort of ambivalence on the part of the judges. One group of judges would find in the sentence 'Jones is experiencing the sensation of bodily suffering' a criterion statement and in the sentence 'Jones shrieks, quivers all over, perspires profusely, grimaces, says with anguish that he is in great pain, and clutches the dagger in his chest' a positive evidence statement and in the sentence 'Jones smiles, laughs, is relaxed, and says calmly that he never felt better in his life' a negative evidence statement.

Another group of experts (the behaviourists), believing that statements about mental states can and must be reduced to statements about bodily states, would take as criteria what the first group took as evidence. For this group, the statement made by 'Jones is in pain' *entails* a long disjunction of statements such as that made by 'Jones shrieks, quivers all over, perspires profusely, grimaces, says with anguish that he is in pain, and clutches the dagger in his chest' and *is incompatible with* such statements as that made by 'Jones smiles, laughs, is relaxed, and says calmly that he never felt better in his life'.

And yet another group of experts (the meta-psychological sceptics) would contend with the first group that it is wrong-headed to propose a reductionist analysis of statements about another person's states of mind to statements about that person's bodily behaviour, but that it follows from this that 'Jones is in pain' is bereft of both criteria and evidence. They would argue that, due to the infinite corrigibility problem confronting statements about a person's bodily behaviour or the type-gap problem confronting the inference from bodily states to mental states or some other standard sceptical gambit (see page 28), bodily behaviour cannot be regarded as genuine evidence for statements about another person's mental states. They would continue to argue that second- and third-person psychological statements are therefore unverifiable and hence (by virtue of the checkability theory of meaning) meaningless and hence (what amounts to the same thing as being meaningless) without criteria either.

The second qualification that must be put on the tidiness of the criteria-evidence distinction in practice is an outgrowth of what Wittgenstein called the 'fluctuation in grammar between criteria and symptoms'.[1] The fluctuation phenomenon can be broken down into three points: (1) the fact that, where the difference between criteria and evidence is hard to discern, sometimes there appears to be nothing but evidence (which is, of course, impossible); (2) the fact that, where for practical purposes certain phenomena are denominated as criteria and the rest as evidence, the decision as to which shall be which appears rather arbitrary; and (3) the fact that what start out

[1] *Philosophical Investigations*, p. 112e.

being regarded as evidence often tend to become associated with the meaning as criteria, and the reverse can also happen.

These three points can be illustrated by means of the sentence 'Jones has measles'. If it were asked, 'How do you know that Jones has measles?', the following answers might be advanced: 'Jones has red spots on his stomach, is running a slight temperature, and says he feels weak and headachey', 'Jones's doctor says that he has measles', and 'Jones has virus x in his bloodstream'. The statement made by the middle sentence ('Jones's doctor says that he has measles') is indisputably an evidence statement and one made (supposedly) either on the basis of the physiological phenomena mentioned in the first sentence or on the basis of the microbiological phenomenon mentioned in the last.

The difficulty is that the statements made by the first and the third sentences also appear at first glance to be evidence statements, which leaves us at a loss for any statement of the criterion or criteria for Jones's having measles. On the other hand, there must be criteria for Jones's having measles. Otherwise 'Jones has measles' would be meaningless, and then it would be wrong-headed to speak of either the physiological or the microbiological phenomena as evidence. If we had some sure way of knowing that the microbiological phenomenon was the criterion, then we could say that the argument stated by the sentence 'The fact that Jones has virus x in his bloodstream proves that he has measles' is an argument from criterion to designation, and that would settle everything. But there are pros and cons to regarding the microbiological phenomenon as the criterion for measles.

The most pressing objection to taking the microbiological phenomenon as the criterion of measles is the fact that the measles virus was isolated just recently, in the summer of 1960. Before this time, the 'cause' of measles was unknown, despite the presumption (based on the general theory of microbiological etiology) that it must be caused by some kind of virus or bacillus in the bloodstream. Are we to conclude, therefore, that 'Jones has measles' became a meaningful sentence only as recently as the summer of 1960? Such a ridiculous conclusion appears to follow, if 'Jones has measles' means that Jones has virus x in his bloodstream. Even if we took 'Jones has measles' to mean that Jones has some virus or bacillus (without knowing or saying which one in particular) in his bloodstream, we do not solve the problem; we only force it back in time to the period when microscopes were invented and the general theory of microbiological etiology formulated.

On the other side of the ledger, if we were to take the microbiological phenomenon as evidence rather than criterion, then we would have no choice but to denominate the physiological phenomena as criteria, and this also leads to troubles. For if the physiological phenomena were the criteria for measles, then the statement made by 'Jones has measles' would have to entail a statement predicating those phenomena of Jones and *vice versa*. But neither the entailment from measles to criteria nor the entailment from criteria to measles holds when the physiological phenomena are taken as criteria.

The statement made by 'Jones has measles' does not entail the physiological phenomena either separately or corporately, for we can imagine conditions (a supra-clinical virus x count in Jones's bloodstream) under which we would want to affirm that Jones has measles even though all of the physiological phenomena were absent. And the physiological phenomena in turn do not entail the statement made by 'Jones has measles', because each of those phenomena are attributable to causes other than measles. If the red spots on the stomach could be the result of some dietary disorder (strawberry rash, say), if the lassitude and headache could have their origin in a frantic day at the office, etc., then red spots plus headache plus lassitude plus temperature, etc., do not *entail* that Jones has measles.

The fact of the matter is that at present we are hard put for assurance on what to say about this problem. The physiological phenomena and the microbiological phenomenon both look like evidence for measles, and there are objections to taking either as criteria. A lack of conceptual tidiness in meta-medicine, however, would be a weak reason for abandoning medicine!

One thing is certain about the relation of the measles virus to measles: It started out as an empirical hypothesis. Diseases were named and identified on the basis of physiological symptoms long before the science of microbiology and the theories of microbiological etiology arrived on the stage of medical history. No doubt, the idea that measles is caused by a germ in the bloodstream was conceived, on analogy with other known microbiological diseases, prior to the discovery that it is. But that is precisely the point: The discovery was a *discovery*, and *empirical* discovery.

Now suppose, under whatever pressures, we are all persuaded to take the microbiological phenomenon as the criterion of measles. This is entirely conceivable. Then we would have a situation in which what started out as an empirical hypothesis became transformed into an entailment-rule. There are many analogues for this process: The boiling point of water was once an empirical discovery but now is commonly considered to be a defining characteristic (a criterion) of water. And conversely, what was once regarded as criteria can in time and as the result of new discoveries come to be thought of as evidence. If the discovery that measles is caused by virus x was once an empirical discovery, there must have been criteria at the time of the discovery for identifying measles as measles apart from its microbiological cause. Supposedly, those criteria were the physiological symptoms. Now if the criterion for identifying measles as measles were to become the microbiological cause, then the physiological symptoms (though once regarded as criteria) would henceforth have to be regarded as evidence.

There is a phenomenon, therefore, which answers to Wittgenstein's description—a fluctuation in grammar between criteria and evidence. Sometimes there appear to be only evidence and no criteria; in such cases, when we are forced to denominate criteria, we must make stipulations that are arbitrary and open to criticism; and even where there are clear and exact rules of language, these rules are subject to change over the years as the result of new empirical discoveries and of the tendency of conclusive evidence to become regarded as criteria.[1] Having now finished with the exposition of the criteria-evidence distinction, we are ready to apply that distinction to judging the checkability theory of meaning.

---

[1] Friedrich Waismann calls this phenomenon the 'open texture' of language. See his article 'Verifiability', in *LL*-I, pp. 119-129.

2. THE CHECKABILITY THEORY OF MEANING

There are three ways of spelling out the possible connections between cognitive meaning and or meaningfulness and checking procedures: (1) The cognitive meaning of a sentence is the method of checking the statement it is used to make; (2) knowing the method of checking a statement is a necessary and sufficient, or a necessary, or a sufficient condition of knowing the cognitive meaning of the sentence used in making that statement; and (3) being used to make a checkable statement (or knowing that a statement is checkable) is a necessary and sufficient, or a necessary, or a sufficient condition of the corresponding sentence being cognitively significant (or knowing that the corresponding sentence is cognitively significant). Let us examine these three possibilities one at a time, to see if they survive scrutiny.

'The cognitive meaning of a sentence is the method of checking the statement it is used to make.' Here we have the checkability theory of meaning in its most problematic form.[1] This version is tantamount to the claim that the meaning of a sentence is equivalent to the meaning of the statement which lays down its checking procedures (or perhaps the statement which records the checking conditions, i.e., the evidence, for it). It is also tantamount to the claim that the statement made by that sentence is reducible to the statement of its checking procedures (or its checking conditions, i.e., its evidence).

[1] Carnap is an example of a theorist who at one time held to this version of the checkability theory: 'If we know what it would be for a given sentence to be found true, then we would know what its meaning is. . . . Thus the meaning of a sentence is in a certain sense identical with the way we determine its truth or falsehood.' Quoted and commented upon in Paul Marhenke, 'The Criterion of Significance', in Linsky, ed., *op. cit.*, pp. 154-156.

With the first sentence of the quotation I fully concur, but hasten to stress that it has to do with truth-conditions (criteria), not verification-conditions (evidence) or verification procedures (test prescriptions). The second sentence of the quotation (the conclusion of the argument), on the other hand, has to do with checking procedures or methods—with evidence rather than criteria—making Carnap's argument a *non-sequitur* rooted in an evidence-criteria conflation.

The frequence of this conflation is amazing and can even be found where it is least expected. Wittgenstein, while distinguishing between evidence and criteria in one passage, obscures that distinction in the preceding passage by saying: 'Asking whether and how a proposition can be verified is only a particular way of asking "How d'you mean?" The answer is a contribution to the grammar of the proposition.' *Philosophical Investigations*, p. 112e.

E

The critics of this version of the theory are legion and their criticisms, most philosophers would now agree, decisive.[1] The answers to the two following questions demonstrate that this version of the theory is unsatisfactory and untenable: 'Is the theory true of *all* cognitive sentences?' and 'Is the theory true of *any* cognitive sentences?'.

One negative instance is enough to prove that the theory is not true of all cognitive sentences, and we have such a negative instance in the cognitive sentence 'Mrs Jones is pregnant'. For the meaning of 'Mrs Jones is pregnant' is equivalent neither to the meaning of the sentence which lays down the checking procedures for the statement made by 'Mrs Jones is pregnant' nor to the meaning of the sentence recording the checking conditions (the evidence) for the statement made by 'Mrs Jones is pregnant'.

Starting with the latter, we may set aside the more ephemeral bits of evidence at once; obviously Mrs Jones being pregnant is not quivalent or reducible to the irregularity in her menstrual cycle, her weight increase and distending abdomen, her morning sickness, or her sudden craving for pickles and ice cream. These are effects of pregnancy rather than the thing itself, and any or all of these effects may fail to occur in a perfectly normal pregnancy. But it is equally obvious that what is true of the ephemeral evidence is just as true for the conclusive evidence: Mrs Jones being pregnant is not equivalent or reducible to the positive results of her rabbit and frog tests nor to the X-ray photograph showing a foetus adhering to the wall of her uterus. 'Mrs Jones is pregnant' does not mean

---

[1] Consult, for example, Carl Hempel, 'Problems and Changes in the Empiricist Criterion of Meaning', in Linsky, ed., *op. cit.*, pp. 163-185; Morris Lazerowitz, 'Strong and Weak Verification I and II', *The Structure of Metaphysics* (London, 1955), pp. 117-143; Marhenke, *op. cit.*, pp. 139-157; Harry Ruja, 'The Present Status of the Verifiability Criterion', *Philosophy and Phenomenological Research*, *XXII* (1961): 216-222; J. O. Urmson, *Philosophical Analysis*, pp. 107-114, 168-172; Friedrich Waismann, 'Verifiability', in *LL-I*, pp. 117-144; John Wisdom, 'Metaphysics and Verification', *Philosophy and Psycho-Analysis*, pp. 51-101; and J. O. Wisdom, 'Metamorphoses of the Verification Theory of Meaning', *Mind*, *N.S. LXXII* (1963): 335-347.

Some philosophers, however, persist in the belief that the theory can sustain itself, at least in the face of objections to date brought against it. See Peter Nidditch, 'A Defense of Ayer's Verifiability Principle Against Church's Criticism', *Mind*, N.S. LXX (1961): 88-89; and Wolfgang Yourgrau and Chandler Works, 'A New, Formalized Version of the Verifiability Principle', *Ratio*, X (1968): 54-63.

the same thing as 'The results of Mrs Jones's rabbit and frog tests were positive, an X-ray photograph of Mrs Jones's abdomen showed a foetus adhering to the wall of her uterus, etc.'.

From the conclusive evidence we can infer the appropriate checking procedures (methods of checking, test prescriptions) for the statement made by the sentence 'Mrs Jones is pregnant'. And here again it is obvious that 'Mrs Jones is pregnant' does not mean the same thing as the sentence stating the appropriate checking procedures, some such sentence as 'Inject a urine sample from Mrs Jones into a rabbit or frog, and that creature will ovulate; take an X-ray photograph of Mrs Jones's abdomen, and it will reveal the presence of a foetus adhering to the wall of her uterus; etc.'.

The cognitive meaning of the sentence 'Mrs Jones is pregnant' is disclosed by the truth-conditions or criteria for the statement that sentence is used to make, the relevant criterion in this case being that there is an embryo or foetus growing in Mrs Jones's womb. That meaning is not disclosed either by the checking conditions (the evidence) or by the checking procedures (the test prescriptions). This one negative instance proves that the version of the theory under consideration is spurious as a general theory; it proves that it is not true for *all* cognitive sentences that their meaning is the method of checking the statements they are used to make.

Granting that the theory is not true of all cognitive sentences, is it nevertheless true of *some*? The so-called 'operationally defined' sentences of science provide a possible test case. For unless they are misnamed, we would expect from the name that the checking procedures for the statements made by those sentences lay down the meaning of those sentences. Let us take 'This liquid is an acid' as an example. It has already been said that 'This liquid is an acid' means the same as 'This liquid can turn blue litmus paper red, is capable of neutralizing alkalis, etc.' If the latter sentence, therefore, were used to list some or all of the operations relevant to verifying the statement made by 'This liquid is an acid', then the present version of the checkability theory would be true for some (though not all) sentences and hence have a limited validity.

But the sentence 'This liquid can turn blue litmus paper red, is capable of neutralizing alkalis, etc.' is used to list the dispositional properties (the potentialities) of the liquid in question, not to list checking procedures or operations relevant to verification. The sentence might *suggest* checking procedures, but it does not *state* any. We might suspect, therefore, that the operationally defined sentences of science are misnamed, since the sentences that actually do function to define them (by listing the truth-conditions for the statements they are used to make) do not in fact state checking procedures or verification operations at all.

This suspicion grows when we look at the sentences which do in fact state checking procedures or verification operations for the sentences in question. Checking procedures are frequently formulated as conjunctions of which the first conjunct is an imperative laying down the test prescription (e.g., 'Put a piece of blue litmus paper in this liquid . . .') and the second conjunct a future-tense sentence predicting the outcome of the test (e.g., '. . . and that blue litmus paper will turn red'). Since the analysis of 'This liquid is an acid' into 'Put a piece of blue litmus paper into this liquid, and it will turn red, etc.' would be patently ridiculous, we can formulate the checking procedures alternatively as hypotheticals and see if the result satisfies the theory.

The proposal here is that we consider the analysis of 'This liquid is an acid' to be given by the sentence 'If a piece of blue litmus paper were put into this liquid the paper would turn red, if an alkali were added to this liquid the alkali would be neutralized, etc.'. Such a sentence surely does lay down procedures, tests, operations for checking the truth of the statement made by 'This liquid is an acid'. But the question is: Does this sentence define, analyse, give the meaning, state the criteria (truth-conditions) of 'This liquid is an acid'? The answer must be negative. For since categorical indicative sentences such as 'This liquid is an acid' and hypothetical subjunctive sentences such as 'If a piece of blue litmus paper were put into this liquid the paper would turn red' are not functionally equivalent (i.e., do not have the same conventional *Use* or *Meaning*), it is incorrect to propose that the former are translatable into or reducible to the latter.[1]

---

[1] For confirmation of this view, see I. Berlin, 'Empirical Propositions and Hypothetical Statements', *Mind*, N.S. LIX (1950): 289-312.

In summary, we may say of the first version of the checkability theory that it is dubious the theory is true of *any* cognitive sentences, and that it is definite the theory is not true of *all* cognitive sentences. This version of the theory fails, plainly enough, through incognizance of the criteria-evidence distinction. If that version asserted that the meaning of a statement-making sentence is identical to its *truth-conditions*, then it would be fully acceptable; it would restate as a handy formula the identification of criteria and meaning (conventional *M*eaning or *U*se). But this is not what that version asserts. It asserts instead that the meaning of a statement-making sentence is identical to its *checking procedures*. It identifies cognitive meaning with evidence rather than criteria, or (what amounts to the same) it conflates criteria and evidence. The examples introduced in the analysis of this first version of the theory prove, however, not only that criteria and evidence are conceptually distinct but also that their application ranges are distinct. Incognizance of these facts about criteria and evidence is bound to result in an aberrant theory of meaning.

'Knowing the method of checking a statement is a necessary and sufficient, or a necessary, or a sufficient condition of knowing the cognitive meaning of the sentence used in making that statement.' This is the second version of the checkability theory of meaning, and it makes a weaker claim than the first version. For knowing the checking procedures for p might be both a necessary and sufficient condition for knowing the meaning of 'p' without those checking procedures being identical with the meaning of 'p'. But I shall argue that knowing the checking procedures for p is neither a necessary nor a sufficient condition for knowing the meaning of 'p'.

In the first place, knowing the checking procedures for p is not a necessary condition for knowing the meaning of 'p'. It is entirely conceivable that we might know the truth-conditions but not the checking procedures for p, and this would prove that knowing the checking procedures for p is not necessary for knowing the meaning of 'p'. For if we knew the truth-conditions for p, we would know the criteria for and hence the meaning of 'p', since knowing the truth-conditions for p is a sufficient (and a necessary) condition for knowing the meaning of 'p'. And if we knew the meaning of 'p' by knowing the truth-conditions of p and apart from knowing the checking procedures for p, then it follows that knowing the checking procedures for p is not a necessary condition for knowing the meaning of 'p'.

The sentence 'Space is relative' provides a ready example. Today we enjoy the historical advantage of knowing not only that the statement made by the sentence 'Space is relative' has checking procedures but also what they are. And yet Leibniz in the eighteenth century certainly understood the meaning of his words when he said that space is ' . . . *that order of things among themselves*',[1] though he said this long before there were known checking procedures for the statement he made. It would be plainly silly to suppose that people could know the meaning of 'Space is relative' only after the Michelson-Morley experiment (1881) or after it occurred to Einstein (1905) that the Michelson-Morley experiment constituted a checking procedure for the hypothesis that space is relative.

In the second place, knowing the checking procedures for p is not a sufficient condition for knowing the meaning of 'p'. We might know the checking procedures for p without knowing that they are checking procedures; we might mistakenly think they are truth-conditions (criteria). Or we might even know that the checking procedures are in fact checking procedures for p and still not understand the meaning of 'p'. These two points need to be illustrated in turn.

Suppose that a young child is told by its mother: 'John from across the street and your big sister Mary are in love.' The child has never known this kind of love and asks searchingly: 'What's it like to be in love?' The mother, not wishing to be obtuse, might well answer in some such fashion as this: 'Just look at John and Mary and you can see. John visits Mary every evening and often brings candy or flowers. Mary scrambles to the phone when John is on the line and often blushes in his presence. They are often caught holding hands on the swing. Etc.' The child now knows the signs or evidence supporting the claim made by the sentence 'John and Mary are in love'. But

---

[1] Philip P. Wiener, ed., *Leibniz: Selections* (New York, 1951), p. 223. This is, of course, not to suggest that Leibniz understood by the relativity of space exactly what Einstein understood by it. There is some common content, however; the denial of Newtonian absolute space is one univocal point.

he may not know that these are signs and not criteria. He may think that 'John and Mary are in love' *means* that John often brings candy or flowers, that Mary blushes in John's presence, that they hold hands, etc. In other words, the child may think that 'in love' is a shorthand description of a particular set of behaviour patterns existing in the relationship between two grown-ups of the opposite sex. Even with this misunderstanding he will be able to use 'in love' on new occasions appropriately, but he still will not know the meaning of 'John and Mary are in love'.

It does not follow that a child cannot correctly understand sentences employing the expression 'in love' before he has himself experienced this kind of love. On the contrary, it is possible to explain the criteria, or some of the criteria, of 'in love' to a child so that he understands them, even before he has experienced the corresponding affection himself. But if the child is given only the signs or evidence for 'in love' and not the criteria, he will not know the meaning of sentences such as 'John and Mary are in love'. He will know *that* they are in love without knowing *what it is* to be in love. Since it is possible for a person to be in a position comparable to the child's, knowing the checking procedures for p is not a sufficient condition for knowing the meaning of 'p'.

But it is also possible for a person to know that the checking procedures are checking procedures rather than criteria and still not know the meaning of 'p'. 'Space is relative' will serve as an illustration again. A person might well understand how to do the Michelson-Morley experiment (having perhaps performed it himself) and know that it is the classical support for the sophis-ticated scientific claim that space is relative, and still not understand the meaning of 'Space is relative'. The experiment does not give the meaning of that claim (although one might fortuitously come to understand that claim while doing the experiment or while pondering it), and a person could under-stand how to do the experiment without understanding the claim prior to doing the experiment and without coming to understand the claim while doing or by doing the experiment. So, knowing the checking procedures for p is neither a necessary nor a sufficient condition for knowing the meaning of 'p'.

A qualification needs to be added to the rejection of the second version of the checkability theory. It sometimes happens that from a knowledge of the checking procedures for p we can guess at least some of the criteria of cognitive meaning for 'p'. From the knowledge that the sentence 'Put a piece of blue litmus paper into this liquid, and the paper will turn red; add an alkali to this liquid, and the alkali will be neutralized; etc.' is used to state the test prescriptions or checking procedures for the statement made by the sentence 'This liquid is an acid', we might readily guess that some such sentence as 'This liquid can turn blue litmus paper red, can neutralize alkalis, etc.' was a statement of the truth-conditions (criteria) for 'This liquid is an acid'. And from the knowledge that an X-ray photograph revealing the presence of a foetus adhering to the wall of Mrs Jones's uterus constituted conclusive evidence that Mrs Jones is pregnant, we might not find it difficult to guess that the claim stated by 'Mrs Jones is pregnant' has something to do with the presence of a foetus in her womb. But since this is frequently not the case (witness the 'Space is relative' example above), no general theory can be built upon the instances where it does happen.

With the disqualification of the first two versions of the checkability theory of meaning, we are obliged to dissociate the meaning of 'p' from the checking procedures (methods of checking, test prescriptions) and the checking conditions (evidence) for p. The remaining version of the theory proposes a connection, not between *meaning* and checkability, but between *meaningfulness* and checkability.

'Being used to make a checkable statement (or knowing that a statement is checkable) is a necessary and sufficient, or a necessary, or a sufficient condition of the corresponding sentence being cognitively significant (or knowing that the corresponding sentence is cognitively significant).' This version of the theory is compound and presents two separate claims—one of them following from a statement's *being* checkable (i.e., having checking procedures) and the other from our *knowing* that a statement is checkable. It will be argued here that p's being checkable is not a necessary condition of the cognitive significant of 'p', and that knowing that p is checkable is also not necessary for knowing that 'p' is cognitively significant. It will also be argued, on the other hand, that p's being checkable is a sufficient condition of the cognitive significance of 'p', and that knowing that p is checkable is also sufficient for knowing that 'p' is cognitively significant. The proof of the latter point forms the climax of this portion of the study, for it states the only connection which obtains between cognitive meaning or meaningfulness and checkability. It states, that is to say, the only tenable version of the checkability theory of meaning.

Let us begin with the easiest portion of the argumentation on this version of the checkability theory—the claim that knowing p to be checkable is a necessary condition for knowing that 'p' is cognitively significant. This claim is false. By analogy with the refutation used on the claim that knowing the checking procedures for p is necessary for knowing the meaning of 'p', we may argue that the present claim is false in view of the possibility of knowing some of the entailments or incompatibles of p (or even knowing *that* p *has* entailments or incompatibles without knowing *what* they are specifically) while being completely ignorant of p's checking procedures (or even ignorant of the fact that p has checking procedures).

It has been shown above that a statement's having entailments and incompatibles is both a necessary and sufficient condition for the cognitive meaningfulness of the sentence used in making that statement. It follows that knowing some of the entailments or incompatibles of a statement (or even knowing that a statement has entailments and incompatibles without knowing what they are specifically) is at least a sufficient condition for knowing that the sentence used in making that statement is cognitively meaningful. So, knowing that p is checkable is not necessary for knowing that 'p' is cognitively significant. This argument needs no illustration.

Secondly, p's being checkable is not necessary to the cognitive significance of 'p'. This point may be more difficult to grasp than the one preceding. As with the entire discussion of the checkability theory of meaning, the present point turns on the criteria-evidence distinction (already elaborated at length) and therefore can be made relatively swiftly. For 'p' to be cognitively significant *means* that there are specifiable criteria of cognitive meaning for 'p', and this in turn *means* that 'p' is used to make a statement p for which there are specifiable truth-conditions, conditions under which p would obtain in reality. There is nothing implicit in the notion of a cognitively significant 'p' about the checking conditions of p, conditions under which it would be known whether or not the truth-conditions for p obtain in reality. To repeat a former emphasis, it is one thing for p to be true and quite another for its truth to be checkable, one thing for p to have truth-conditions (for 'p' to have criteria of cognitive significance) and quite another for it to have checking-conditions (evidence). The idea, therefore, of p's being indeed true but in principle uncheckable is completely coherent and its corollary—that 'p' is cognitively significant while p is in principle uncheckable—internally consistent. Since ' "p" is cognitively significant' does not entail 'p is checkable', it is no contradiction to assert the former while denying the latter. Checkability, in short, is not a semantically necessary condition of cognitive significance. Unless I am missing an undetected sense of 'necessary condition' (But what could it be?), it follows immediately that the checkability of p is not a necessary condition of the cognitive significance of 'p'.

This would hold even if it were to prove impossible to cite examples of cognitively significant sentences which were used to make in principle uncheckable statements. For the point here is purely theoretical and abstract and has to do strictly with the inter-conceptuality of cognitive significance and checkability. Even if there were for every cognitively significant 'p' a checkable p, even if in other words there were a constant conjunction or correlation between cognitively significant sentences and checkable statements, it could not be concluded therefrom that the checkability of p is a necessary condition of the cognitive significance of 'p'. The constant conjunction of x and y does imply the dependence of one upon the other; other features explaining such a correlation could be appealed to. Cognitive significance, to reiterate, is a matter of criteria not evidence, and criteria are quite independent of evidence. To be sure, when 'p' is cognitively significant, in all probability there *will* be some way of determining the truth or falsity of p. But it is not the case that there *must* be. A cognitively significant 'p' must have *criteria*, but the corresponding p need not have *evidence*.

We come now to the climax of our investigation of the checkability theory of meaning. It would be pointless duplication to prove separately that p's having checking procedures or being checkable is a sufficient condition of the cognitive significance of 'p' and that knowing that p is checkable is sufficient for knowing that 'p' is cognitively significant.[1] These two points can be proved together with a single, brief argument: When we say of a statement that it has checking procedures or is checkable, we have already said that the sentence used in making it is cognitively significant. On pages 32–33, we saw that 'cognitively significant' could be explicated in terms of 'true' and 'false' among other explicata. To establish that a statement is true or false (the work of checking procedures), therefore, is *ipso facto* to establish that the sentence used in making that statement is cognitively significant. This is so because of the relation of *presupposition*: 'p is checkable' presupposes ' "p" is cognitively significant', that is to say, the question of the checkability of p fails to arise unless 'p' is antecedently (in the logical sense) cognitively significant. How could p be checkable unless 'p' were cognitively significant? If p is in fact checkable, therefore, 'p' must be cognitively significant. Cognitive significance is a precondition, a presupposition, of checkability, making the latter a sufficient condition of the former. And with this argument, it has been demonstrated that there is (and what it is) a connection between cognitive meaning and/or meaningfulness and checkability.

3. CHECKABILITY AND 'G'-SENTENCES

The question remains: 'Does the fact that checking procedures for p is a sufficient condition of the cognitive significance of "p" sustain the metatheological sceptic's prime argument?' That argument, to repeat, contends that 'G'-sentences are not cognitively significant because G-statements are not checkable. It is easily seen that our discussion of the actual connexion between checkability and cognitive meaningfulness does not

---

[1] This does not imply that everyone who knows that p is checkable also knows that 'p' is cognitively significant, of course. For a person may know that p is checkable but not understand the meaning of 'cognitively significant'. That understanding is presupposed by my thesis, and so the difficulty mentioned is averted.

sustain the metatheological sceptic's argument. For that argument holds only if checkability is a necessary condition for cognitive meaningfulness. On the basis of previous argumentation, it is legitimately contended that G-statements need not be checkable in order for their corresponding 'G'-sentences to be cognitively significant.

From this we can conclude that there is no obligation to show G-statements in principle or in fact verifiable or falsifiable in order to prove that their corresponding 'G'-sentences are cognitively significant. If it can be shown that those G-statements have entailments and incompatibles reflecting their truth- and falsity-conditions, that would suffice. But if it can be shown that G-statements have checking procedures as well as entailments and incompatibles, then the basis will be twice as strong for asserting that G-statements are actual in contrast to merely putative statements and that their corresponding 'G'-sentences are in fact cognitively significant.

Since two grounds for a claim are better than one, and since the metatheological sceptic might be expected to acquiesce more readily to the argument from the checkability of G-statements to the cognitive significance of 'G'-sentences, and since this entire study is conceived as a dialogue with the metatheological sceptic, we must embark on an exploration of the question of the checkability of G-statements. In Chapters III and IV, we shall see what the metatheological sceptics (two of them, at any rate, but these two are typical) have said against the checkability of G-statements. Then in Chapters V and VI, we shall learn what can be said on behalf of the checkability of G-statements.

CHAPTER III

THE CHALLENGERS (I)

———————

Are G-statements checkable? The minor premise in meta-theological scepticism's prime argument, denying the check-ability and hence the actuality of G-statements, must now be confronted and tested. Though the major premise—that checkability is *sine qua non* for cognitivity—has already been diagnosed at the level of generality, it too must now be coped with concretely, in the writings of its actual advocates.

Two metatheological sceptics whose contributions have elicited a great deal of comment—Antony Flew and R. B. Braithwaite—have been selected to represent the position of metatheological scepticism and to open up the falsifiability and verifiability debates respectively in this chapter and the next. The most intense and sustained debate in the recent meta-theological literature has focused on the falsifiability issue: Are G-statements falsifiable or not?[1] Flew's article on theology

———————

[1] Wisdom's 'Gods' provided the seminal idea for a symposium (in the now defunct periodical, *University*) which included papers by A. Flew, Fr. Corbishley, P. Nowell-Smith, R. M. Hare, M. Foster, B. Mitchell and Dom Illyd Trethowan. All of these papers are conveniently summarized in H. D. Lewis, 'Philosophical Surveys X: The Philosophy of Religion, 1945-1952', *Philosophical Quarterly*, IV (1954): 167-168. The articles by Flew, Hare, and Mitchell, together with a rejoinder to Hare and Mitchell by Flew and an incisive supplement by I. M. Crombie, have been reprinted in *New Essays*, pp. 96-130.

Quite a following has consolidated around the viewpoint Flew expressed on falsification in the seminal article. His supporters include: William T. Blackstone, *The Problem of Religious Knowledge*, pp. 20-21, 47-54, 73-76, 167; R. B. Braithwaite, *An Empiricist's View of the Nature of Religious Belief*, pp. 1-8; Gerald F. Downing, *Has Christianity a Revelation?*, pp. 171-175; D. R. Duff-Forbes, 'Theology and Falsification Again', *Australasian Journal of Philosophy*, XXXIX (1961): 143-154; Ronald W. Hepburn, *Christianity and Paradox*, pp. 11-15; and Kai Nielsen, 'Can Faith Validate God-Talk?', *Theology Today*, XX (1963): 158-173, 'On Fixing the Reference Range of "God" ', *Religious Studies*, II (1966): 13-36, and 'Wittgen-steinian Fideism', *Philosophy*, XLII (1967): 191-209. The second article of Nielsen's mentioned here is answered by Illyd Trethowan, 'In Defence of Theism—A Reply to Kai Nielsen', *Religious Studies*, II (1966): 37-48. Flew undertakes on behalf of Mitchell and Crombie to straighten Duff-Forbes out on a point or two in 'Falsification and Hypothesis in Theology', *Australasian Journal of Philosophy*, XL (1962):

and falsification has had a catalytic effect upon the thinking of practically every theorist who has participated in this debate since the publication of that article. While praising the article for promoting discussion, its contents must be disputed on three counts: the assumption that the meaning of a sentence is equivalent to the empirical expectations of the statement it makes, the identification of the 'counts against' relation with the 'is incompatible with' relation (i.e., the conflation of falsifiability with incompatibility), and the concluding suggestion that G-statements are in principle unfalsifiable.

1. THE PARABLE OF THE GARDENER

In his adaptation of Wisdom's (in 'Gods') parable of the two explorers, with which he opens his paper, Flew assumes that the meaning of a sentence is equivalent to the empirical expectations of the statement it makes. The parable goes like this: Two explorers, one a believer and the other a sceptic, come across a clearing in the jungle in which many flowers and weeds are growing. The sceptic queries the believer's assertion

---

318-323, and is countered by Duff-Forbes in 'Reply to Professor Flew', *Australasian Journal of Philosophy*, XL (1962): 324-327. Flew has reaffirmed his original stand on theology and falsification (albeit in a *seemingly* more lenient formulation) in *God and Philosophy*, pp. 22, 39-40, 144-145, though in this book his emphasis shifts from the falsification problem to proving that there are no criteria for singling out the reference to 'God', that the predicates applied to God are unintelligible, and that there are logical inconsistencies within the notion of God. Among those who agree with Flew that G-statements are unfalsifiable but disagree with his inference that 'G'-sentences are therefore cognitively meaningless are John Hick, *Faith and Knowledge*, pp. 145-148, 156, *Philosophy of Religion*, pp. 94-106, and 'Theology and Verification', *Theology Today*, XVII (1960): 15-17; and A. MacIntyre, 'The Logical Status of Religious Beliefs', in MacIntyre, ed., *Metaphysical Beliefs*, pp. 180-182.

Flew's basic position of falsifiability has been attacked by Frederick Copleston, *Contemporary Philosophy*, pp. 99-101; A. C. Ewing, 'Religious Assertions in the Light of Contemporary Philosophy', *Philosophy*, XXXII (1957): 214-216; A. Boyce Gibson, 'Empirical Evidence and Religious Faith', *Journal of Religion*, XXXVI (1956): 24-35; Gareth B. Matthews, 'Theology and Natural Theology', *Journal of Philosophy*, LXI (1964): 99-108; Thomas McPherson, *The Philosophy of Religion*, pp. 185-186, 195-196; and Schubert M. Ogden, 'God and Philosophy: A Discussion with Antony Flew', *Journal of Religion*, XLVIII (1968): 161-181. Flew exchanges views with Ogden in 'Reflections on "The Reality of God"', *Journal of Religion*, XLVIII (1968): 150-161. McPherson's remarks are to my way of thinking particularly adroit, for he is cognizant of the negative implications for Flew's position of a strict criteria-evidence distinction.

that a gardener must tend the plot, demanding of the believer that empirical expectations be stipulated and that tests be made. They set up a watch, they encircle the clearing with an electric fence, they patrol with bloodhounds. But they see no one, hear nothing and the bloodhounds never give indication that a scent has been picked up. As the empirical expectations are unfulfilled one by one, the believer qualifies his original assertion, maintaining first that the gardener is invisible, then that he is intangible, then that he is inaudible, etc., until the sceptic finally exclaims in exasperation: ' "But what remains of your original assertion? Just how does what you call an invisible, intangible, eternally elusive gardener differ from an imaginary gardener or even from no gardener at all?" '[1]

The sceptic's question is quite obviously Flew's own, and its implications reveal the presuppositions in Flew's approach to the problem of the falsifiability of G-statements and the cognitive significance of 'G'-sentences. First, the question implies that there is no difference in cognitive meaning among 'An invisible, intangible, eternally elusive gardener tends this plot', 'An imaginary gardener tends this plot', and 'No gardener tends this plot'. Secondly, the parable and the question suggest that checking out the empirical expectations prompted by the statements these three sentences are used to make is the only checking procedure relevant to those statements. And thirdly, Flew's question would carry no weight at all unless one were willing to grant that only a difference in empirical expectations (and hence in checking procedure) marks off two or more sentences as making different assertions. So the question bears the implication also that the empirical expectations as well as the meaning of these three sentences are the same for each, indeed that the meaning is the same expressly *because* the empirical expectations are the same.

The whole parable illustrates Flew's commitment to the position that the meaning of a cognitive sentence is equivalent to the empirical expectations of the statement that sentence makes. For he claims by implication that two sentences have the same meaning if and only if the statements they make have the same empirical expectations and different meaning if and only if those statements have different empirical expecta-

[1] *New Essays*, p. 96.

tions. His implicit identification of empirical expectations and checking procedures constitutes this claim as a corollary of the theory (rejected in the preceding chapter) that the meaning of a cognitive sentence is equivalent to the checking procedures for the statement it makes. It is hardly necessary to reaffirm against this theory and its corollary that identity of criteria (not evidence) proves identity of meaning between two sentences, and difference of criteria (not evidence) proves difference of meaning.

Inasmuch as Flew's parable must be understood as a meta-theological sceptic's commentary on the unfalsifiability of G-statements and the cognitive meaninglessness of 'G'-sentences, and inasmuch as his commentary is predicated upon a version of the checkability theory of meaning (i.e., the meaning of a sentence is equivalent to the empirical expectations of the statement it makes), his position can be attacked on two fronts: The theory behind the position (the checkability theory of meaning) can be attacked by reference to the critique of it worked out in Chapter II. And the application of that theory in the parable can be attacked by taking issue with Flew's insinuations that 'An invisible, intangible, eternally elusive gardener tends this plot', 'An imaginary gardener tends this plot', and 'No gardener tends this plot' all have the same meaning, empirical expectations, and checking procedures. Since the first line of attack has in effect already been secured, we shall pursue the second.

Can a case be made for the synonymity of 'An invisible, intangible, eternally elusive gardener tends this plot', 'An imaginary gardener tends this plot', and 'No gardener tends this plot'? We shall see presently that no such case can be made even with the help of the checkability theory (for the statements these sentences make do in fact differ in checking procedures). How much less of a case can be made when we approach the meaning of these sentences without any preconceived notions about meaning and checkability! Setting aside the second of the three sentences momentarily, a close look at 'An invisible, intangible, eternally elusive gardener tends this plot' and 'No gardener tends this plot' discloses that the two have different criteria (as reflected by their presuppositions and entailments) and hence different meanings.

To begin with, the first sentence makes a statement which presupposes commitment to the existence of a gardener, though it places him outside the empirical domain of discourse. 'No gardener tends this plot', on the other hand, makes a statement which presupposes denial of the existence of a gardener without specifying the empirical domain of discourse or some other. If the statement made by 'No gardener tends this plot' presupposes denial of the existence of an empirical gardener, then that statement and the statement made by 'An invisible, intangible, eternally elusive gardener tends this plot' have compatible existential presuppositions, which in no way is tantamount to admitting that the two sentences involved have the same meaning. If, on the other hand, the statement made by 'No gardener tends this plot' presupposes denial of the existence of any sort of gardener empirical or non-empirical, then this presupposition is radically incompatible with the existential presupposition of the statement made by 'An invisible, intangible, eternally elusive gardener tends this plot'. Since a difference in existential presuppositions (even when compatible) indicates a difference in meaning between two sentences, we have one good reason for denying the proposed synonymity of the two sentences involved.

In the second place, the statement made by 'An invisible, intangible, eternally elusive gardener tends this plot' entails a causal hypothesis, due to the fact that 'tends' is a causal verb. That entailment might be expressed by the sentence 'An invisible, intangible, eternally elusive gardener causes this plot to be the way it is'. The entailment makes clear that 'An invisible, intangible, eternally elusive gardener tends this plot' is an attempt to account causally for the phenomenon that the two explorers encounter in the jungle clearing. The statement made by 'No gardener tends this plot', however, entails a denial of that causal hypothesis, if its reference extends beyond the empirical domain of discourse. If that statement applies only the the empirical domain, of course, though it still entails the denial of a causal hypothesis (i.e., the denial that an empirical gardener causes this plot to be the way it is), it does not entail the denial of the causal hypothesis which is entailed by the statement which 'An invisible, intangible, eternally elusive gardener tends this plot' is used to make. The entail-

F

ments of the statement made by the two sentences in question are different entailments even under that interpretation of the two sentences which renders those entailments compatible. Compatibility of entailments is in no way tantamount to the synonymity of the sentences making the statements which have those entailments. 'An invisible, intangible, eternally elusive gardener tends this plot' and 'No gardener tends this plot' make statements which, even when compatible (and under one interpretation they are not), have different existential pre-suppositions and entailments, hence different criteria, and hence different meanings.

Another status altogether must be accorded to 'An imaginary gardener tends this plot'. The first two sentences we considered, though different in meaning, were both intelligible. The remaining sentence of the three differs from the first two by lacking any straightforward cognitive sense. It could perhaps be used to make a joke, but it could not be used to make a serious assertion. The explanation for the inability of this sentence to make a serious assertion is to be found in the fact that it violates certain semantical type-restrictions governing the sorts of subject-expressions that will combine with causal predicate-expressions to form cognitively significant sentences.[1] The subject-expression in this case, 'an imaginary gardener', belongs to the imaginary or fictional domain of discourse, whereas the predicate-expression 'tends this plot' belongs to the empirical domain of discourse. The combination of the two fails to make sense, because it makes no sense to attribute a phenom-enon in the empirical world to a causal agent in the fictional or imaginary world.

Flew would probably retort that the same criticism holds for 'an invisible, intangible, eternally elusive gardener' if it holds for 'an imaginary gardener' and that his ultimate point in the parable was to bring out this criticism. But the two cases are not really parallel. The problem inherent in 'An invisible, in-tangible, eternally elusive gardener tends this plot' is explaining *how* a causal agent outside the empirical world can bring about a phenomenon in the empirical world (compare the mind-body

---

[1] See pp. 180–183 for an elaboration of the role of type-restrictions in deter-mining the sense or lack of sense in grammatically well-formed English sentences.

problem). Inasmuch as the invisible, intangible, eternally elusive gardener is a stand-in for God, however, there is no question of a violation of type-restrictions in 'An invisible, intangible, eternally elusive gardener tends this plot', because God *in concept* is an agent who can interact causally with the empirical world, though it is difficult to elaborate a theory explaining how he can do this. An imaginary gardener, on the other hand, is *in concept* unable to effect causal action in the empirical world. What the semantical type-restrictions allow to God (and by extension to an invisible, intangible, eternally elusive gardener) they forbid to the imaginary gardener.

Flew asks just how an invisible, intangible, eternally elusive gardener differs from an imaginary gardener or even from no gardener at all. The first part of the answer to his question is that when 'an invisible, intangible, eternally elusive gardener', 'an imaginary gardener', and 'no gardener' are put into grammatically well-formed English sentences, 'An invisible, intangible, eternally elusive gardener tends this plot' and 'No gardener tends this plot' differ in meaning because the statements they make have different existential presuppositions and entailments, and 'An imaginary gardener tends this plot' fails to make any straightforward cognitive sense at all. As we go on to inquire about the sameness or difference of the empirical expectations and other (if any) checking procedures for the statements made by these sentences, 'An imaginary gardener tends this plot' will drop out of the discussion. If a sentence has no cognitive meaning, it goes without saying that it cannot be used to make a statement which is checkable by empirical expectations or any other sort of checking procedure.

Can a case be made for the claim that the statements made by 'An invisible, intangible, eternally elusive gardener tends this plot' and 'No gardener tends this plot' have the same empirical expectations? The answer to this question is a qualified 'yes': They have the same empirical expectations, but only if a particular construction is put on 'No gardener tends this plot' rather than another possible construction, and only if the statement made by 'An invisible, intangible, eternally elusive gardener tends this plot' is subject to verification by some type of evidence other than empirical expectations apropos the gardener.

It is significant that Flew suggests, not that 'An invisible, intangible, eternally elusive gardener tends this plot' is meaningless because bereft of empirical expectations (though that may be his thrust in the last analysis), but that this sentence is equivalent in sense to 'No gardener tends this plot' because the statements made by both have the same empirical expectations. Evidently he has in mind the expectation that the routine empirical expectations for the statement made by 'An empirical gardener tends this plot' (i.e., seeing, hearing, smelling, touching an empirically real gardener, or perhaps receiving reliable reports from someone who has) will not be fulfilled, which expectation itself can be fulfilled. For Flew, therefore, both sentences make statements which give rise to the same empirical expectations, namely the negative expectation that something (an empirical gardener) will not be sensed, that certain empirical tests (such as setting a watch, posting bloodhounds, rigging an electric fence, etc.) will fail.

Flew is correct in this estimate, as was stated above, only if two qualifications are added. The two sentences in question make statements which share the same negative empirical expectations in the first place only if 'No gardener tends this plot' is taken to mean 'No *empirical* gardener tends this plot' rather than 'No *real but non-empirical* gardener tends this plot'. For the latter makes a statement which has no negative empirical expectations at all, and therefore differs in empirical expectations from the statements made by 'An invisible intangible, eternally elusive gardener tends this plot' and 'No empirical gardener tends this plot'. That is to say, if a person asserts 'No invisible, intangible, eternally elusive gardener tends this plot' he does not expect that the absence of the sights, sounds, smells, etc., relevant to testing for a *visible, tangible* (i.e., empirical) gardener will count *for* his assertion. But the person who says 'No empirical gardener tends this plot' *does* expect that the absence of the empirical cues relevant to an empirical gardener will corroborate his claim and corroborate it conclusively.

The two sentences in question make statements which share the same negative empirical expectations in the second place only if the statement made by 'An invisible, intangible, eternally elusive gardener tends this plot' draws positive support from some source. For the absence of the empirical cues for an empirical gardener counts for that statement only inconclusively and provisionally, and unless there is independent evidence arguing for the presence of a real (in contrast to an imaginary) gardener of some sort these negative empirical expectations do not count for the statement at all. This is in effect to say that the statement made by 'An invisible, intangible, eternally elusive gardener tends this plot' must have support from some source other than empirical expectations about an empirical gardener before the absence of such expectations can in fact count for it. And this point leads us to question Flew's implication that empirical expectations are the only checking procedure relevant to the statements made by the sentences in question.

Can a case be made, in other words, for the implicit claim that the statements made by 'An invisible, intangible, eternally elusive gardener tends this plot' and 'No empirical gardener tends this plot' have the same checking procedures when checking procedures are not necessarily limited to empirical expectations apropos the gardener? The answer here is plainly 'no', even if we concede that those empirical expectations (i.e., the negative expectation that the positive empirical expectations for an empirical gardener will be unfulfilled) are the same. For certain features of *the plot itself* are relevant to the determination of the truth or falsity of the statements made by the sentences in question, features which would have to be entirely different when each of these statements was judged true.

Consider the description we are given of the plot itself. Flew makes his case easier for himself by taking a situation which is ambiguous to begin with. The two explorers come across a clearing in the jungle in which both flowers and weeds are growing. Why *both* flowers *and* weeds? One might expect to discover clearings in the jungle, to find weeds growing in those clearings, even to find a few scattered flowers growing among the weeds—all this without being particularly struck by the notion that maybe a gardener was responsible for the situation.

But suppose one chanced across a clearing in the densest part of the jungle and found in it no weeds at all, but only flowers planted in neat, geometrical, carefully cultivated rows— flowers indigenous to an entirely foreign locale and which had never been found growing in this area before. Suppose further that there were irrigation ditches extending from the river, that weeds never appeared nor did the jungle ever require to be trimmed back, that the whole plot was surrounded by a white picket fence that never needed fresh paint. What would one want to say then? These are all features of the plot, but do they not form a garden-pattern signifying the agency of a gardener of some sort? Given a plot in the jungle manifesting the garden-pattern that clearly, would it be irrational to infer that some sort of gardener tended the plot?[1]

Only under circumstances something like this and in conjunction with them would the absence of the cues and empirical expectations for an empirical gardener count for the statement made by 'An invisible, intangible, eternally elusive gardener tends this plot'. If at the conclusion of Flew's gardener parable we feel uneasy (Flew wants us to feel uneasy and has constructed the parable so that it will make us feel uneasy) about uttering the sentence 'An invisible, intangible, eternally elusive gardener tends this plot', we are uneasy not because that sentence is *meaningless* but because the statement it expresses is *unwarranted* given the ambiguous flowers-and-weeds situation Flew presents us with as original data. Implausibility is one thing, unintelligibility quite another.

If the claims made by 'An invisible, intangible, eternally elusive gardener tends this plot' and 'No gardener tends this plot' are to be checked not only by looking for an empirical gardener (and expecting to be disappointed) but first by looking at the plot to see whether or not it manifests a garden-pattern, then we must conclude that the specific checking procedures or test prescriptions for these two claims are diametrically opposed. The test prescription for the statement made by 'An invisible, intangible, eternally elusive gardener tends this plot' would read: 'Look at the plot, and the garden-pattern will be definitely *present*.' But the test prescription for the statement made by 'No gardener tends this plot' would read: 'Look at the plot, and the garden-pattern will be definitely *absent*.' The claims made by the two sentences in question,

---

[1] For an extensive elaboration of the philosophical rationale for such inferences, see the discussion of sign reasoning in Chapter VI, pages 205–212 and 217–244 especially. See also the trenchant remarks of John Wisdom in *Paradox and Discovery*, pp. 20–22, as well as his article 'Gods', *op. cit.*

therefore, differ in their primary checking procedure (expecting the garden-pattern to be present in the original data as opposed to expecting that pattern to be absent from the data), even though they might agree in their secondary checking procedure (expecting not to find an empirical gardener).

Flew asks how an invisible, intangible, eternally elusive gardener differs from an imaginary gardener or even from no gardener at all. The answer implicit in the question is that there is no significant difference at all. His conviction that the sentences formulated from these three subject-expressions have the same meaning results from his convictions that the statements made by the three sentences have the same checking procedures (which for him means the same empirical expectations) and that the meaning of a sentence is equivalent to the checking procedures for the statement it makes (a version of the checkability theory of meaning with the criteria-evidence conflation built in).

Over against Flew's position in the gardener parable, it has been urged that 'An imaginary gardener tends this plot' lacks straightforward cognitive meaning and that 'An invisible, intangible, eternally elusive gardener tends this plot' and 'No gardener tends this plot' have different cognitive meanings because they are governed by different criteria as reflected by differing existential presuppositions and entailments. It has been urged also that the primary checking procedures for the statements made by these two sentences differ and that their secondary checking procedure (looking for an empirical gardener) agree only provisionally. These findings should suffice to show up the basic faults in Flew's employment of the gardener parable. The gardener/God parable is, nevertheless, ingenious and useful, and the analysis here of empirical checking procedures for the statement made by 'An invisible, intangible, eternally elusive gardener tends this plot' adumbrates the discussion of the verifiability of G-statements in Chapter VI.

2. FALSIFIABILITY AND INCOMPATIBILITY

We have just seen how the criteria-evidence conflation, Flew's root error, manifests itself in his conviction that the meaning of a sentence is equivalent to the empirical expectations of the statement it makes. That error manifests itself again in his identification of the 'counts against' relation with the 'is incompatible with' relation—the conflation of falsifiability and incompatibility. After developing the parable of the two explorers for the purpose of suggesting that affirmations about God differ in no significant respect from affirmations about imaginary entities or even from denials about God, he proceeds to expound in terms of a figure what he calls 'the endemic evil of theological utterance': 'A fine brash hypothesis may thus be killed by inches, the death by a thousand qualifications.'[1] It is his contention that every qualification ('invisible', 'intangible', etc.) which is added to the sentence 'A gardener tends this plot' erodes away its cognitive meaning.[2]

That the doctrine underlying the figures of killing a hypothesis and of eroding away the meaning of a sentence is the version of the checkability theory of meaning which maintains that the meaning of a sentence is the method of checking the statement it makes is obvious from what Flew says in the same general context:[3]

---

[1] *Ibid.*, p. 97.

[2] It is worth noting that Karl Popper would take issue with Flew on his use of falsifiability as a criterion of meaning. Popper is adamant in his belief that falsifiability is useful only as a criterion of demarcation for distinguishing scientific theories from non-scientific theories (i.e., metaphysical theories), but not as a criterion of meaning. See *The Logic of Scientific Discovery*, English Edition (London, 1959), pp. 35-37, 40-42.

I certainly agree with Popper, over against Flew, that falsifiability is not a criterion of meaning. But at the same time I disagree with Popper's view that falsifiability is the criterion for demarcating scientific theories from non-scientific. I hope to show in Chapter V that at least some G-statements are conclusively falsifiable on empirical grounds alone. If that is so, then on Popper's premises these G-statements would have to be put into the category of 'scientific theories', an arrangement which would displease the theologian as much as the scientist. Of course, Popper could by stipulation *make* falsifiability the criterion of demarcation, but this would result in stretching the meaning of 'scientific' way out of shape by including in that category statements which we do not *ordinarily* regard as having anything to do with science, unless 'scientific' were taken in its generic sense to mean simply 'cognitively meaningful'. But even if 'scientific' were taken by Popper in its generic sense, falsifiability would still not qualify as the criterion of demarcation. For falsifiability is only a sufficient and not a necessary condition of cognitive meaningfulness, as we saw in the preceding chapter. Popper, on the other hand, requires a condition which is both necessary and sufficient to serve as the criterion of demarcation. There are pressing objections, therefore, to regarding falsifiability as either a criterion of meaning with Flew or as the criterion of demarcation with Popper.

[3] Passmore, *op. cit.*, p. 127, brings this out. He also thinks that Flew's adherence

Now to assert that such and such is the case is necessarily equivalent to denying that such and such is not the case. Suppose then that we are in doubt as to what someone who gives vent to an utterance is asserting, or suppose that, more radically, we are sceptical as to whether he is really asserting anything at all, one way of trying to understand (or perhaps it will be to expose) his utterance is to attempt to find what he would regard *as counting against, or as being incompatible with, its truth.* For if the utterance is indeed an assertion, it will necessarily be equivalent to a denial of the negation of that assertion. *And anything which would count against the assertion, or which would induce the speaker to withdraw it and to admit that it had been mistaken, must be part of (or the whole of) the meaning of the negation of that assertion.* And to know the meaning of the negation of an assertion, is as near as makes no matter, to know the meaning of that assertion. And if there is nothing which a putative assertion denies then there is nothing which it asserts either: and so it is not really an assertion.[1]

This is the decisive passage in Flew's essay, and it reveals two things. It reveals, first of all, that Flew is incognizant of any difference whatsoever between falsifiability and incompatibility or between the meaning of the expressions 'counts against' and 'is incompatible with' (which he equates by means of an epexegetic 'or' in the passage quoted). He is absolutely right when he says that if we know the incompatibles of a statement we know part or all of the meaning of the sentence which states the negation of that statement. That is, if we know that the statement made by 'Mrs Jones does not have an embryo or foetus in her womb' is incompatible with the statement made by 'Mrs Jones is pregnant', then we know part or all of the meaning of 'Mrs Jones is not pregnant'. But when he makes the

---

to the checkability theory assumes a milder (though still unsatisfactory) form at the end of the essay. When Flew asks in closing, ' "What would have to occur or to have occurred to constitute for you a disproof of the love of, or of the existence of God?" ', Passmore sees in the question that modification of the theory which says that a proposition is meaningless unless its proponent will admit that in certain circumstances it can be falsified. This weakened version of the checkability theory is still unsatisfactory, because, as stressed before, falsifiability is a sufficient but not a necessary condition of cognitive meaningfulness. It follows that unfalsifiability is necessary but not sufficient for cognitive meaninglessness.

[1] Flew, *op. cit.*, p. 98 (Italics mine).

same allegation for negative evidence (that which would count against a statement), saying that it gives part or all of the meaning of the sentence which states the negation of the statement that evidence counts against, he is patently wrong. Negative results from the rabbit and/or frog test(s) do not give part or all of the meaning of 'Mrs Jones is not pregnant'.

The passage reveals, in the second place, what was only dimly apparent in the passages we considered in the previous section of this chapter: When Flew speaks of a method for exposing the meaninglessness of certain sentences in the context of a discussion of whether or not 'G'-sentences are cognitively meaningful, there is the very strong suggestion (though he never comes right out with it) that he believes 'G'-sentences are cognitively meaningless because the statements they make are in principle unfalsifiable. This suggestion becomes even stronger as we approach the end of the paper.

3. CHECKING ON THE LOVE OF GOD

Flew closes his paper with an expression of at least provisional belief that G-statements are unfalsifiable in principle. He finds himself unable to specify any falsification procedures, and by concluding with the following question he challenges his fellow symposiasts to specify some: ' "What would have to occur or to have occurred to constitute for you a disproof of the love of, or the existence of, God?" '[1] The question seems to connote that Flew thinks the challenge cannot be met.

Without elaborating in full detail my theory of the falsifiability of G-statements (the project of Chapter V), I would like to take up Flew's challenge for someone to attempt to specify falsification procedures for the statements made by the sentences 'God loves all human beings' and 'God exists' as they are understood within the context of classical Christian theism. I shall not contend that these two G-statements are in practice either verified or falsified, but only that they are in principle falsifiable (with some qualifications in the case of the latter G-statement). And while specifying the falsification procedures, it will be convenient to delve into their verification procedures as well.

[1] *Ibid.*, p. 99.

'God loves all human beings' poses the God problem compounded with the other minds problem: The statement this
sentence is used to make is at once a G-statement (because of
'God') and an other-minds statement (because of 'loves'). The
entailments and incompatibles which can be used as criteria for
laying down the meaning of 'God loves all human beings' are
also both G-statements and other-minds statements. 'God is
aware of humans as existing beings, is interested in humans and
their destiny, has a benevolent concern for human well-being,
wills their well-being and happiness (salvation), desires to
give something of himself toward that well-being'[1] would
state entailments of and hence could be used as positive criteria
of 'God loves all human beings', while 'God wills the eternal
damnation and misery of all human beings'[2] would state an

[1] Each conjunct of this sentence states a separate entailment of the statement
made by 'God loves all human beings'. Taken together those conjuncts pretty well
exhaust the meaning of 'God loves all human beings', so that the two sentences are
for all intents and purposes synonymous or equivalent in meaning. It remains true,
however, that the longer sentence explicates the meaning of 'God loves all human
beings', detailing as it does the separate entailments of the statement that God loves
all human beings. The point, of course, is that we can explicate the meaning of 'God
loves all human beings', that we can list the entailments of the statement that
sentence makes, without delving into checking procedures.

[2] The logical incompatibility of the statements made by 'God loves all human
beings' and 'God wills the eternal damnation and misery of all human beings' is
recognized and made explicit by Copleston, *op. cit.*, pp. 99-101.
Though my account of the falsifiability of G-statements parallels Copleston's in
many respects, and though I am indebted to him for both ideas and examples, I
believe that in two passages he has fallen prey to Flew's error of conflating evidence
with criteria: (1) 'Now, it has been argued that a statement like "God loves all
human beings" *excludes* no other factual statement, and that on this account it has
no positive meaning. The Christian, it is said, will not allow that any other factual
statement *counts or can count against the truth of* the statement that God loves
human beings.' (2) 'But suppose that one asks the Christian theologian *why* he
makes the statement that God loves human beings. He may answer that he says this
because he believes that God offers all men through Christ the grace to attain eternal
salvation. *So interpreted*, the statement is incompatible with, and therefore excludes,
the statement that God wills the eternal damnation and misery of all human beings.'
Ibid., p. 100 (Italics mine).
In the first passage, the identification of the 'is incompatible with' (i.e., 'excludes') and the 'counts against' relations might possibly be excused on the ground
that here Copleston is simply aping Flew's idiom (it is quite likely that Copleston
has Flew in mind at this juncture). But in the second passage, where Copleston
identifies the 'is a reason for' and the 'is an interpretation of' relations, the conflation of evidence and criteria is patent. The statement made by the sentence 'God
offers all men through Christ the grace to attain eternal salvation' is in fact a
reason for the statement made by the sentence 'God loves all human beings', but
the former sentence is certainly not an interpretation of (i.e., equivalent in meaning

incompatible of and hence could be used as a negative criterion of 'God loves all human beings'. Since making a statement which has entailments and incompatibles is a necessary and sufficient conditions of cognitive meaningfulness, Flew's insinuation that 'God loves all human beings' has no cognitive meaning is refuted short of showing what would have to occur or to have occurred to constitute a disproof (or a proof) of the statement that God loves all human beings. If, however, checking procedures for that statement could be specified also, then we would have an additional reason for affirming the cognitive meaningfulness of 'God loves all human beings' (and a reason more acceptable to Flew, presumably), for checkability is a sufficient (though not a necessary) condition of cognitive meaning. What, then, would have to occur or to have occurred to constitute either a disproof or a proof of the statement that God loves all human beings?

It should come as no surprise, in view of our understanding of the workings of other-minds statements, that the evidence statements for and against the statement that God loves all human beings are not themselves other-minds statements. But it might seem strange that at least some—the crucial ones, in fact, from the standpoint of the actual reasoning processes of most classical Christian theologians—of the evidence statements for and against the statement of God's love for man are themselves G-statements, though not statements about bodily states. The evidence statements for and against other-minds

---

to) the latter. And the statement made by 'God wills the eternal damnation and misery of all human beings' is in fact incompatible with the statement made by 'God loves all human begins', but it certainly is not incompatible with the statement made by 'God offers all men through Christ the grace to attain eternal salvation'. That is to say, it is *logically* possible (though theologically preposterous) for God to *will* man's eternal damnation and still *offer* him eternal salvation. Language has not been misused or abused in asserting a conjunction of these two claims.

There is this further shortcoming to Copleston's account: Though he lists some of the evidence statements (mistakenly conflated with criteria) for the statement made by 'God loves all human beings', he leaves unanswered the pressing question of what in turn would count for these evidence statements. The statement made by 'God offers all men through Christ the grace to attain eternal salvation' counts for the statement made by 'God loves all human beings', it is true, but what would count for the former statement? Copleston leaves us with the uneasy feeling that possibly the system of G-statements in classical Christian theism is a closed circle, i.e., that only other G-statements can serve as evidence for G-statements. Since this is not the case, as will be shown in the present chapter and in Chapters V and VI, Copleston's account is critically deficient.

statements are ordinarily statements about bodily states, but God (in the sense in which 'God' is used in these evidence statements) is not a bodily being.[1]

Why should it seem strange, however, that some of the evidence statements for and against the statement of God's love for man are themselves G-statements? The primary and direct evidence statements for statements about Jones's mind are also statements about Jones (his bodily states) though not about his mind. Similarly, the primary and direct evidence statements for statements about God's mind are also statements about God (his actions in history, for example) though not about his mind. There are, of course, other evidence statements (secondary and indirect) for statements about Jones's mind which are not also statements about Jones's bodily states. E.g., the statement made by 'Smith, who visited Jones in the hospital, reports that Jones is in severe pain' has some bearing upon the acceptance of the statement made by 'Jones is in pain'. But the former statement, though the report it contains is doubtless based upon observations of Jones's bodily behaviour, is about Smith's bodily behaviour rather than Jones's. There are evidence statements for G-statements which are not also G-statements. However, just as the primary and direct evidence statements for statements about Jones's mind are also state-

---

[1] 'God' in classical Christian discourse is used in the incarnation strand as well as in the numinous strand. In the incarnation strand, 'God' *does* refer to a bodily being, specifically Jesus of Nazareth, as in 'God died for us on the cross'. See Ninian Smart, *op. cit.*, pp. 108-126. But the evidence statements at point here are part of the numinous rather than the incarnation strand.

The claim that 'God' in the numinous strand names a bodiless being undergoes a modification in the neoclassical theism of Charles Hartshorne. Hartshorne and his theological followers, seeking to establish a viable option between classical Christian theism and pantheism, contend that there is a pronounced analogy between the human mind-body relation and the God-world relation, so that in a sense the world functions as God's body. Since Hartshorne offers a conceptuality of God decidedly different from the one presupposed in this study, since in other words he rejects classical Christian theism in favour of his own neoclassical theism (alternatively described by him as dipolar theism and as panentheism), his analysis of the logic of G-statements must of necessity differ sharply from the one I shall work out in the remaining chapters of this study. For a brief explanation of panentheism and its logic see pp. 1-15 and 499-514 of Charles Hartshorne and William L. Reese, eds., *Philosophers Speak of God* (Chicago and London, 1953). Schubert M. Ogden does an admirable job of putting Hartshorne's viewpoint into the perspective of contemporary theological discussion in his book, *The Reality of God*.

ments about Jones, so too the primary and direct evidence statements for statements about God's mind are also G-statements.

We must first specify some of the G-statements which constitute direct and primary evidence for and against the statement of God's love for man. Then we can consider some of the evidence statements for and against that statement which are not also G-statements and how they might bear upon the truth or falsity of that statement. Since the statement that God loves all human beings is an other-minds statement, and since we ordinarily look to the actions of the individual in question for patterns of behaviour signifying the mental states referred to by other-minds statements, it seems quite natural and appropriate to fix on the statements declaring what classical Christian theologians refer to as 'the mighty acts of God' as the primary and direct evidence statements for the statement of God's love for man. If this be a defensible procedure, then the statements made by the sentences 'God delivered the children of Israel from bondage in Egypt' and 'God has provided all men, through the life, death, and resurrection of Jesus of Nazareth, the grace sufficient for eternal salvation' can be specified as primary evidence statements bearing directly upon the truth of the statement that God loves all human beings.

The inference here from evidence to conclusion can be warranted by analogy, as inferences often are. If the action of the men who piloted the little boats across the English Channel to and from Dunkirk could and should be interpreted as manifestation of their concern for preserving the lives of the men in the BEF, and if the moves of Lincoln as a nation's leader toward providing liberty and equal rights for the Negroes could and should be taken as signs of his goodwill towards those people, then we are warranted in finding in the Exodus and in the Christ-event evidences of the love of God. Rescue-action and provision-action, whether by God or men, can under suitable conditions form part of the pattern symptomatic of love or of other mental states cognate with love. Included under suitable conditions would be the presence of other parts of the pattern signifying love and the absence of symptoms which, together with rescue-action or provision-action, might form a pattern signifying something else.

Though parts of a pattern individually can be said to provide evidence for that which is signified, actually it is the pattern as a whole which so signifies. Jones's grimacing, together with his groaning, sweating, clutching the dagger in his chest and screaming 'I'm in pain', would signify that Jones is in pain. Together with actor's makeup and his presence on a commercial stage, despite the groaning and screaming, the grimace would indicate that Jones is play-acting. At the end of a ball game in which he had just missed the tying score, or after receiving a telegram from a young lady responding negatively to his proposal of marriage, the grimace would indicate extreme disappointment due to physical or romantic ineptitude.[1]

It will be obvious to all that neither of these evidence statements (the statements about the Exodus and about the Christ-event) is an empirical statement,[2] since 'God' in both of them is in the numinous strand and does not name an empirical referent. Consequently, neither 'delivered' nor 'provided' refers to a strictly empirical action. At least some of their entailments are non-empirical, in other words.

What may not be evident to all, on the other hand, is that both of these statements have *empirical* entailments as well. The statement made by 'God delivered the children of Israel from bondage in Egypt' has as an empirical entailment the historical statement made by 'The children of Israel, who were in bondage in Egypt at t_1, escaped from bondage in Egypt at t_2'. Again, the empirical entailments of the statement made by 'God has provided all men, through the life, death, and resurrection of Jesus of Nazareth, the grace sufficient for eternal salvation' would include such historical statements as that made by 'Jesus of Nazareth was alive at t_1, dead both clinically and biologically at t_2, and alive again in bodily form at t_3'. Empirical entailments such as these, since they themselves are conclusively falsifiable

[1] This account of how *patterns* of evidence form the grounds for G-statements will be expanded in pp. 205–212.

[2] Let me lay down a precising definition of 'empirical statement' which I believe makes sense of our linguistic practices: An empirical statement is one which has empirical criteria only, empirical evidence only, and contains no expressions which refer to non-empiricals. It would follow, of course, that the statement made by 'Jones is in pain' is not an empirical statement, for 'Jones's pain' does not have an empirical referent. And G-statements in the numinous strand are also without exception non-empirical. Though some of them have some empirical entailments and perhaps only empirical evidence, 'God' does not name an empirical referent.

on empirical grounds alone, provide the possibility (on analogy with *modus tollens*) of the conclusive falsifiability on empirical grounds alone for those statements of which they are entailments.

On the negative side of the ledger, such statements as those made by 'God has condemned or will condemn innocent men to eternal damnation' and 'God, though able, has done or will do nothing to save guilty men from eternal damnation' can be taken as evidence statements arguing against the truth of the statement that God loves all human beings. The line of reasoning may be traced out as follows: Both of the above statements argue for the statement made by 'God desires the eternal damnation of at least some human beings', which in turn is incompatible with the statement of God's love for man. If these two evidence statements are true, then the statement for which they are evidence is true, and then the statement of God's love for man must be ruled out on analogy with *modus ponendo tollens*, since the meaning of 'God desires the eternal damnation of at least some human beings' *excludes the meaning of* 'God loves all human beings'.

Hence, we have specified what would have to have happened or to happen in order to constitute a disproof of the love of God. There are several lines of reasoning that might lead to a rejection as false of the statement that God loves all human beings; the specification of one of them is sufficient to prove that the falsification of this statement is in principle possible and that therefore 'God loves all human beings' is cognitively significant.

So far, four statements related to the statement that God loves all human beings (either for or against it) as evidence to conclusion have been suggested. All four are G-statements. We may anticipate from Flew, therefore, the perfectly legitimate demand that evidence and criteria be specified for each of these four evidence statements. The sceptic would certainly feel that the account so far given did not solve the problem of the falsifiability of the statement that God loves all human beings, but rather only pushed the problem still unsolved back a step. He must be made to see, however, that it is in no way implicit in this account either that these evidence statements are without problems of their own (centring around the conceptual intricacies in 'God', 'grace', 'salvation', 'damnation', 'eternity', etc.) or that they are in some mysterious way 'basic' or 'protocol' statements in religious language and hence exempt from the need to have criteria and checking procedures specified for them too. All that the account as given entails so far is that believing the four statements mentioned serves to strengthen or to weaken, as the case may be, one's belief in God's love for man. They therefore must figure somehow into the checking procedures for the statement of that love.

The concession that these evidence statements are themselves neither unproblematical nor 'basic' statements might remove some of the sceptic's uneasiness. But since that uneasiness is due at heart to the omission so far of any mention of how *empirical* evidence figures into the checking procedures for the statement that God loves all human beings, something along that line must now be said. We have already seen that the statements about the Exodus and the Christ-event have empirical entailments, and it has been suggested that these empirical entailments provide the avenue along which empirical data can have a bearing upon the verification or falsification of the statements having those empirical entailments. It may be said further that the same empirical data will also have a bearing, though indirectly rather than directly, upon the verification or falsification of the statement of God's love for man, since the G-statements upon which those data bear directly are evidence statements for the statement of God's love for man.

What of the two statements which have been said to count against the statement that God loves all human beings? Let us take 'God, though able, has done or will do nothing to save guilty men from eternal damnation' for an instance. Since the statement which this sentence makes is radically incompatible with the statement made by 'God has provided all men, through the life, death, and resurrection of Jesus of Nazareth, the grace sufficient for eternal salvation', whatever counts directly for the latter will count directly against the former, and whatever counts conclusively for the latter will count conclusively against the former, again on analogy with *modus ponendo tollens*. If empirical evidence can count directly and conclusively for the latter, then we automatically know what empirical evidence counts against the former statement and

G

why it counts against that statement. But the converse is not the case: Any empirical evidence which might count directly and conclusively against the latter statement would not automatically count directly and conclusively for the former statement, since both the former and the latter statements might be false. Their incompatibility guarantees only that both of them cannot be true and that if one of them is true then the other must be false, but it does not guarantee that one of them must be true. The sketch has been rough, but it should nevertheless be clear in a general way how empirical evidence figures into the checking procedures for the statement that God loves all human beings.

No discussion of the bearing of empirical data upon the statement of God's love for man would be complete, however, without some mention of statements reporting the existence of evil in the world, physical (in contrast to moral) evil in particular. The question is: What bearing, if any, would such statements as are made by 'Approximately one-third of the population of western Europe perished in the Black Death of 1348–50', 'Thirty thousand lost their lives in the Lisbon earthquake of 1755', and 'Johnny Jones (aged 9) is dying of inoperable throat cancer' have upon the falsification of the statement that God loves all human beings, if we had reason to take these statements as true?

Such statements would have bearing upon the falsification of the statement that God loves all human beings if and only if credence could be given to certain subjunctive conditionals needed to link up such statements with the statement of God's love for man. To be more specific, it would have to be shown that the statements made by 'If God loves all human beings, then God would want to spare them physical suffering and unnatural death' and 'If God wants to spare all human beings physical suffering and unnatural death, then God would do everything in his power so to spare them' are acceptable. Everything depends upon the acceptability of these subjunctive conditionals, because if they are denied, then the statement of God's love for man and the empirical reports about the Black Death, the Lisbon Earthquake, and Johnny Jones can all be maintained together without the latter three counting against the former in the slightest. But if these subjunctive conditionals are granted, then the empirical reports about the Black Death, the Lisbon Earthquake, and Johnny Jones (either singly or corporately) count conclusively for the statement 'God has not done everything in his power to spare all men physical suffering and unnatural death'. It is easy to see that from here a double application of *modus tollens* results in the denial of the statement that God loves all human beings. For anyone who grants these two subjunctive conditionals, therefore, physical evil has a definite though indirect bearing upon the falsity of the statement of God's love for man.

There are those who would be willing to grant the first of these two subjunctive conditionals but who would argue that the second is too strong. They would correct it to read: 'If God wants to spare all human beings physical suffering and unnatural death, then God would do *something* (rather than everything) in his power so to spare them.' Such a revision is important, for it renders impossible the falsification of the statement about God's love by a few empirical reports. If we were to insert this revision into our line of reasoning, then we would have to be able to assert not 'God has not done everything in his power to spare all men physical suffering and unnatural death' but the stronger statement 'God has done *nothing* in his power to spare all men physical suffering and unnatural death', in order to arrive at the falsification of the statement of God's love for man through a double application of *modus tollens*. Nothing short of a completely evil empirical world, however, would serve to verify conclusively the statement made by the sentence 'God has done nothing in his power to spare all men physical suffering and unnatural death'.

The point stands, nonetheless, that many thinkers, religious as well as non-religious, see a definite rational connexion between empirical reports of physical evil and the statement of God's love for man and are able to spell out that connexion in terms of the mediating steps. The question of whether one maintains with Ivan Karamazov that the suffering of just one innocent child is sufficient to falsify the statement that God loves all human beings or whether one sides with Ewing in saying that only a totally evil empirical world would be sufficient to falsify that statement is irrelevant to the present question of whether or not empirical data can in principle have any bearing upon the truth or falsity of the statement of God's love for man.[1] It can if and only if a good case can be made for accepting the connecting subjunctive conditionals, and such a case can be made.

'If God loves all human beings, then God would want to spare them physical suffering and unnatural death' seems to be a

---

[1] A. C. Ewing, 'Religious Assertions in the Light of Contemporary Philosophy', *Philosophy*, XXXII (1957): 214-216, states that a totally evil empirical world would count conclusively against the statement that God loves all human beings.

Not all of the other Christian philosophers in the falsification disputes would agree with Ewing. R. M. Hare, *New Essays*, pp. 99-103, concedes Flew his point about the unfalsifiability of G-statements, then attempts to supersede him by maintaining he misconceives the nature of religious belief, which is said by Hare to be not ultimately a matter of verifiable or falsifiable assertions at all. Religion, as Hare understands it, belongs to a special kind of belief for which there was no commonly known designation until Hare himself baptized them '*bliks*'.

What is a *blik*? Belief is both a psychological and a logical category, and so *bliks* like other sorts of beliefs have both dimensions. As a psychological category, a *blik* is an attitude, feeling, or conviction deeply rooted in the sub-rational mind; it is a mind-set or mentality formed in a person by processes other than those of consciously rational persuasion or proof, even though it may come to conscious expression in highly rational form as a carefully articulated and defended position. (Here I have gone beyond Hare's actual words in an effort to explicate him.) Hare sharply demarcates *bliks* as a logical category from assertions, although he everywhere hints that *bliks* have cognitive import. He who holds a certain *blik* posits that an intelligible state of affairs obtains in the world; those who hold conflicting *bliks* think about the world in mutually exclusive terms. A *blik*, then, must be like an assertion in at least one important respect: The sentences which state both kinds of belief—the *blik* as well as the assertion—are cognitively significant sentences. (That this point does not emerge in Hare's essay with sufficient clarity has proved to be a snare and a deception to Hare's critics, many of whom misinterpret him as a non-cognitivist metatheologically.) And yet Hare is insistent that a *blik* is not an assertion and that Flew is right about religion not being a set of genuine assertions.

What differentiates for Hare a *blik* from a assertion as two varieties of cognitively significant beliefs is precisely the checkability component: Whereas assertions are susceptible to falsification, *bliks* are immune to it; whereas it is of the nature of assertions to stand or fall on the basis of evidence, it is of the nature of *bliks* not only to be compatible with all conceivable counter-evidence but even to either explain it away or convert it into positive evidence. It is in this sense that paranoia and sanity, inductive science and Humean scepticism about induction, are all *bliks*. Conflicting *bliks* can sustain themselves nicely in the face of what their adversaries throw up as 'negative evidence', which is another way of saying that for them there can be no counter-evidence. The issue between any pair of them, though rational in the sense that they project mutually exclusive states of affairs in the world, is non-rational in the sense that you cannot pronounce one of them true and the other false on the basis of rational argumentation. It is not so with assertions; the issue between contradictory assertions has to be at least in principle decidable on the ground of factual evidence.

Religion for Hare is that *blik* which imputes a structure of justice to the world, predicts the triumph of good over evil, and finds morality to be the best policy.

perfectly rational and theologically unobjectionable hypothesis
about God's love on the proviso that the evils mentioned are
taken to be senseless or at least out of proportion to any good
they might occasion. Evil possibly purposed by God to produce
greater good must be excluded from the hypothesis. Those who
would raise objection to this hypothesis on the grounds that

Religion and its opposite (nihilism?), therefore, are not two contradictory assertions but two conflicting *bliks*, which do not stand or fall on the basis of evidence as
assertions must. Still, it is possible according to Hare to judge between opposing
bliks on pragmatic grounds. Religion is the right *blik* and nihilism the wrong of this
pair, because the religious *blik* is life affirming and facilitating whereas the nihilistic
is life negating and stultifying.

But for his stipulation of falsifiability as a defining property of assertions, Hare
could have subsumed *bliks* under assertions as a special exception. But this does not
discount the fact that Hare has in his notion of *blik* given us an intelligible (albeit
vaguely established) category. The question is, whatever we may choose to think
about Hare's other examples of *bliks*, whether or not in the last analysis religious
belief deserves to come under that category. Surely religious belief is rooted in the
sub-rational mind and usually comes upon people or leaves them by virtue of
processes other than rational deliberation upon the positive and negative evidences.
Surely, too, religious assertions are logically compatible with their potential
counter-evidence, as is the case with all assertions; positive evidence does not entail
conclusion and negative evidence is not incompatible with conclusion, by virtue of
the meaning of 'evidence'. Still, it remains dubious that religious believers, however clever their apologetic manoeuvring, can *successfully* explain away or convert
all *conceivable* counter-evidence to religious belief. The logic of G-statements is
intricate, making it difficult in practice to decide their truth or falsity. The issue
before us in this study, however, is the *theoretical* checkability of G-statements, not
their actual truth or falsity. G-statements *need* not be checkable for their corresponding 'G'-sentences to be cognitively significant, but that does not mean that they
are not checkable. Showing that they are and how they are is one of the major aims
of this study. In this connexion, surely a world that was totally and senselessly evil
would count decisively against classical Christian theism. Telling whether or not
the world in actual fact is totally and senselessly evil is another matter.

Another participant, Basil Mitchell (*New Essays*, pp. 103-105), argues that
events in the empirical world which men agree are evil *do* count against the statement that God loves all human beings but not *decisively* or *conclusively*. The only
reason he gives for claiming that G-statements are in principle inconclusively
falsifiable is theological rather than logical: 'For he (the believer) is committed by
his faith to trust in God.' (p. 103)

Mitchell's argument is not to the point, because he has overlooked the difference
between psychological falsification (the mental act of a person in rejecting a belief)
and logical falsification (the demonstration on logical grounds alone that a proposition is false). Religious commitment may account for a believer's not *regarding*
anything as counting conclusively against his belief, but this has little or nothing
to do with the question of whether or not there are rules (procedures) which
determine under what circumstances a G-statement *must be regarded* as conclusively
falsified, the latter being the issue at stake for Flew and for us. Any sort of rule can
be disregarded, including the rules of evidence. It does not follow that such rules
therefore do not exist or are faulty.

God's love pertains to man's soul and its eternal salvation but not to man's body and its temporal needs have an inadequate grasp of biblical anthropology, in which man is essentially and not accidentally a bodily being. Many would find the concept of a God whose concerns did not extend to the whole bodily existence of man theologically objectionable.

Furthermore, 'If God wants to spare all human beings physical suffering and unnatural death, then God would do something (everything) within his power so to spare them' also seems to be a perfectly rational way of hypothesizing about how God's love would manifest itself, on analogy with human love. The idea of a limited God is attractive to those who want to hold to the ethical perfections of God while believing that the fact of physical evil necessitates the sacrifice of his omnipotence. Most classical Christian theologians would approve this second subjunctive conditional (in one or the other of the two versions suggested), by virtue of finding the notion of a limited God theologically objectionable. The price, of course, of holding theologically both to the moral perfection and to the omnipotence of God is that one must then allow the relevance of empirical reports of senseless physical evil to the falsification of the statement that God loves all human beings. Many, if not most, classical Christian theologians would upon reflection consider that price well worth the theological gains. Affirming the weaker of the two alternative subjunctive conditionals most probably, they would stand firm on the claim that the positive evidence for that statement has more merit than the negative evidence thus recognized. Assigning weights to various pieces of conflicting evidence is never an easy matter but has constantly to be done in all spheres of intellectual endeavour. Here again there are rules and principles that govern, but they are seldom neatly formulatable or universally indisputable.

Having touched on the matter of the positive evidence for the statement of God's love for man, it deserves further amplification here. It has been said that the primary and direct evidence for that statement are such G-statements as is made by 'God has provided all men, through the life, death, and resurrection of Jesus of Nazareth, the grace sufficient for eternal salvation'. It has been said also that, since such G-statements have empirical entailments, they provide an avenue along which empirical data can have some bearing upon the truth or falsity of the statement about God's love. What needs to be said in addition is that the subjunctive conditionals just discussed open up yet another avenue along which another sort of empirical evidence can have bearing upon the verification of that statement, namely empirical reports of physical *good* in the world.

It would be anomalous if empirical reports of physical evil in the world could in theory count against the statement that God loves all human beings but empirical reports of physical good could not in theory count for that statement. Yet there are many who regard the statement either as tremendously weakened or as conclusively falsified by the fact of physical evil without recognizing that for this to be possible the fact of physical good must be given some weight in its behalf. This is an odd commutation of the predicament with which Flew confronts the religious believer who allows good things to strengthen his beliefs while refusing to allow evil things to weaken them. If the problem of evil must be taken seriously as a threat against the grounds of classical Christian theism, then the 'problem of good' must be respected as a challenge against the case for non-theism.

Among those who insist upon an 'is evidence for' connexion between the statement of God's love for man and empirical reports of physical goodness in the world, there are differences of opinion about what kind of empirical experiences actually deserve consideration. Some believe that such phenomena as the rainfall and the fertility of the soil, under the label of the general providence of God, strengthen the backing for the statement about God's love. Others would add to these phenomena, or substitute for them, events distinguishable as the special providence of God: finding a good job in the midst of a desperate depression, receiving an unexpected honour, making an important scientific discovery, surviving a severe automobile collision without a scratch, or, perhaps better yet, undergoing complete and permanent recovery from some hopeless disease (inoperable throat cancer, say) totally apart from the instrumentality of medical science.

The fact that some of these phenomena, all of which can and do happen, can be given explanations under readily acceptable laws of one sort or another, and the fact that none of them appears to be *in principle* inexplicable on natural laws alone (the lack of sufficient advancement in scientific research—a purely technical matter—being the only handicap) in no way damage the claim that such phenomena have a positive bearing upon the statement of God's love for man. After all, we have (and have had for some time) scientific explanations for earthquake, tidal wave, drought, famine, automobile accidents, physical pain, and most varieties of disease, but these explanations have not taken the edge off of the theological problem of evil.

The plain fact of the matter is that if God is to be held accountable (with aspersions upon his moral character) for famine, drought, disease, and unnatural death, then God must also be made responsible (with credit to his moral character) for those 'natural' events (both ordinary and extraordinary) upon which we place the contrary value. If that line of subjunctive reasoning which allows us to link empirical reports of senseless physical evil to the denial of the statement about God's love is theologically and logically sound, then that reasoning which links empirical reports of physical good to the affirmation of that statement must also be sound, for the subjunctive reasoning is the same in both cases. To stand by both (or neither) is just to be consistent.

Of course, some would prefer to reject both, denying that either class of empirical event (the physical goods and the physical evils) has any bearing upon the truth-value of the statement in question. Such a stand would be prompted, no doubt, by the critical ambiguity of the evidence: The evil events and the good events of the empirical world are an extremely mixed lot, and it seems completely futile to try to formulate a calculus for weighing and tabulating the evils over against the goods in order to reach some final estimate as to whether the empirical world is predominantly evil or good and as to whether the statement about God's love is predominantly disconfirmed or confirmed. In light of the mixed state of this sort of evidence, it emerges that it is impossible to decide the truth-value of the statement that God loves all human beings on this basis alone.

Two things which qualify this stand must be borne in mind, however. In the first place, it is impossible to make the decision on these grounds in practice only but not in principle. It has already been said that if the empirical world were totally evil, then this would be sufficient to falsify the statement about God's love conclusively (but still only if the mediating subjunctive conditionals are theologically and logically acceptable). Conversely, a totally good empirical world would conclusively verify that statement (under the same proviso). So, the difficulty is not with the relevance of such evidence in principle but with the ambiguity of the evidence in practice.

Secondly, it would follow that the statement of God's love for man is in practice undecidable on empirical grounds only if the sort of empirical evidence we have presently been considering is the only sort of empirical evidence which in principle has bearing upon that statement. But it has already been outlined how another sort of empirical evidence not having to do with physical goods or evils has bearing upon the statement about God's love through the empirical entailments of the G-statements which constitute the primary and direct evidence for or against that statement. It is pointless, therefore, either to say that empirical reports of physical good or evil have no bearing upon the truth-value of the statement in question or to say that, though this sort of evidence is in principle relevant, one must be agnostic about God's love for man due to the ambiguous state of the evidence available. The only conclusion that follows from such ambiguity is that the statement that God loves all human beings is in practice not decidable on this sort of ground.

Though the entire discussion above has been metatheological in character, it is strongly hoped that the implications of these remarks for the theological problem of evil will be clear. It is further hoped that this single example will bear testimony in behalf of the more general claim that metatheological endeavour has much to contribute toward the resolution of problems and difficulties on the theological level. No contention has here been advanced that the statement of God's love for man is either conclusively (or inconclusively) verified or falsified in actual fact. The only contention at the conclusion of this entire discussion is that rules of evidence and checking procedures for determining what *in principle* would have to occur or to have occurred to constitute a disproof (or proof) of the love of God have been successfully outlined. Flew's meta-doubts apropos of

'God loves all human beings' should, therefore, have been put
to rest.

4. CHECKING ON THE EXISTENCE OF GOD

Flew also asks what in principle would have to occur or to
have occurred to constitute a disproof of the existence of God.[1]
It is relatively simple to outline what would have to happen or
to have happened in order to constitute a proof, rather than a
disproof, of the existence of God. We shall start with the proof
of the existence of God and take up the disproof afterwards.

In establishing a checking procedure for the statement made
by 'God exists', the first step that must be accomplished is the
rejection of any untoward strictures on 'exists'. Keeping the
full range of actual applications of 'exists' in mind, we must
oppose the demand that 'exists' be limited in application to
what is empirical or to logical constructions out of empiricals.
For it surely makes sense to assert that there exists a prime
number between 1 and 5. Yet the prime number 3 is not
empirical, nor is talk about it reducible to talk about numerals,
which are empirical. And, again, it surely makes sense to say
that the state exists for the benefit of its citizens. The state,
however, is not empirical, and talk about the state is not
logically equivalent to talk about the citizens who comprise the
state. Within their proper universes of discourse, we may
meaningfully speak of Huckleberry Finn existing (in the world
of fiction), of fairies and elves existing (in the world of make-
believe, which is like the world of fiction in some respects but

---

[1] There has been an abundance of metatheological discussion on the existence of
God, some of it directed to the analysis of 'God exists', but much of it dealing with
the question 'Is "God" a referring-expression of any sort (proper name, definite
description, etc.)?'. Since stating procedures for referring to God in discourse is
integrally bound up with specifying a set of directions for picking out, singling out,
distinguishing in thought God from everything else, the problem of identification
(so-called) is one of the most critical in metatheology. Unless directions can be
given for identifying God in thought, it is senseless to say that God exists or that
'God' refers to anything. Unless it is possible to list the properties which define
God in concept, it is impossible to give the criteria of meaning for 'God exists' and
hence the truth-conditions for the statement that God exists. For the truth-conditions for that statement are simply that there be something in reality answering to
just that set of identifying or defining properties. And without truth-conditions
already in mind, there would be no point in inquiring into what would constitute
a proof or a disproof of the existence of God (checking procedures). Hence the
importance of the problem of identification for the present discussion.

different in other respects), of motives and wishes and even suppressed or unconscious desires existing (in the world of the mind), of tautologies and hence also of self-contradictions existing (in the world of statements, not to be confused with the world of sentences), and even of nothingness existing (cf. a void in memory, a vacuum in space, a silence that deafens, the null class, oblivion that the mystic experiences, anti-matter—all these negatives are subjects of true and hence genuine assertions and therefore must exist).

What is there then to prevent our speaking meaningfully of the existence of God? 'God', in the numinous but not in the incarnation strand, does not name anything empirical or any logical construction out of empiricals. But all that follows from this observation is that the numinous strand of 'God'-talk is not part of the empirical universe of discourse, that God has an existence-status quite different from that of empirical objects, and that if we are to think and speak properly of God we must disobjectify our thought and speech about God, i.e. free them from the forms, associations, and demands which control thought and speech about empirical or physical objects. It does not follow from the above observation that 'God'-talk is ruled out as meaningless discourse or that the assertion of God's existence understood disobjectifyingly is some sort of logical monstrosity. Granted, if God is meaningfully to be said to exist disobjectifyingly (with an existence-status other than that of empirical objects), then it must be possible to say clearly what this disobjectified existence-status is like and in what sense of 'exists' God exists. But this is merely an invitation to character-ize the universe of discourse to which the numinous strand of 'God'-talk belongs by stating what sort of existent God is, what the key properties are which single out, distinguish, and identify God uniquely in thought.

The metatheological problem of identification is bound to arise—so dominated are we by empirical forms of thinking and speaking— wherever it is acknowledged (as it certainly is in classical Christian theism) that God is not empirically indicatable and talk about God not reducible to expressions denoting only empiricals.[1] That certain metatheological sceptics find the

---

[1] Among those who draw negative conclusions to this problem are A. J. Ayer, *Language, Truth and Logic*, p. 116; Antony Flew, *God and Philosophy*, pp. 30-36,

problem intractable derives partially from general empiricist predilections and partially from a confusion—the confusion of the problem of identifying God *in experience* with the problem of identifying God *in thought*. It is the former problem which they end up discussing, whereas it is the latter alone which has pertinence to the investigation of the cognitive significance of 'G'-sentences.

The confusion manifests itself in the attempt to assimilate the problem of identification to the problem of checkability by implying that an absence of checking procedures for the assertion that God exists would be tantamount to an absence of directions for identifying God in thought. But the two are quite different indeed. To attempt to assimilate them is another instance of the evidence-criteria conflation, a root mistake in much metatheological scepticism. One could without contradiction insist that God is identifiable in thought but not in experience, though the converse would not hold (if God is identifiable in experience he must be identifiable in thought, for being able to identify God in thought is a precondition for being able to identify any experience as an experience of God). And one could maintain without contradiction that there are truth-conditions (criteria) but no checking procedures (evidence) for the statement that God exists. In short, because of the clear difference between criteria and evidence, between truth-conditions and checking procedures, and between identification in thought and identification in experience, failure to be able to identify God in experience would not be equivalent to and would not entail failure to be able to identify God in thought.

66, 74, 193; Stuart Hampshire, 'Identification and Existence', in H. D. Lewis, ed., *Contemporary British Philosophy*, Third Series, pp. 195-198; Ronald W. Hepburn, *Christianity and Paradox*, and 'From World to God', *Mind*, N.S. LXXII (1963): 40-50; H. Hudson, 'Is God an Entity?', *Australasian Journal of Philosophy*, XLII (1964): 35-45; T. R. Miles, *Religion and the Scientific Outlook*, pp. 38-46, 137, 140-145, 157-161, 176; and Kai Nielsen, 'On Fixing the Reference Range of "God" ', *Religious Studies*, II (1966): 13-36.

Representing the view that the identification problem can be solved are William A. Christian, *Meaning and Truth in Religion*. pp, 28-31, 185-209; I. M. Crombie, 'Theology and Falsification', in *New Essays*, pp. 109-131, and 'The Possibility of Theological Statements', in *Faith and Logic*, pp. 31-83; D. Z. Phillips, 'Philosophy Theology, and the Reality of God', *Philosophical Quarterly*, XIII (1963): 344-350; Ninian Smart, *Reasons and Faiths*, p. 166; and Illyd Trethowan, 'In Defence of Theism—A Reply to Kai Nielsen', *Religious Studies*, II (1966): 37-48.

I hold, contrary to the metatheological sceptics, that both the problem of identifying God in thought and the problem of identifying God in experience are tractable. Since it ties in with the verification problem, the latter will be confronted systematically in Chapter VI, pages 217-244 especially, where the notion of the model G-configuration is set forth as the key to identifying God in experience. The model G-configuration is a theoretical construction prescribing what syndrome of characteristics an experience must have to identify it as an experience of God. As a theoretical construction, the model G-configuration is a clear function of some concept of God, definition of God, or formula for identifying God in thought. Once God has been identified in thought as this or that sort of something, it then becomes possible to specify the model G-configuration. (God concepts, of course, do not spring from pure thought. A set of experiences latent with a certain G-configuration comes first, and the God concept is distilled from that.) Which brings us back to the former problem—identifying God in thought.

One way of looking at certain aspects of theology—those aspects which speak of the nature, essence, or being of God— is in terms specifically of the function of defining or identifying God in thought. Theology tells us what sort of a something God is and in so doing gives us a set of directions for thinking and speaking about God.[1] Each and every theology enshrines its own unique concept of God. The dipolar, panentheistic God of Hartshorne and Tillich's ground of being differ conceptually from the God of classical Christian theism, with which we are primarily concerned. Classical Christian theism down through the centuries has embodied a consensus (albeit a somewhat fluid one) on how God ought to be defined. This consensus on how believers ought to think and speak of God is manifested clearly enough in the history of Christian creedal and confessional formulations and of Christian systematic theology. Within Christianity itself, Schleiermacher of the early nineteenth century stands as the first major dissenter to this consensus and as the first major reformulator or reinterpreter of the Christian definition of God.

In what terms does classical Christian theism identify God

---

[1] 'Grammar tells what kind of object anything is. (Theology as grammar.)' Ludwig Wittgenstein, *Philosophical Investigations*, p. 116e.

for thought and speech? Witness the following sample of confessional formulae: 'We believe and confess that there is but
one God, who is one sole and simple essence, spiritual, eternal,
invisible, immutable, infinite, incomprehensible, ineffable,
omnipotent; who is all-wise, all-good, all-just, and all-merciful.'
'We all believe with the heart, and confess with the mouth,
that there is one only simple and spiritual Being, which we call
God; and that he is eternal, incomprehensible, invisible,
immutable, infinite, almighty, perfectly wise, just, good, and
the overflowing fountain of all good.' 'We believe and teach
that God is one in essence or nature, subsisting in himself, all
sufficient in himself, invisible, incorporeal, immense, eternal,
Creator of all things both visible and invisible, the greatest
good, living, quickening and preserving all things, omnipotent
and supremely wise, kind and merciful, just and true.' 'God is a
Spirit, infinite, eternal, and unchangeable in his being, wisdom,
power, holiness, justice, goodness, and truth.'[1]

Insofar as these formulae define the God of classical
Christian theism, the metatheological problem of identifying
God for thought and speech (apropos this one theological viewpoint at any rate) is solved. Of course, the metatheologian, be
he non-cognitivist or cognitivist on the question of the meaning
of 'God'-talk, would and rightly should want to press for a
closer definition of some of the components of these formulae,
spirituality especially since it is crucial to all of them. Classical
Christian theists are agreed that the spirituality of God has a
dual thrust. Negatively it signifies the immateriality of God
and the need for radical disobjectification of all thought and
speech about God. In the positive vein, spirituality is taken to
bespeak personality (including simplicity and continuity),
awareness (including self-awareness), intelligence, affection,
volition, moral character, and agency or the power to act. How
these components are to be further defined and the special
qualifications upon their application to God are legitimate
concerns but need not detain us here.

[1] These formulae are taken in that order from the French Confession of Faith
(1559), the Belgic Confession of Faith (1561), the Second Helvetic Confession
(1566), and the Westminster Shorter Catechism (1647). Although these formulations happen all to be Protestant and come from one period of church history, they
would be generally acceptable to Catholics and Protestants alike up until recent
times.

It can be said that spirituality, thus explicated, is the quin-
tessence of the God of classical Christian theism, for so many of
the details (but not all, e.g., infinity, eternality, immutability,
self-sufficiency) of the several formulae flow from this one
concept, and the others are really qualifications upon this one.
It can further be said that if one can comprehend the phrase
'infinite, eternal, immutable, self-sufficient spirit' one can *ipso
facto* identify in thought the God of classical Christian theism.
To assert that such a God exists is to assert that there is in
reality a something to which this phrase accurately refers. To
identify such a God in experience (to state what would constitute a proof that such a God exists) is to derive from that
definition a model G-configuration which can be applied to
single out those experiences (if any) which can reasonably be
regarded as experiences of such a God. So much for the metatheological problem of identification.

   With the empiricist's strictures out of the way, the next
step is to counter, briefly, the view that the statement made by
the sentence 'God exists' is objectionable for theological
reasons. The theological paradox which denies God's existence
(e.g., Tillich's claim that 'God exists' is meaningless because
God is not *a* being[1]) certainly serves a useful function, for if

---

[1] Paul Tillich, *Systematic Theology* (Chicago, 1951), I, 205, 236, 261-266, has
maintained that God is not *a* being, in favour of saying that God is the ground of
being or being-itself. How could the ground of all beings be itself *a* being (in
which case it too would require a ground for its being)? Such considerations led
Tillich, who associated existence with beings in his conceptual lexicon, away from
the appropriateness of saying that God exists. Without denying that propriety,
Thomas Aquinas approximated Tillich's point in his claim that God is not in any
genus, not even the genus of substance (*Summa Theologica* I, Q. 3, Art. 5). That
Aquinas' point is convertible into the formal mode as ' "God" is not a substance-
word' is, along with other shrewd metatheological observations, remarked by
G. E. Hughes, 'Critical Notices: *Religious Belief* by C. B. Martin', *Australasian
Journal of Philosophy*, XL (1962): 212-219. R. F. Holland, 'Religious Discourse
and Theological Discourse', *Australasian Journal of Philosophy*, XXXIV (1956):
147-163, has rejected all talk *about* God including the existential assertion.
A. MacIntyre, 'The Logical Status of Religious Belief', in *Metaphysical Beliefs*, pp.
202-203, has declared that the concepts both of existence and of non-existence are
inapplicable to God. J. J. C. Smart at one time entertained the view that 'Does
God exist?' is an improper question, because it has no clear meaning for the un-
converted and it fails to arise for the converted for whom it does have meaning. See
'The Existence of God', in *New Essays*, pp. 28-46 (p. 41 esp.). Rejoinders by
A. B. Gibson, John Passmore, and H. D. Lewis prompted some retractions and
re-evaluations from Smart in 'Philosophy and Religion', *Australasian Journal of
Philosophy*, XXXVI (1958): 56-58. B. A. O. Williams, 'Tertullian's Paradox', in

taken seriously it blocks certain lines of faulty thinking about
the nature of God: God certainly does not exist in the same way
that tables and chairs exist, he is not another piece of furniture
in the time-space universe, 'God'-talk is not part of the empirical
universe of discourse—all of this is perfectly well taken. But at
the same time the paradox is dangerously misleading, for it
reinforces the empiricist's strictures on the application of 'exists'.
From the standpoint of the full and actual range of application
of 'exists', the paradox is surely false, as false for Tillich's
theism-beyond-theism (say) as for classical Christian theism,
for the ground of all being has an existential status, albeit one
differing considerably from that of empirical objects. The
paradox is surely dispensable, if we are careful to distinguish
(through a complete description of the differences) God from
other sorts of existing things, and 'God'-talk from empirical
language. If precautions against the possible category-mistakes
(especially the category-mistake of conceiving of God in the
thought-forms of physical objects) are vigilantly preserved,
there is no good reason why the sentence 'God exists' or the
statement it is used to make should be theologically objectionable. Granted, as Tillich, Bultmann, Bishop Robinson and
others have pointed out, there is a tendency within classical
Christian theism toward the objectification of thinking about
God, toward thinking of God in the thought-forms appropriate
to physical objects. But for a carefully articulated classical
Christian theism, that tendency is as much a category-mistake to
be avoided as it is for the newer theologies. The fact remains,
every theology be it classical or modern needs some way of

New Essays, pp. 192-193, has declared that the statement made by 'God exists' is
extremely untypical of religious statements and has invoked Collingwood's
authority for denying that it is a religious statement and taking it instead as the
presupposition of any religious statement.

Others oppose the theistic disavowal of the existence of God. S. Coval, 'Worship,
Superlatives and Concept Confusion', Mind, N.S. LXVIII (1959): 218-222, has
insisted that repudiation by the theist of the existential claim for God is self-
defeating, since 'what I worship' or 'God' is a concept to which 'Being' is essential
for religious purposes. Worship of a non-entity, in other words, is inconceivable.
David Cox, 'The Significance of Christianity', Mind, N.S. LIX (1950): 209-218,
has held that the statement made by 'God exists' is a straightforward empirical
proposition. He has been opposed by T. McPherson, 'The Existence of God',
Mind, N.S. LIX (1950): 545-550; and by T. R. Miles, 'A Note on Existence',
Mind, N.S. LX (1951): 399-402.

affirming the reality of God. That need seems best served by the simple sentence 'God exists'.

With the preliminary problems disposed of, a sketch of the proof procedure for the statement made by 'God exists' may now be given. The position taken here is that existential statements are verified *through* the verifying of attributive statements with existential import. That is to say, the verification of an attributive statement with existential import suffices to prove the statement is genuine rather than spurious, i.e., that the statement presupposes only fulfilled existential commitments.[1] And if a statement is genuine as opposed to spurious, it goes without saying that its existential presuppositions are true. To verify an attributive statement with existential import, therefore, is to verify its existential presuppositions.

For example, if we know that El Dorado is a *legendary* city of gold, then we know *ipso facto* that the statement made by the sentence 'El Dorado is located in Antarctica' is a spurious statement, in contrast to being a false statement. The statement that El Dorado is located in Antarctica would be a false statement, if El Dorado were in fact located in Australia (say). To say that the statement made by 'El Dorado is located in Antarctica' is a spurious statement is simply to say that there is no such city as El Dorado anywhere on earth, which would be the case if El Dorado were a legendary earthly city. But suppose that the question of whether or not El Dorado is a legendary earthly city is an open question. Suppose further we hear that El Dorado is located in Antarctica and decide to check that statement. If we were to go to Antarctica and there found a golden city named 'El Dorado', then a number of things would have been accomplished: The statement made by the sentence 'El Dorado is located in Antarctica' would have been verified, and at the same time it would have been proved that the statement in question is a genuine statement (i.e., a statement presuppos-

---

[1] See P. F. Strawson, 'On Referring', in Flew, ed., *Essays in Conceptual Analysis*, pp. 33-40. The distinction between genuine and spurious statements is Strawson's, and so is the notion that existential commitment is a presupposition rather than an entailment of genuine statements. 'The present king of France is bald', though meaningful, makes a spurious statement since there is no longer a king in France. A spurious statement presupposes *unfulfilled* existential commitments, and hence can be neither true nor false. 'The present president of France is tall' makes a genuine statement, because there is a president of France.

H

ing only fulfilled existential commitments) or, in other words, that the statement that El Dorado exists (or that there is an El Dorado) is true.

This example suggests a verification procedure for existential statements: Try to verify any attributive statement which presupposes the existential statement you are interested in verifying, and if that attributive statement is verified (or can be verified) then *ipso facto* the existential statement presupposed by it is verified (or can be verified).

The theological application is a matter of course, given this general theory for the verification of existential statements. In order to verify the statement that God exists, we need to verify some attributive G-statement. Whatever would count for any given G-statement with existential import, therefore, would *ipso facto* count for the statement that God exists. For if there is anything which counts for a given statement, the fact of its counting for that statement argues at the same time for the genuineness over against the spuriousness of the statement. It follows that if there were only one attributive G-statement with existential import which was conclusively verifiable (even in principle only), then this fact alone would be sufficient proof that the statement that God exists was conclusively verifiable in principle. And if there were only one attributive G-statement with existential import which was in fact conclusively verified, then this would suffice to prove that God in fact exists.

The statements made by 'God loves all human beings' and 'God raised Jesus of Nazareth from the dead' are normal G-statements with existential import; if verification procedures for these G-statements can be specified, then *ipso facto* verification procedures can be specified for the statement that God exists. Since verification procedures for the statement of God's love for man have in fact just been specified, and since verification procedures for the statement that God raised Jesus of Nazareth from the dead will be specified in Chapter VI, it is possible to say that we know what would constitute a proof of the existence of God. A proof that God loves all human beings or that God raised Jesus of Nazareth from the dead or of any other G-statement with existential import would constitute a proof of the existence of God. Given the fact that the verification of a G-statement is proof of its genuineness, and given the fact that being a genuine statement is tantamount to presupposing only fulfilled existential commitments, the above account of what would constitute a proof of God's existence is entirely adequate.

Care must be exercised in distinguishing this view from the view that one must *first* establish that God exists before one can know whether a genuine rather than a spurious use is being made of a 'G'-sentence such as 'God loves all human beings' and before one can even speak of verifying the G-statement which that 'G'-sentence makes. My view is that one verifies the statement made by some such 'G'-sentence as 'God loves all human beings' *and* establishes the genuineness of that G-statement *and* proves the existential presupposition of that G-statement all in one movement, all concurrently. How could any existential statement be established if not through the establishing of some attributive statement?

As an exercise proving the point, one might try manufacturing checking procedures for the statement made by 'The Taj Mahal exists' without at the same time (and not incidently, but as the fundamental part of the first) manufacturing checking procedures for the statements made by such sentences as 'The Taj Mahal is a mausoleum in Agra, India, built in the seventeenth century by Shah Jehan for his dead wife', 'It is made of white marble', 'It has four minarets and is flanked by red sandstone buildings', etc. Of course, if nothing could in practice count either for or against these attributive statements, it would not necessarily follow that they were spurious. But if, on the other hand, there are data which in fact do provide grounds for these attributive statements, then these same data and these data alone (not some other, entirely independent data) furnish all the proof of the statement made by 'The Taj Mahal exists' that the latter statement is capable of. Existence is not another property over and above the other properties of the existent. Consequently, verifying an existential statement is not something over and above verifying one or more of the attributive statements which presuppose it.

The same is true of the statement that God exists. It is not the case that God must exist in order for us to say anything significant about him, for 'God loves all human beings' would be perfectly meaningful even if it were used to make a spurious assertion. Nor is it the case that we must know that God exists *before* we know whether 'God loves all human beings' makes a genuine rather than a spurious assertion, i.e., before we can know whether that G-statement has only true existential presuppositions. For the knowledge that God exists and the knowledge that some such assertion as that made by 'God loves all human beings' is a genuine assertion are acquired simultaneously, i.e., when conclusive evidence for this G-statement is forthcoming. The proof of the existence of God, therefore, is completely contingent upon the proof of any G-statement (with existential import) amenable to proof. The proof of that G-statement would inevitably include the proof that it was a genuine assertion (How else could it be proved that it was a genuine assertion?) and hence that God exists.

The disproof of the existence of God, on the other hand, is not as simple. It has been said that singular existential statements are never conclusively falsifiable (though they are conclusively verifiable), even as universal statements are never conclusively verifiable (though they are conclusively falsifiable). If this were so, then, even though proving just one attributive G-statement is sufficient for proving that God exists (as has just been shown), disproving all attributive G-statements would not be sufficient for falsifying the statement made by 'God exists'.[1]

But such a claim about the unfalsifiability of singular existential statements must be qualified in certain important respects

---

[1] In the light of the strategy already adopted for proving God's existence, it might seem that, ironically enough, a real disproof of any attributive G-statement would also *prove* the statement that God exists. For a false or disproved statement must (just like a true or proved statement) be genuine, and a genuine statement must have true existential presuppositions. It might seem, then, that the disproof of any attributive G-statement would *ipso facto* be a proof of the statement that God exists. But such is not and could not be the case. Intuitively, a disproof of one G-statement could not automatically be converted into the proof of another, namely the existential presupposition of the first. More will be said on this problem in pages 186–192, since it has far-reaching implications for my whole scheme for the falsification of G-statements. In brief, the analysis of genuine and spurious statements adopted from Strawson generates two paradoxes requiring solution: the one already mentioned (that the disproof of any attributive G-statement yields the proof of its existential presupposition) and one more germane to my scheme, namely that if the existential presupposition of all attributive G-statements is open to question (as it surely is for many people), then the genuineness of G-statements cannot be vouched for or their falsifiability be proved.

in order to be made acceptable. And once these qualifications have been recognized, the claim is no longer of any service to Flew's scepticism. For singular existential statements fail to be conclusively falsifiable only when they lack time and place indicators. Furthermore, even when they lack such indicators, some of them fail to be conclusively falsifiable only in practice rather than in principle.[1] And those which fail to be conclusively falsifiable even in principle are still conclusively disverifiable, which is the next best thing to their being conclusively falsifiable. Being disverifiable means that they can be shown to be groundless and hence outside the scope of serious consideration. Disverifiability is not inconsistent with cognitive meaningfulness; on the contrary, it requires cognitive meaningfulness. That is to say, a statement is disverifiable only if it is cognitively significant—another way of making the point that disverifiability (like falsifiability and verifiability) is a sufficient condition for cognitive meaningfulness. It would not make sense to speak of invalidating the supports for a statement unless there were something which could (in theory at least) count for that statement. And if there is something which could in theory count for a statement, then the sentence used in making that statement would have to be cognitively significant.

Some comparisons will bring out these points. Take for instance the singular existential statement made by 'There is a

---

[1] The distinction between checkability *in practice* and checkability *in principle* requires some explanation. A statement is checkable in practice if and only if there are checking procedures for it which are clearly conceivable to the imagination and transgress no limitation of the logically possible, *and* if and only if we have at our disposal now all of the physical and technical means of actually applying those checking procedures. The statement made by 'There are mountains on the other side of the moon' has become checkable in practice only within our own times, due to technological advancement in the field of space satellites. On the other hand, a statement is checkable in principle if and only if the first of the two conditions for checkability in practice is met, i.e., if and only if there are logically possible checking procedures for it, procedures which do not violate the law of contradiction. A statement can be checkable in principle even if there are physical and/or technical limitations which make it impossible to actually apply its checking procedures now. The statement made by 'There is life on Venus' is an example of a statement which is checkable in principle but not now in practice. The fact that some statements will at no future time become checkable in practice (e.g., the statement made by 'The last dinosaur on earth during the Mesozoic period was a crippled male') is no argument against their being checkable in principle. We can imagine within the limits of logical possibility checking procedures for the dinosaur statement, for example.

human corpse in that closet now'. Because the criteria for identifying something as a human corpse are relatively precise, and because of the presence of definite time ('now') and place ('that closet') indicators, this statement is conclusively falsifiable in practice as well as in principle. Any novice, much less any trained investigator, could open the door of that closet now and make the simple perceptual tests which would yield a definitive verification or falsification of the statement in question. There might be no body in that closet at all, or the body that is there might not be a dead body, or the dead body might not be human. These matters are readily determinable. The complete failure of those tests which would confirm the statement made by 'There is a human corpse in that closet now' would constitute a conclusive falsification of that statement.

Of course, if the time-place indicators were either less exact or removed altogether, then the situation would be altered. The statement made by 'There is a human corpse in *a* closet somewhere now' could be conclusively falsified only if it were possible to apply to every closet in the universe all at once the tests requisite for establishing the existence of a human corpse, a highly impractical task. Such high-order impracticality, however, does not void or diminish the fact that a thoroughly perspicacious falsification procedure for the statement made by 'There is a human corpse in *a* closet somewhere now' can be given which would render that statement conclusively falsifiable in principle.

The statement made by 'There is a human corpse somewhere sometime' is even more difficult but still manageable. With the time-place indicators removed altogether, a checking procedure would have to be worked out by which, at a single point in time and space, knowledge could be had of every other point in time and in space apropos of the results of applying the tests requisite for establishing the existence of a human corpse. Granted, the difficulties to be overcome in setting up a checking procedure for the statement made by 'There is a human corpse somewhere sometime' are compounded by several orders of magnitude over the difficulties encountered for setting up a similar checking procedure for the statement made by 'There is a human corpse in *a* closet somewhere now'. But such difficulties, great as they certainly are, still render the statement made by 'There is a human corpse somewhere sometime' unfalsifiable only in practice but not in principle.

I have been attempting to show that one sort of singular existential statement, namely one about a physical object, fails to be conclusively falsifiable only when it lacks time and place indicators, and that even then the unfalsifiability is only in practice and not in principle. The fact that we have been dealing in our example with a physical object—a human corpse—is important. We have clear-cut empirical expectations apropos of claims about phsycial objects, and when all of the empirical expectations apropos of any given physical object fail to actualize, a more complete disproof of the claim could not be imagined.

If we are told, however, that the corpse in question, though somehow still present in the physical world, is an *invisible, intangible, empirically elusive* corpse (like Topper, who, though visible on the screen to the movie-goer, is invisible to the other people in the world the screen depicts), then a whole new dimension of the falsifiability problem has been introduced. And, of course, such a corpse, as Flew's parable of the gardener suggests, is much more like God (in the numinous strand) than its visible counterpart. In order to cope with the problem of falsifying existential claims about things which are in concept not exposed to direct knowledge by the senses, further comparisons will be necessary.

Consider the statement made by the sentence 'There is an electric current in that wire now'.[1] This example is instructive, because an electric current is like God in that both are invisible, intangible, and in that sense empirically elusive. Neither are physical objects; neither are exposed to direct knowledge by the physical senses. There is no way to bisect the wire so as to lay bare the current to sight by the naked eye or by a scientific instrument which extends the power of sight. When a scientist looks into an electron microscope or at a cathode-ray tube, what he sees is not the electron itself but a trace (a manifestation) left by the electron in course. Nor is there any way one can take ahold of an exposed portion of a hot wire to apprehend an electric current by the sense of touch. Were one to do this, one would feel the wire and its properties (hot/cold, smooth/rough,

[1] An example borrowed from John Wisdom, *Other Minds.*

thick/thin, etc.); one might also feel an electric shock, an effect in the nerves and muscles caused by the electric current. But one would not feel the electric current itself. Feeling an electric current, if there were such a thing, would be feeling a flow of electrons passing along its conductor, rather like feeling a string of beads passing through one's fingertips. When one takes hold of a hot wire in which the electric current is weak enough that feeling is not obliterated by the shock, one does not feel in addition to the properties of wire something like a string of beads passing through one's fingertips. Electrons are as elusive to the sense of touch as to the sense of sight. They are by nature unavailable to the physical senses.

Certain electrical phenomena are, of course, exposed to direct knowledge by the physical senses. We can see the visible results of a current passing through a wire—sparks, flashes, the moving needle on the face of an amperage meter, the light emitted from the bulb of a common lamp. We can hear the sound of a buzzer or bell connected to a wire when the current is on. We can feel the heat or the shock produced by the current. But electrical phenomena such as these are not to be confused with the electric current itself. The effect is not to be mistaken for the cause. There can be an electric current present where there are no electrical phenomena accompanying, but no phenomena where there is no current. Electrical phenomena, therefore, as empirical manifestations of the presence of a non-empirical electric current, mediate to us the knowledge of such a presence. An electric current, itself by nature unavailable to the physical senses, becomes available to them through the electrical phenomena it might produce.

Our statement about an electric current in that wire now is by virtue of this fact susceptible to complete falsification via the physical senses. That statement gives rise to empirical expectations about electrical phenomena, that shocks will be felt, amperage meter needles move, lights glow, bells ring, etc., if the appropriate things are done with the wire. Consequently, if those expectations are unfulfilled subsequent to performing the proper operations, then a more thorough falsification of the statement could not be imagined.

What happens when the time and place indicators are removed and we ask about the falsifiability of the statement made by 'There exists an electric current somewhere sometime'? Since we have apparatuses for testing the presence or absence of electric currents at any point in space, it is in principle possible at any one time to determine decisively either the truth or falsity of the statement made by 'There exists an electric current somewhere now'. The obstacles preventing the actual check are all practical, as are those encountered in extending the investigation into the past and future in order to check the statement made by 'There exists an electric current somewhere sometime'. It would seem, therefore, that the complete falsification (in principle if not in practice) of the existential claim about something by nature invisible, intangible, and empirically elusive is well within range.

We may turn now to the question of the falsifiability of the existential claim for God. As might be expected from the preceding discussion, when time and place indicators are included in that existential claim, it is conclusively falsifiable in practice as well as in principle. When for example the claim is made, 'God was in Jesus reconciling the world unto himself', certain empirical expectations apropos of Jesus arise, just as certain empirical expectations of electrical phenomena in the wire arise when it is claimed that there is an electric current in that wire now. And, to hark back to Flew's parable of the gardener, the claim that an invisible, intangible, eternally elusive gardener tends this plot gives rise to empircal expectations of garden-like characteristics apropos of the plot together with the absence of empirical expectations apropos an empirical gardener.

The complete absence of garden-like characteristics from the plot (which means the presence of ungarden-like characteristic) and/or the presence of an empirical gardener would be sufficient to falsify conclusively the claim that an invisible, intangible, eternally elusive gardener tends that plot, even as the absence of all electrical phenomena from the wire is all it takes to disprove completely the assertion made by 'There is an electric current in that wire now'. And the complete and total absence of the anticipated G-configuration (whereby the presence of God is identified in experience) in the personality, teachings, and deeds of Jesus would conclusively demolish the claim made by 'God was in Jesus'. The fact that God is in concept empirically elusive, and that hence his non-existence in Jesus would have to be inferred from Jesus' bodily behaviour, is beside the point. We know roughly what bodily behaviour Jesus would have to manifest in order to indicate that God was in him, and we know perfectly well what bodily behaviour he would have to manifest in order to signify that God most certainly was not in him. As long as time and place indicators are included in an existential claim for God, that claim is conclusively falsifiable in practice as well as in principle.

When the time and place indicators are removed from the existential claim for God, however, an entirely new situation is created. For then not only must tests be devised for checking on the absence of God at every point in time and space (let us suppose that such tests, though of a high order of impracticality, could be devised), tests must also be devised for checking on the absence of God *beyond* time and space. The God of classical Christian theism is in concept infinite and transcends the time-space universe, requiring that time-space transcending tests be devised if a complete check on his possible non-existence is to be made. It does not take much thinking to see that such tests are in principle out of the question. The transcendent existence of God, in sharp contrast to his immanent existence, fails in principle to be conclusively falsifiable.[1]

But it surely is disverifiable nonetheless: If any evidence is advanced in behalf of the transcendent existence of God, we know what it would take to disqualify it. And if after much searching no evidence in behalf of it turns up, the very failure of an extensive attempt to discover positive evidence defeats the purpose of the assertion. A sentence which states a disverifiable assertion is still a cognitively significant sentence, however. The fact that God's transcendent existence cannot be conclusively falsified does not help the cause of Flew's scepticism, therefore, since the claim for God's transcendent existence is in principle both verifiable and disverifiable.

This concludes the discussion of Flew's position on the

---

[1] Perhaps it might be added 'for us human beings under the time-space terms of our existence'. It has been assumed throughout this discussion that checkability by human beings specifically was the frame of reference and that the conditions of human existence set a definite limit on what is in principle possible by way of checkability. For beings with natures other than ours or even for ourselves under changed conditions of existence, the falsifiability of the transcendent existence of God might well be possible in principle and even in practice.

falsifiability issue. In summary, he has been charged with three important mistakes: the assumption that the meaning of a sentence is equivalent to the empirical expectations of the statement it makes, the identification of the 'counts against' and the 'is incompatible with' relations, and the suggestion that G-statements expressing the love of God and the existence of God are in principle unfalsifiable. The first two mistakes are manifestations of commitment to the checkability theory of meaning and in combination with the third yield Flew's implicit disbelief in the cognitive significance of 'G'-sentences. The attempt has been made in this chapter to defend the metatheological cognitivist's thesis by showing Flew to be wrong on all three of these counts, but especially on the third. For if Flew's challenge to stipulate falsification procedures for the statements of God's love and existence has been successfully met, then on Flew's own grounds (checkability) the cognitive significance of at least two 'G'-sentences will have been upheld.

CHAPTER IV

THE CHALLENGERS (II)

Just as the Flew article was helpful in opening up the issues of the falsifiability controversy, an examination of R. B. Braithwaite's Eddington Lecture[1] will set the stage for a discussion of the verifiability problem.[2] Though Braithwaite is concerned in this lecture with both aspects of the general problem of checkability, including falsifiability as well as verifiability, his specific focus is upon the latter. Because verifiability intersects with epistemology as well as logic, it will be impossible to avoid taking up some vital questions of epistemology in the process of meeting Braithwaite's challenge for someone to outline the logic of G-statements (i.e., stipulate checking procedures for G-statements).

---

[1] *An Empiricist's View of the Nature of Religious Belief* (Cambridge, 1955). This lectureship honours Sir Arthur Eddington, the famous Cambridge physicist.

[2] Among those who join Braithwaite in denying the verifiability of G-statements are: A. J. Ayer, *Language, Truth and Logic*, pp. 114-120; Ronald W. Hepburn, *Christianity and Paradox*, and 'From World to God', *Mind*, N.S. LXXII (1963): 40-50; and Paul F. Schmidt, *Religious Knowledge*.

Included on the positive side of the ledger are: John Baillie, *The Sense of the Presence of God* (New York, 1962), pp. 64ff.; Kent Bendall and Frederick Ferré, *Exploring the Logic of Faith*, pp. 163-181; Joseph M. Bochenski, *The Logic of Religion*, pp. 106-108 especially; William A. Christian, *Meaning and Truth in Religion*, pp. 238-269; David Cox, 'The Significance of Christianity', *Mind*, N.S. LIX (1950): 209-218; Frederick Copleston, *Contemporary Philosophy*, pp. 41-60 *passim;* I. M. Crombie, 'Theology and Falsification', in *New Essays*, pp. 109-130; Frank B. Dilley, *Metaphysics and Religious Language;* Frederick Ferré, *Basic Modern Philosophy of Religion*, pp. 371-407, and *Language, Logic and God*, pp. 159-166; F. B. Fitch, 'On God and Immortality', *Philosophy and Phenomenological Research*, VIII (1948): 688-693; A. Boyce Gibson, 'Empirical Evidence and Religious Faith', *Journal of Religion*, XXXVI (1956): 24-35; John Hick, *Faith and Knowledge*, pp. 134-165, *Faith and the Philosophers*, pp. 235-250, *Philosophy of Religion*, pp. 94-106, and 'Theology and Verification', *Theology Today*, XVII (1960): 12-31; Ninian Smart, *Reasons and Faiths*, pp. 127-159; W. J. Wainwright, 'Religious Statements and the World', *Religious Studies*, II (1966): 49-60; John Wilson, *Language and Christian Belief*, pp. 1-15, and *Philosophy and Religion*, pp. 34-95; and John Wisdom, 'Gods', in *Philosophy and Psycho-Analysis*, pp. 149-168, and *Paradox and Discovery*, pp. 1-22, 43-56.

Braithwaite believes that 'G'-sentences are not cognitively significant because G-statements are in principle not verifiable, and he believes that G-statements are in principle not verifiable because the verification procedures for certain paradigm cases of cognitive discourse (particular and general empirical statements and logically necessary statements) do not seem to him applicable to G-statements. Braithwaite's general approach, therefore, is at one with Flew's and true to form for metatheological scepticism: Checkability is chosen as the battlefield upon which to decide the issue of cognitive significance precisely because of a prior commitment to the checkability theory of meaning. The place to begin the analysis of Braithwaite's thought, consequently, is with his underlying assumption about checkability and meaning.

1. THE UNDERLYING ASSUMPTION

The checkability theory of meaning forms the backbone of the first (and negative) part of Braithwaite's lecture. But with which version of the theory he is working is a matter of some confusion. He starts by his own declaration with the version originally propounded by logical positivists: 'The meaning of any statement is given by its method of verification.'[1] In the very next paragraph he states an implication of this general theory which makes a related but separate and weaker claim as to the nature of the connexion between checkability and meaning, i.e., the claim that knowing the checking procedures for a statement is a necessary condition for knowing the meaning of the sentence used in making that statement.[2] Lastly, through-

---

[1] *Op. cit.*, p. 2. Since Braithwaite does not incorporate the sentence-statement distinction, this formulation needs to be converted into the terms employed throughout our study: 'The meaning of any sentence is given by the method of verification for the statement it makes.'

[2] 'The implication of this general principle for the problem of religious belief is that the primary question becomes, not whether a religious statement such as that a personal God created the world is true or is false, but how it could be known either to be true or to be false. Unless this latter question can be answered, the religious statement has no ascertainable meaning and there is nothing expressed by it to be either true or false. Moreover a religious statement cannot be believed without being understood, and it can only be understood by an understanding of the circumstances which would verify or falsity it.' *Ibid.*, pp. 2-3. 'The meaning of a religious statement has to be found by discovering the steps which must be taken to ascertain its truth-value.' *Ibid.*, p. 3.

out the early portion of the lecture there are suggestions of sub-
scription to a later version of the checkability theory: A sentence
is cognitively significant if and only if it is used to make a
statement which is either analytic or empirically verifiable.[1] So
here we have three different versions of the checkability theory.
Which does Braithwaite espouse?

The easy answer would be that he espouses the first, as he
clearly states and that the others are applications or corollaries
entailed by the first. It is true, of course, that the second version
is entailed by the first: If it is the case that the meaning of a
sentence is given by the method of verification for the statement
it makes, then it must follow that knowing the method of
verification for that statement is a necessary (and sufficient, for
that matter) condition for knowing the meaning of the corresponding sentence. It is not true, however, that the second
version is necessarily tied to the first. The truth of the second is
compatible with the falsity of the first, which is another way of
saying that the second could be affirmed while rejecting the first.
Other grounds might be found for maintaining the second apart
from its being entailed by the first. For Braithwaite, though, it
does seem that he affirms the second version precisely because
it is a corollary entailed by the first. So we need not trouble with
the second version as an independent option for Braithwaite.

The third version, on the other hand, is not an entailment of
the first. Suggestions of its presence in Braithwaite's thinking
cannot be justified on the basis of its being a corollary of the
first version. These two versions are quite independent
logically. The third lays down (supposedly) the necessary and
sufficient conditions for membership in a class of sentences, i.e.,
the class of all cognitively significant sentences. The first, on the
other hand, proposes a formula for ascertaining the meaning of
any specific sentence (and perhaps also an explanation of how
any sentence gets its meaning). It is not a matter of these two
versions being incompatible. They are logically independent,
and they can consistently be held together. But historically the

---

[1] Braithwaite says that if religious statements fall into any of three classes, i.e.
'statements about particular matters of empirical fact, scientific hypotheses and
other general empirical statements, and the logically necessary statements of logic
and mathematics (and their contradictories)', the problem of the *meaningfulness* of
the sentences used in making them is solved. *Ibid.*, p. 4.

third version was offered as an important revision of the first.[1] Historically men turned to the third upon becoming aware of the shortcomings of the first. It is for this reason that their dual presence in Braithwaite's framework of thought is a source of confusion.

It is, however, of little practical consequence in appraising the merits of his results as to whether he espoused the one or the other or both. The flaws and faults of the first version (that the meaning of a sentence is given by the method of verification for the statement it makes) and of its corollary (that knowing the method of verification for a statement is a necessary condition for knowing the meaning of the corresponding sentence) were established in Chapter II. These versions are beyond redemption. If it is with these versions of the theory that Braithwaite operates, the proof status of his results is a foregone conclusion. Those results may be true (I shall offer arguments to the contrary), but we know from the start that he will not succeed in *showing* that they are, for the theory which forms the backbone of his proof is unacceptable.

The third version (that a sentence is cognitively meaningful if and only if it is used to make a statement which is either analytic or empirically verifiable) is redeemable if some drastic alterations on it are permitted. If we dismiss the proviso that *empirical* verifiability is the only kind of verifiability that establishes cognitive significance and if we erase the 'only if' (the necessary-condition indicator) from the formulation, then we come up with the acceptable revision: If a statement is either analytic or verifiable (by empirical or any type of established procedure) the sentence used in making it is cognitively meaningful. Surely either analyticity or verifiability is a sufficient condition for cognitive meaningfulness, as was shown in Chapter II. The only drawback of this revision for Braithwaite is that it certainly is not powerful enough to yield his results.

---

[1] For remarks on the transformations (and reasons for them) of the checkability theory of meaning over the past thirty years, see A. J. Ayer, *Language, Truth and Logic*, Second Edition (London, 1946), pp. 5-16, 36-39; C. Hempel, 'Problems and Changes in the Empiricist Criterion of Meaning', in Linsky, ed., *op. cit.*, pp. 163-185; H. Ruja, 'The Present Status of the Verifiability Criterion', *Philosophy and Phenomenological Research*, XXII (1961): 216-222; and J. O. Wisdom, 'Metamorphoses of the Verifiability Theory of Meaning', *Mind*, N.S. LXXII (1963): 335-347.

Braithwaite approaches the position that religious sentences cannot be used to make actual in contrast to apparent statements (i.e., are not 'cognitively significant', though he nowhere uses this term) by way of the process of trying and failing to fit G-statements somewhere into a trichotomy of preferred statements 'whose method of truth-value testing is in general outline clear: statements about particular matters of empirical fact, scientific hypotheses and other general empirical statements, and the logically necessary statements of logic and mathematics (and their contradictories).'[1] My strategy in opposition to Braithwaite's approach will be two-fold. Negatively, I shall criticize Braithwaite's trichotomy of cognitive categories one by one, contending that these categories do not exhaust the class of all cognitive sentences, and that puzzles and oversights within the three categories themselves raise doubts about their internal consistency. Positively, I shall undertake a comparative study of the logic of G-statements, the logics of the three categories of statements in Braithwaite's trichotomy, and the logics of other classes of cognitively significant statements excluded from Braithwaite's scheme, insisting that there are stronger affinities between G-statements and the paradigm cases of cognitive discourse than Braithwaite is prepared to acknowledge.

2. STATEMENTS OF PARTICULAR EMPIRICAL FACT

Do G-statements qualify for membership in the class of statements about particular matters of empirical fact? Braithwaite answers in the negative, explaining that statements in this category must be testable by direct observation, a criterion which restricts the category to statements predicating observable properties or relations to observable entities.[2] Theologians who hold that the existence of God is known by observation in the 'self-authenticating' experience of 'meeting God' are in

---

[1] *Op. cit.*, p. 4. Preference for these three types of statements is the strongest manifestation of the presence of that version of the checkability theory which reads: A sentence is cognitively significant if and only if it is used to make a statement which is either analytic or empirically verifiable. Compare this with A. J. Ayer's formulation of the theory: 'A simple way to formulate it would be to say that a sentence had literal meaning if and only if the proposition it expressed was either analytic or empirically verifiable.' *Language, Truth and Logic*, p. 5.

[2] *Op cit.*, p. 4.

reality merely using the word 'God' to give dramatic description to an unusual experience, we are told by Braithwaite. For
no 'interesting theological proposition' attributes an observable
property to God, and so none can qualify for the present
category as testable by direct observation.[2]

Such theses throw up some fundamental barriers which must
be torn down if the view is to be defended that at least some
G-statements are actual rather than merely apparent. Braithwaite has missed some of the tricks in the expressions 'directly
known by observation' and 'testable by direct observation',
tricks that make a big difference both to metatheology and to the
analysis of statements of other types. Here again it will be to the
advantage of the theologian to make common cause with the
historian, the psychologist, and the scientist against a scepticism which threatens them all. For none of these investigators
deals exclusively or even primarily in particular facts (whether
or not we call them also 'empirical' facts) which are allowable
under Braithwaite's strictures. All that needs to be said about
G-statements *vis-à-vis* Braithwaite's first category will come
out in the process of working through three epistemological
puzzles connected with Braithwaite's use of 'direct'.

The first thing that must be pointed out is that Braithwaite's
use of 'direct' renders his trichotomous analysis of cognitive
sentences non-exhaustive, for it puts all but one type of statement about particular facts in a bad light by forcing paradoxical
constructions upon the expressions 'testable by direct observation' (to be understood liberally as 'testable by direct
sensory experience') and 'directly known by observation' (to
be taken as meaning 'directly known by sensory experience').
As stated above, Braithwaite wields 'testable by direct sensory
experience' as the criterion or defining characteristic of the class
of all statements about particular facts (Braithwaite follows the
empiricist dogma of identifying 'fact' with 'empirical fact').
This is tantamount to saying, as Braithwaite himself says, that
a statement is a statement of particular fact if and only if both
the thing referred to and the property or relation attributed to
that thing are amenable to examination directly by sensory
experience of one sort or another. Paradoxically, many (if not
most) of the statements of particular facts in which the historian

[1] *Ibid.*, pp. 4–5.

I

or the psychologist (excluding the behaviourists) or the scientist or the theologian are ultimately interested fail to qualify under this ruling.

Let us therefore first examine some examples which demonstrate how Braithwaite's use of 'direct' leads him into the paradox of having to deny sentences which are certainly cognitive a place in his scheme of cognitive sentences. Then let us pose common sensical interpretations of 'testable by direct sensory experience' and 'directly known by sensory experience' which removes the paradox and allows a place in the category 'statement of particular fact' for all the statements which surely are statements of particular fact.

Under Braithwaite's ruling, no other-minds statement such as that made by 'Jones has a headache' is a statement of particular fact, because none is testable by direct sensory experience. We can see and hear the symptoms of Jones's headache, but we cannot (logical 'cannot') observe or even feel *that* headache itself. Any headache which I might directly (in Braithwaite's sense of 'directly') feel or in any way experience has to be my own headache and not Jones's. This is one of the logical demands of being myself rather than someone else.

How about the Corsican brothers then? If Corsican brother-A is stabbed in the chest and brother-B miles away feels sudden pain and instantaneously develops a 'stab wound' at just that spot in his chest without having been stabbed there, what then do we say? Does brother-B directly feel brother-A's pain in the sense of 'directly' requisite to establish under Braithwaite's ruling that the statement made by 'Brother-A feels pain from his stab wound' is a statement about a particular fact because testable by direct experience? No. Though the pain the two brothers feel is identical in quality, intensity, location in each one's chest, time of occurrence, duration, etc., it is not the same pain. There are still differences in spatial location and in possession: Brother-A's pain occurs in his (A's) chest and is his pain, whereas brother-B's pain occurs in his (B's) chest and is his pain, not A's. The most that can be said is that brother-B's pain is evidence for the statement made by 'Brother-A feels pain from his stab wound', and this only if past experience has established a solid correlation (a strange kind of psycho-physiological *sympatico*) between B feeling pain and suddenly develop-

ing unimplemented wounds and A feeling pain from imple-
mented wounds.

It should be evident that the type of thing required by
Braithwaite's ruling ('testable by direct sensory experience') is
impossible to satisfy in the case of other-minds statements,
impossible in concept not just in practice. The consequence is
that either something is drastically wrong with other-minds
statements such that they are not really statements about
particular facts after all, or else something is drastically wrong
with Braithwaite's ruling and especially with his use of 'direct'
in that ruling.

To cite another example, under Braithwaite's ruling no
statement about the past, such as the statement made by
'Hannibal and his army crossed the Alps in the second century
B.C.', can be permitted entry into the class of statements about
particular matters of fact. The present-tense statement made by
'Hannibal and his army are now crossing the Alps' is testable by
direct experience in Braithwaite's sense of 'direct', but its past-
tense counterpart is not. What now presents itself as evidence
to our direct observation twenty-one centuries after the event is
a few artifacts dug up by archaeologists perhaps and some
ancient manuscripts (or photostatic copies of them), probably
none of them written by eye-witnesses and certainly none of
them autographa. But the event itself, i.e., the men bearing
swords and shields, the elephants fitted out for war, with the
snowy mountains in the background, is no longer available for
direct inspection. If it were, it would be a present rather than a
past event. This is true even for statements about the very
recent past, such as the statement made by 'The cat was on the
mat ten minutes ago'. My direct observation, that the cat is on
the mat now, does not count for the statement made by 'The
cat was on the mat ten minutes ago'. And my direct observation
of ten minutes ago to the effect that the cat was on the mat then
is now no longer direct; it is now mediated by memory.

History does not (and cannot) repeat itself in the sense
requisite for the satisfaction of Braithwaite's demands. Not even
a time machine (were there such a thing) could bring the past
right into the present and still have it be the past. (The machine
is in concept modelled on the spatialization of time and seems to
work only insofar as it is able to make a simple transference

from place to place appear to be a conceptually impossible transference from one time to another.) We cannot have the past over again in the present, with the consequence that none of the historian's statements make the grade as 'statements about particular facts' under Braithwaite's ruling. Either that, or else something is amiss with his ruling.

Yet one more example. Under Braithwaite's ruling no statement about the future, such as the statement made by 'There will be a lunar eclipse at 10:32 p.m. tomorrow night', can pass for a statement of particular fact. This statement is testable against the table of past lunar eclipses (or else formulae, derived from past observations, about the relative movements of the sun, moon, and earth) plus some mathematical calculations and calendar work. That statement is not testable the way that its present-tense counterpart (the statement made by 'A lunar eclipse is taking place now') is, i.e., by direct observation in Braithwaite's sense of 'direct'. Knowledge of the future by scientific prediction, therefore, is under Braithwaite's ruling doomed to the same fate as statements about the past and about other minds.

Small wonder that G-statements are also found wanting under this same ruling. As we have already seen, G-statements are often compounded with other-minds statements (e.g., the statement made by 'God loves all human beings') or with statements about the past (e.g., the statement made by 'God raised Jesus of Nazareth from the dead'). But apart from the troubles inherent in such compounding, G-statements could not possibly meet Braithwaite's standards for admission into the category of statements about particular matters of fact. Take a G-statement which is not also either an other-minds statement or a statement about the past or future, such as the statement made by 'God is raising Jesus of Nazareth from the dead now': Though it is certainly possible to experience directly (in Braithwaite's sense) the event of Jesus rising from the dead (however you may care to imagine it), it is certainly not possible in concept to experience directly (in Braithwaite's sense again) God while the raising is being done. In the very best of recent theological jargon (it was Luther's as well), God remains hidden even where and when he is most fully revealed.

This puts G-statements in the same plight, not a whit better or worse, with the other classes of statements, examples of which we have been considering. None can qualify as statements about particular facts, because none are testable by direct sensory experience in Braithwaite's rendition of that ruling. Other-minds statements name observable subjects but attribute unobservable properties to them (e.g., the statement made by 'Jones has a headache'). G-statements name an unobservable subject while attributing to him observable properties on certain occasions (e.g., the statement made by 'God is raising Jesus of Nazareth from the dead now') but unobservable properties on other occasions (e.g., the statement made by 'God is love'). Statements about the past and future refer to events which are not now observable. Their present-tense counterparts refer to events now observable and hence qualify under Braithwaite's ruling. But those counterparts are not the statements we are concerned with. G-statements share with other-minds statements the stigma of being unable to qualify even in the present tense. It is obvious that Braithwaite is involved in paradox here.

When 'testable by direct sensory experience' and 'directly known by sensory experience' are taken as pointing to the primary and ultimate data for any given statement, rather than in the sense Braithwaite imputes to those expressions, however, an entirely new complexion adorns those classes of statements which appeared cognitively worthless under Braithwaite's ruling. The paradox evaporates. For then it makes perfectly good sense to speak of some G-statements (e.g., 'God is now raising Jesus of Nazareth from the dead'), other-minds statements in the present tense, and statements about the past and future as being testable by direct sensory experience, even though all of these types of statements refer to substances or properties which themselves are not available to sensory experience.

The primary and ultimate data for the statement made by 'God is now raising Jesus of Nazareth from the dead' is first-hand empirical information corroborating that the corpse is biologically dead one minute (listening for a heartbeat and not hearing one, feeling for a pulsebeat and failing to find one, smelling the fetid flesh, etc.) and that it is alive the next minute (listening for a heartbeat and hearing one, feeling for a pulse-beat and finding one, observing autolocomotion, hearing the voice, etc.). The primary and ultimate data for the statement made by 'Jones has a headache' is seeing him holding his head glumly, taking ergot pills, and hearing him groan and say, 'This migraine is killing me!'. The primary and ultimate data for the statement made by 'Hannibal and his army crossed the Alps in the second century B.C.' is a first-hand examination of the artifacts and the documents, and the same for the statement made by 'There will be a lunar eclipse at 10:32 p.m. tomorrow' is a first-hand study of the tables for lunar eclipses (reporting past instances) plus doing the mathematics and calendar work therefrom oneself. Each of the classes of statements, therefore, which was cast away under Braithwaite's ruling is recoverable under the acceptable ruling, 'Every statement which has sensory experience as its primary and ultimate data is a statement of particular fact.'[1]

We may terminate the discussion of the first point about the trickiness of 'direct' and 'indirect' in epistemological contexts by confronting Braithwaite with the following dilemma: Either he must remain true to the construction he puts on the expressions 'testable by direct sensory experience' and 'directly known by sensory experience' (the construction which requires that the statement to be tested have subject and predicate which name substances and properties exposed to knowledge by the senses), in which case statements which obviously belong to the category of statements about particular matters of fact (statements about other minds, the past, the future, etc.) have to be excluded from that category; or he must revise his interpretation of these expressions (taking them to mean that sensory experience is the primary and ultimate data for the statements in question), in which case at least some G-statements must be included in the first category along with statements about other minds, the past, the future, etc. There is no third alternative. If he were to

---

[1] I say 'statement of particular fact' rather than 'statement of particular *empirical* fact' (a la Braithwaite), because a statement (or class of statements) receives its character from the nature of its entailments, not from the nature of its checking procedures. The statements made by 'God is now raising Jesus of Nazareth from the dead' and 'Jones has a headache', to cite the most obvious examples, have empirical checking procedures exclusively but mostly non-empircal entailments. Why then call them 'empirical'? There may be conflict on this point, but I believe that the recommendation to save 'empirical' for those statements which have only subjects and predicates accessible to the senses will avoid confusion.

choose the first, he would fall into paradox and lose his case that way. And if he were to choose the second alternative, he would lose his case against 'G'-sentences by admitting the falsity of the minor premise in his basic argument (the claim that G-statements are in principle uncheckable). In either event the speciousness of Braithwaite's case against the checkability of G-statements becomes transparent at this point.

The first point leads naturally to the second, that knowledge can be direct and yet inferred at the same time. The incubus that gives rise to Braithwaite's paradox is hard to dispel, and those still under its influence will find the present point difficult to accept. Nevertheless, everyone would agree that other-minds statements must be inferred from evidence statements about bodily symptoms, that statements about the past must be inferred from evidence statements about historical records and reports, and that G-statements must be inferred from evidence statements about historical events or psychological experiences or natural phenomena or whatever.[1] No one disputes the need for these odd inferences in achieving knowledge of other minds, of the past, or of God. The question is: If such statements have to be inferred, how can the knowledge derived therefrom be direct knowledge?

Let us take the other-minds statement made by 'Jones has a headache' as the test case. It has been claimed above that sensory experience is the primary and ultimate data for other-minds statements. Imagine Smith sitting directly across the table from Jones in a well-lit room watching Jones hold his head glumly, watching him take ergot pills, hearing him groan and say 'This migraine is killing me tonight!'. Since the statement made by 'Jones has a headache' is about Jones's headache and not about his bodily behaviour, we must admit that the statement about Jones's headache is inferred from the evidence given by his bodily behaviour. But then how can Smith's knowledge of Jones's headache be direct knowledge?

It would seem that we are confronted by a dilemma: Either the knowledge is really direct (in which case it must be un-inferred), or it is really inferred (in which case it must not be really direct). But neither of these alternatives is satisfactory.

---

[1] The question of the validity of these trans-type inferences will be discussed on pages 244–248. It is one of the central problems in this study.

For if the knowledge were direct and uninferred, Jones's headache would be nothing more or less than that syndrome of symptoms which Smith observes across the table, which is patently absurd. And if the knowledge were inferred but indirect (some would then no longer want to call it 'knowledge'), then it is incumbent upon the person who takes this option to make 'indirect' in this context applicable by specifying what the primary and ultimate data for the statement about Jones's headache would be if not his bodily symptoms. Such a use of 'indirect' cannot be made applicable, with the result that this alternative in the dilemma is also unsatisfactory. The obvious solution is to take the dilemma by both horns, maintaining that Smith's knowledge of Jones's headache is a case of direct *and* inferred knowledge.

A word of explanation is called for apropos the claim that 'indirect' is inapplicable to the case of Smith's knowledge of Jones's headache. When we admit that we did not until now know directly that there are mountains on the other side of the moon or even that there are craters on this side of the moon, we speak the truth. 'Indirect' was applicable as a description of the state of our knowledge of these situations, because the statements made by 'There are mountains on the other side of the moon' and 'There are craters on this side of the moon' were not then testable by direct sensory experience. We relied upon radio messages from a space satellite for the information confirming the first and upon the use of telescopes for the second. Such checking procedures, though the best we had until space travel facilitated flying trained observers to the moon, are not the primary and ultimate data for their respective claims. But we knew and could specify—this is the point—exactly what checking procedures would provide the primary and ultimate data for these claims, i.e., travelling to the moon and seeing the mountains and craters as mountains and craters (in contrast to hearing radio impulses which are interpreted as mountains or seeing images in telescopes which are interpreted as craters). 'Indirect' was truly applicable to the state of our knowledge derived from radio messages and telescopes.

It remains to extend the present point to our knowledge of God, which even when based upon direct sensory experience must by the very nature of the case be also inferred. Consider the resurrection claim of the Christian gospel, for example: 'God raised Jesus of Nazareth from the dead.' In order to circumvent the knowledge-of-the-past complication, it is better to work from the present-tense counterpart: 'God is now raising Jesus of Nazareth from the dead.' It is one of the major contentions of this study that the present-tense version of the resurrection claim, as understood in classical Christian theism, finds its primary and ultimate data in the pattern or configuration of sensory experiences featuring the memory of having heard (first-hand) Jesus predict his resurrection when pressed for a sign of his authority, the performing of the tests (first-hand) establishing the biological death of Jesus, and the experience of finding him alive subsequent to his biological death. It will not be disputed (except by the reductionist) that there is an inference, valid or invalid, involved here. The inference is of that odd, trans-type variety, since the evidence is entirely empirical whereas the conclusion (though it has some empirical entailments) is basically non-empirical. The inference acknowledged, what will seem strange is that the knowledge of God's action in Jesus' resurrection be thought to be direct knowledge and the knowledge-claim be thought to be testable by direct sensory experience. Since God himself is not apprehended empirically in the event of Jesus' resurrection, something essential seems to be lacking.

A dilemma emerges similar to the one attending the other-minds parallel: Either the knowledge is really direct (in which case it must be uninferred), or it is really inferred (in which case it must not be really direct). Again the dilemma must be firmly grasped by both horns. If the knowledge that God is raising Jesus of Nazareth from the dead were both direct and uninferred, then 'God raises Jesus of Nazareth from the dead' would *mean* no more and no less than 'I heard Jesus predict that he would rise, and I established by medical tests just a few minutes ago that he was biologically dead then, and now I behold him before me alive'. Semantical manoeuvring like this would please the reductionist, but it would leave most of the rest of us grossly dissatisfied purely on conceptual grounds.

On the other hand, if the knowledge that God is raising Jesus of Nazareth from the dead were both inferred and indirect, then it must be possible to specify what (if not the evidence already outlined) constitutes the primary and ultimate data for the statement. But the application of 'indirect' to this knowledge-claim cannot be justified, for no more direct checking procedure can be specified. It is not just a matter of there not *in fact* being such a thing as seeing God raise Jesus in the same sense of 'see' as one could see Jesus rising; there could not *conceivably* be such a thing. God is in concept, to use Luther's phraseology again, *deus absconditus*. The application of 'indirect' to this knowledge-claim is therefore inappropriate with the consequence that the knowledge-claim is both direct and inferred.

The third point follows as the answer to a question emerging from the second: Is direct but inferred knowledge really know-ledge? Can a trans-type inference from empirical data to a conclusion about something in principle non-empirical yield genuine knowledge?[1] Since the present point has more to do with the meaning of 'know' than 'direct', it bears repeating that we apply the word 'know' in common speech when our claim is true and we are sure it is true and we have the right to be sure.[2] The question then becomes: Do we ever have the right to be sure when in principle we cannot confront the object of our knowledge itself with the physical senses?

There is full authorization in contemporary speech practices for saying that from the pain syndrome in his bodily behaviour we know Jones is in pain, that from the artifacts and reports we know Hannibal crossed the Alps in the second century B.C., that from the table of lunar eclipses we know there will be a lunar eclipse at 10:32 p.m. tomorrow night, and even that from the G-configuration in the data we know that God is raising Jesus of Nazareth from the dead. Everyday language, allowing such things to be meaningfully said (whether truly or falsely is another matter), seems to acknowledge the legitimacy of knowledge of unobservable things inferred from observable things. Neither Jones's pain nor Hannibal's army nor tomorrow night's lunar eclipse nor the God of classical Christian theism can be confronted by the physical senses. Yet would anyone using 'know' in its everyday sense deny that we can know of such

---

[1] The question of the validity of trans-type inferences will be taken up systematically on pages 244-248.

[2] This follows A. J. Ayer's account of the rules for the use of 'know' in everyday speech. *The Problem of Knowledge*, pp. 31-35.

things when the primary and ultimate data are sufficiently complete to give us the right to be sure?

A sophisticated objector, however, might concede that in the everyday sense of 'know' we can know such things and that by the everyday criteria for having the right to be sure we can have the right to be sure about them. He might concede this but hasten to add that the everyday use of 'know' is too loose to be the proper or true use and that the everyday criteria for having the right to be sure are too weak to insure real knowledge. The expression 'in the *strict* sense of "know"' has an important history in epistemological disputes. What is this strict (and supposedly proper) sense of 'know', and should it be taken to heart as much as some people urge?

The objector can give a perfectly clear meaning to ' "know" in the strict sense'. It differs significantly from the everyday meaning of 'know'. 'Know' in the everyday sense means 'has the right to be certain'; 'know' in the so-called strict sense means 'has the right to be logically certain'. The strict senses reveals itself in the way in which the objector would no doubt attempt to justify his reservations about our knowledge of Jones's pain, Hannibal's expedition, tomorrow night's lunar eclipse, or the God of classical Christian theism. The objector would point to the perfectly indisputable fact that even though we had considerable evidence and it all pointed uniformly in one direction our 'knowledge'-claims nevertheless have infinite corrigibility, so that it is logically possible to contemplate the discovery of negative primary evidence, evidence which surely would deprive us of the right to use 'know'. For the only kind of knowledge-claim which does not possess infinite corrigibility is the logically certain knowledge-claim. And the only criterion strict enough for having the right to be sure is logical necessity (the entailment of the conclusion by the data).

A tempting question asserts itself at this juncture: 'Which of these two meanings of "know", the strict or the everyday, is correct?' Though the answer will seem *ad hoc* to some (resorting as it must to some very fundamental linguistic considerations), there is a way out of the present impasse. Several factors argue that the ordinary use of 'know' should (a recommendation) remain normative: (1) The ordinary sense of the word is not misleading, nor is it loose or vague or imprecise. The rules governing this use have been clearly exhibited above, and they are precise. To be sure, when we have the right to be certain and when we do not will in some cases be a disputed question. But this is not a difficulty in the meaning of (the rules for the use of) 'know'; it is a practical difficulty for those cases. Judging the truth of the statement made by 'I know that p' is often precarious work, but judging its meaning is quite a different and less disputable matter. (2) If the strict sense of 'know' were to become the standard use in place of the present everyday use, not only would the word virtually drop out of common parlance (How often do we engage in conversation about logically certain matters?), but we would also be deprived of our most effective expression for putting the complete force of our authority behind a claim. No other word in English does double duty for 'know' in its everyday sense, and if that sense were lost English would become to that degree less potent. (3) Contemplating the logical possibility of discovering compelling negative evidence is false ground for doubt in cases where the positive evidence leaves nothing practical to be desired. It is true that for contingent claims the evidence is never all in. But when considerable evidence has accumulated for a contingent claim and it is all positive, what are the dangers of backing that claim with one's full authority by saying 'I know that p'? Are the risks real? And what of the normal life-processes which would be stultified if we were deprived by linguistic rule from girding up contingent claims with the necessary assurances and guarantees that only 'know' in its everyday use provides? These factors may appear inconclusive to some, but they are the sorts of things that must be appealed to in making a decision such as the one confronting us.

We may conclude, therefore, that the 'correctness' of the ordinary sense of 'know' has been upheld against those who claim to take a 'strict' view of its meaning. Contingent claims are dubitable only on contingent grounds; the ever-present logical possibility (conceivability) of the discovery of compelling negative evidence is to be discounted as a solid ground for doubting contingent claims. It follows that nothing substantial bars the genuineness of the sort of direct but inferred knowledge we are concerned with, even though the objects known (e.g., Jones's pain, Hannibal's expedition, tomorrow night's lunar eclipse, and the God of classical Christian theism) cannot be confronted by the physical senses. Not all matters of particular fact are matters of particular *empirical* fact, despite Braithwaite's confining equation of the two categories.

This completes the discussion of the misleadingness of 'direct' and 'indirect' in epistemological contexts. If G-statements are to be barred from the first category in Braithwaite's trichotomy (statements about particular matters of empirical fact) by his formidable phrase 'testable by direct observation', well and good.[1] No doubt they should be excluded (if only because of the implications of the word 'empirical' which occurs in the category name), an exclusion which reflects the non-exhaustiveness of Braithwaite's scheme of cognitive sentences and the para-doxicalness of the construction he puts on 'testable by direct observation'. But they remain in the good company of statements about other minds, the past, the future, and scientific unobserv-ables, to mention a few. The exclusion of any or all of these types of statements from Braithwaite's first category in no way jeopardizes their status as genuine statements or as statements about particular facts or as verifiable statements or even as statements verifiable directly by sensory experience. Because of the misleadingness of 'direct' in Braithwaite's formulations and the way statements which are indisputably about particular

[1]Braithwaite's choice of an example to prove the exclusion of G-statements from his first category is a poor one. He says, 'If it is maintained that the *existence* of God is known by observation, for example, in the "self-authenticating" experience of "meeting God", the term "God" is being used merely as part of the description of that particular experience.' *Op. Cit.*, p. 4. First, anyone with a firm conceptual grasp on 'God' knows that 'observation' in Braithwaite's sense is unthinkable with reference to what the theologian speaks of as the experience of meeting God. Secondly, 'self-authenticating' (a term which, with good historical reason, tends to irritate the philosopher) is dispensable in theology and often means to the theologian simply that the experience under consideration contains at least some of the cues for its own interpretation as in truth an experience of God. The theologian may well concede that the experience is subject to certain checks and is corrigible in the light of further experience of the same or another order, and if he does not concede this he deserves censure. But the term need not for the theolo-gian entail that the experience is intuitively and indubitably veridical and beyond the province of testability. Thirdly, 'meeting God' does not function (for the theologian) to describe the experience in dramatic and pious language; it functions to interpret the experience as an experience of God and to claim what the experience is an experience of. Braithwaite's suggestion here smacks of the phenomenalist's claim that talk about external objects is really (means the same as, must be reduced to) subtlely disguised talk about sense-data. The moves behind the reductionist analysis and the antidote for them are by now familiar.

matters of fact are excluded from the first category (with no claim to a position in either of the other two) of cognitive sentences, it is difficult to see that he has achieved anything significant for his main thesis by the way he argues his first supporting point.

3. GENERAL EMPIRICAL STATEMENTS

Do G-statements qualify for membership in the class of scientific hypotheses and other general empirical statements? After what has already been said about the inapplicability of 'empirical' to G-statements, the immediate reaction on that count alone is to answer negatively. Though Braithwaite ultimately agrees with this answer, he sees more promise in the present possibility than in the first: 'The view that would class religious statements with scientific hypotheses must be taken much more seriously. . . . There is no prima facie objection to regarding such a proposition as that there is a God who created and sustains the world as an explanatory scientific hypothesis.'[1] The possibility that God is 'an empirical concept entering into an explanatory hypothesis' cannot be ruled out on the grounds that God is not directly observable, for neither are electric fields of force or Schrödinger wave-functions.[2] Such theoretical concepts receive their meaning from the roles they play in deductive systems of hypotheses in which the least general are generalizations of observable facts deducible from the more general ones.

But if any or all G-statements are to be regarded as scientific explanations or as psychological explanations or as historical explanations of facts in the empirical world, they must be refutable by experience. 'A hypothesis which is consistent with every possible empirical fact is not an empirical one. . . . If there is a personal God, how would the world be different if there were not? Unless this question can be answered God's existence cannot be given an empirical meaning.'[3] Thinking G-statements to fail on the falsifiability requirement, Braithwaite exludes them from the present category—the class of scientific hypotheses and other general empirical statements.

[1] *Ibid.*, pp. 5-6.
[2] *Ibid.*, p. 5.
[3] *Ibid.*, p. 6.

Nothing in addition to what has been said already need be said at this point in refutation of the claim that G-statements are in principle unfalsifiable. That refutation was put under way in the preceding chapter and will be brought to conclusion in the next. Setting that matter to one side then, there still remain a number of objections to Braithwaite's attempt and failure to qualify G-statements for membership in another class to which again by its very name they obviously do not belong.

In the overview, the objection to Braithwaite's handling of G-statements relative to the category of scientific hypotheses and other general empirical statements is two-fold: He excludes G-statements from that category for the wrong reason, and he completely overlooks the salient logical features which some G-statements share with some of the fully participating members of that category. G-statements should be excluded from the category of scientific hypotheses and other general empirical statements not because they are in principle unfalsifiable (which is false), but because many are singular in quantification (having 'God' for their subject) rather than general, because God is not a theoretical construct, and even more so because the word 'empirical' would have to be stretched in order to afford G-statements at best an awkward fit in the category (since 'God' does not name an empirically indicatable referent). And some G-statements have salient logical features in common with some members of the category of scientific hypotheses and other general empirical statements in that some G-statements have empirical entailments (as will be shown in the following chapter), some of them are verifiable and falsifiable on empirical grounds alone (as will be shown in the two following chapters), and some of them can be used in suitable contexts to explain psychological or historical facts (but not scientific facts in the standard sense of 'scientific'). It is with this last point that we shall concern ourselves during the remainder of this section, contrasting G-statements with scientific explanations and comparing them with historical explanations.

Do any G-statements double for scientific explanations of facts in the empirical world? Braithwaite is of the opinion that at an earlier stage in the history of religion G-statements were regarded as scientific explanations, that most educated believers at the present do not in point of fact regard them that way, and that at no time ought G-statements to have been classed with scientific explanations since they are not refutable by experience.[1] It is hardly necessary to reaffirm once more the falsehood of the claim that no G-statements are refutable by sensory experience. But if Braithwaite's reason for exclusion is not a sound one, should any G-statements then be classed under scientific explanations? By no means. Even to suggest the possibility is to misconstrue the nature of G-statements or of scientific explanations or both. The word 'God' is not in the vocabulary of science *qua* science.

That G-statements cannot be classed under scientific explanations follows from the explication of 'scientific explanation'. To give a scientific explanation in most cases (typically) is to bring a phenomenon under law, i.e., to use a universal description about some aspect of the empirical world to answer a why-question where that question is not an inquiry into purposes or a request for a justification.[2] This means that no G-statement can be used to do the proper job of a scientific explanation, because G-statements by nature are not themselves and do not entail universal descriptions of aspects of the empirical world, nor are they nomological (i.e., law-like) in the sense requisite for scientific explanations. When they are nomological, they are nomological after the manner of legal laws in that they have prescriptive force in directing and guiding human behaviour, not after the manner of scientific laws.

An objection to this bifurcation of G-statements and scientific explanations might arise on account of the fact that classical Christian theism attempts explanations of the origin, preservation, and orderly operation of the physical universe. Does not the doctrine of creation address itself to some interests shared by scientists? G-statements may differ in form from scientific hypotheses (which are typically, we have just seen, universal and nomological in character), but don't some of them focus on the same field of phenomena-to-be-explained as scientific hypotheses?

Theology is interested in the why of the sheer existence of the

[1] *Ibid.*, pp. 6-8.
[2] See John Hospers, 'What Is Explanation?', in Flew, ed., *Essays in Conceptual Analysis*, pp. 98-99, 117-118 especially.

physical universe. 'Why does the physical universe exist at all? Why is there something rather than nothing?', where these why-questions are requests for information on efficient rather than final causes, arise genuinely in theology. 'The physical universe exists, because God created it' is something the theologian—classical or modern—wants to assert, it is an answer to the above why-questions, and it is at least putatively an explanation of some sort (Shall we call it a 'G-explanation'?). But these same questions do not arise in astronomy, physics, chemistry, or geology. The scientist *qua* scientist is not equipped to answer them. They do not fall within the province of direct experimentation or of mathematical theorizing with experimental consequences. The sciences take for granted the sheer existence of the physical universe; they do not explain it.

But there may be more to the question of the origin of the physical universe than its sheer existence. If creation is construed as an initiating event or series of events that took a specifiable amount of time and followed a specifiable sequence, then theology might conceivably be competing with science in the same arena. Classical Christian theism, it is true, has taken the theological phrase *'creatio ex nihilo a deo'* to mean that the physical universe had a set beginning in time, that creation was an event of absolute initiation.[1] The doctrine so interpreted would surely be quasi-scientific and come into logical contact with scientific cosmogony. For it would entail a denial of the eternality of the cosmos that would conflict with the theory of

---

[1] The tendency in the modern theologies is away from this interpretation of the phrase *'creatio ex nihilo a deo'* and toward an interpretation allowing for or even requiring the eternality of the physical universe. Friedrich Schleiermacher, *The Christian Faith*, English Translation of the Second German Edition, ed. by H. R. MacKintosh and J. S. Stewart (New York and Evanston, 1963), I, 142-156, 170-193, teaches that the doctrines of creation and preservation have the exact same content—to maintain that all that is has its ontic ground or source in God alone—though the force of the creation doctrine is to make the point negatively by ruling out any suggestion of ultimate dualism or any possibility of something existing outside the ontic power of God, while the force of the preservation doctrine is to state the common content positively. Paul Tillich, *Systematic Theology*, I, 252-254, denies that the creation doctrine gives the cosmos a beginning in time; what it claims instead is that everything that is, though it might not be, *is* by virtue alone of its participation in the divine ground of being. Schubert Ogden, *The Reality of God*, pp. 62-63, 213, working in the Hartshorne tradition, holds that God was never without some actual world of creatures, and that the doctrine of creation is simply the teaching that God is the necessary ground of whatever cosmos does in fact exist at the moment.

K

the endlessly continuous creation of the physical universe (Fred Hoyle) and would harmonize with certain aspects of the 'big bang theory'. Though the creeds and confessions of classical Christian theism are innocent of it, some classical Christian theists have attempted to make the celebrated creation passages in Genesis out to be a quasi-scientific report, repleat with details of the temporal length and exact sequence of the creative process. Such attempts surely come into logical contact, for good or ill, with paleontology and evolution theory. But these adventures of theology into the sphere of scientific explanation —in field of focus though not in form—are not necessarily normative for theology, not even for classical Christian theism.

'Why is the physical universe the way it is rather than some other way?' is another question which arises for theology but not for science. Classical Christian theism explains the orderly operation of the cosmos in terms of the governance of an intelligent God. How God is thought to keep order in his universe is a difficult matter leading into the issue between those theologians who believe that every instance of every sort of natural phenomenon is occasioned by a direct effort of the divine will (making the scientific laws of nature to be reports of the divine activity and making the scientist willy-nilly a kind of theological investigator) and those who believe that God created natural laws which operate on their own as secondary causes or determinants of natural phenomena (putting God at one remove from the actual scene of the everyday cosmic process). But we need not become embrangled in this debate. Suffice it to say that the scientist can explain much by reference to such principles as the speed of light or the law of gravity. But he has no answers to the very questions the theologian finds interesting, such questions as 'Why does light travel at 186,000 miles per second rather than (say) at 200,000?' or 'Why do falling bodies accelerate at 32 feet per second per second rather than at 30 or 35, and why doesn't a ten pound weight fall faster than a one pound weight?'. Though the theologian might not wish to undertake to answer such questions one by one, he surely does wish to pronounce on the whole lot at once in terms of the sovereign will, intelligence, and faithfulness of God, i.e., in terms of God's nature. Science and theology are surely thinking on different levels with reference to the way things are in the physical universe.

G-statements, therefore, are for all intents and purposes not to be regarded as scientific explanations. By and large even those G-explanations which refer to phenomena occurring in the physical universe do not coincide in specific focus with or meet the formal specifications of scientific explanations.

Are then any G-statements to be regarded as historical explanations? Though this possibility contains more promise than the one preceding, Braithwaite dismisses it almost peremptorily, in a single sentence. At the conclusion of his rejection of the psychological explanation possibility, he adds: 'And a metaphorical description is not in itself an explanation. This criticism also holds against attempts to interpret theism as an explanation of the course of history, unless it is admitted (which few theists would be willing to admit) that, had the course of history been different in some specific way, God would not have existed.'[1]

In order to appraise the present option and Braithwaite's rejection of it, we must understand something about the nature of historical explanation. One way of approaching the nature of historical explanation is to provide the differentiae between it and scientific explanation. Both types of explanation perform their function of answering why-questions (where these are requests for information about efficient causes rather than for final causes or rational justifications) by grouping the phenomenon in question together with certain other phenomena. It is the way the grouping is constituted, i.e., the other phenomena in the group, which spells the difference.

The phenomenon which the historian is interested in explaining is the *individual* event, and so he groups the individual event together with other individual events which he discovers to be in the same temporal (and perhaps spatial) sequence with it. The properties of the individuals in the grouping may (and probably will) differ radically, for their temporal (and perhaps spatial) proximity is all that matters in constituting the grouping. The phenomenon which the scientist is interested in explaining, by and large is a *class* of events rather than the individual event. Even when the scientist concentrates upon explaining a single phenomenon, it is really the explanation for

[1] *Op. cit.*, p. 7.

the whole class to which that phenomenon belongs that he is after. Such a class is constituted on the basis of properties belonging in common to the individual members (e.g., the class of all falling bodies, the class of all instances of ionization or of oxidation or of combustion), and the scientist groups such a class of events together with another class of events with which it is constantly conjoined. He is oblivious to the temporal (and spatial) context of any of the individual events in either of the correlated classes of events, for he is concerned only with the correlation.[1]

Since the scientist is interested in explaining classes of events, scientific explanations are always formulated in universal statements, and universal statements of a special cast. For only those universal statements which have achieved nomological status (and how this is accomplished is a matter of dispute among philosophers) qualify for employment in scientific explanations. Historical explanations, on the other hand, may be formulated in singular statements or (if general) in particular statements, but never in timeless universal statements. This is due to the preoccupation of historical explanations with groups of individual events with nothing but temporal context in common: These events have nothing in common to universalize about in a nomological fashion.[2]

The historian is interested in explaining individual events, but what constitutes an individual event may differ widely in generality (not in the sense of quantification, but in the sense of the amount of specific detail comprehended) depending upon the historian's purpose and principle of selectivity. The statement made by 'The Byzantine Empire ceased to flourish,

[1] When the distinction between science and history and between scientific explanation and historical explanation is drawn in this fashion, the work of people like Toynbee constitutes a conflict case. Toynbee is known professionally as a historian, he deals strictly in the realm of human events (avoiding scientific concepts and mathematical formulations), and yet his purpose is to discover universal laws about the rise and fall of civilizations in general. Following the criteria we have set up, Toynbee's work would have to be placed in the category of scientific explanation. Perhaps Toynbee and his kind are best described as historical sociologists.

[2] See A. M. MacIver, 'Historical Explanation', in LL-II, pp. 192-193. This is not to deny, of course, that the historian at times may fall back on scientific laws in the process of qualifying or disqualifying a given historical explanation. There can be interaction, in other words, between science and history without obscuring the distinction between scientific explanation and historical explanation.

because Constantinople fell to the Turks in A.D. 1352' offers an historical explanation. But the decline of the Byzantine Empire is a considerably larger slice of the total span of history than is encompassed in the explanation stated by 'Constantine was victorious at the Milvian Bridge in A.D. 313, because the vision of the Cross and the command ("In this sign conquer!") inspired him and his army to greater efforts'.

With the differentiation between historical and scientific explanations as background, it is now possible to state that some G-statements in appropriate contexts may be used to do the job of historical explanation, i.e., that some G-explanations are historical explanations. 'God raised Jesus of Nazareth from the dead', for example, can be used in suitable contexts to state a historical explanation. In the context of the why-question, 'Why was the tomb of Joseph of Arimathea (in which the dead body of Jesus of Nazareth had been interred) empty on Easter morning?', we might be told, 'The tomb of Joseph of Arimathea was empty on Easter morning, because God raised Jesus of Nazareth from the dead'. A catechism class might provide the context for the asking of such a why-question.[1] 'God raised Jesus of Nazareth from the dead', when used to state a historical explanation (as well as in its other uses), makes a singular rather than general statement. It is not itself a nomological statement, nor is it deduced from a nomological statement together with other singular or particular historical statements. Tombs become vacant for a variety of reasons and as a result of God's action only rarely (according to actual claims). So the vacancy of this particular tomb could hardly be explained by bringing the event to be explained under a universal law based upon consistent correlation between two event-classes (empty tombs and divine resurrections). This explanation is to be labelled 'historical', because it is accomplished by grouping the

---

[1] 'God raised Jesus of Nazareth from the dead' is not used in the New Testament to state a historical *explanation*. We are reminded on all hands by contemporary theologians of the kerygmatic nature of the New Testament documents. The 'kerygma' was the preaching of the early church, and when it is said that the New Testament is 'kerygmatic', it means that it was written not to explain historical phenomena but rather to preach and proclaim a message directed toward the conversion of men. This is not to say that the G-statements of the kerygma could not be used as historical explanations in the context of why-questions; it is only to say that in the context of preaching their purpose is different—to persuade rather than explain.

individual event to be explained together with another individual event some aspects of which were purportedly contiguous in space and time with it.

Granting that some G-explanations are historical explanations, is there any limit to the size of the slice of history they can explain? The question is germane, since Braithwaite suggests that there have been 'attempts to interpret theism as an explanation of the course of history'.[1] Due to the limited context, it is uncertain what Braithwaite means by 'the course of history'. Suppose 'God directs the whole course of history' is taken as a sort of shorthand for 'The specific character (not just the power of being) of every event within history can be explained exhaustively by means of a G-statement'. (I dismiss from the outset the plausibility of saying that God directs the whole course of history if no event receives its specific historical character from God.) The obvious objection dawns: That which explains everything explains nothing. If there were no difference between Christ's resurrection and the Exodus on the one hand over against the burning of the Reichstag and Khrushchev's antics at the May 1960 Summit Conference on the other, i.e., differences from the standpoint of their historical causality, then G-statements would lose their point when used as historical explanations. They would sacrifice their function of marking off those events in which God can be 'seen' from those in which he cannot, unless it be true (which it surely is not) that every historical event bears equally the marks of divine action. If a G-explanation were proposed for each of the heterogeneous lot of historical events, it would soon cease to be clear what exactly it is to give a G-explanation for any event whatsoever.

Suppose, however, that 'God directs the whole course of history' is taken to mean 'God causes certain key events in

[1] Op. cit., p. 7.

[2] Along this line might be mentioned the widely-discussed recent work of the German theologian, Wolfhart Pannenberg. Pannenberg departs from certain aspects and goes beyond other aspects of traditional salvation-history theology (heilsgeschichtliche Theologie), as exemplified in Oscar Cullmann's recent Book Heil als Geschichte (Tübingen, 1965). Salvation-history theology bases its theological conclusions solely on the redemptive events of sacred history as reported in the Bible and interpreted by the witness of faith. Pannenberg, for his part, finds God's redemptive activity revealed in the promise-fulfilment structure inherent in the macro-'event' of total world history (Universalgeschichte), open to secular vision apart from any faith assumption. Of course, this revelatory structure cannot yet be

history which in turn shape its entire course'.[2] This interpretation allows the believer to indicate God as the source, guide, and goal of history without obscuring the difference between those historical events which God causes and those which he does not cause (though he may influence even these events indirectly through the events which he does directly cause). And it does not require for its intelligibility that we know for certain which are the key events through which God shapes the entire course of history. Some of the events which should be designated as key events (e.g., the incarnation, crucifixion, and resurrection of Jesus of Nazareth) are obvious to anyone who agrees with the lead claim. Others will give rise to a great deal of disputation.

For example, believers might quarrel over whether or not the collapse of the crusading movement of the twelfth century is to be explained as a judgement of God upon western Europe. But due to the known operation of ordinary historical causation in the situation, this difference of opinion would have to be fought out on a much more rudimentary level. We know that the crusading movement of the twelfth century collapsed due to the indecisive outcome of the Third Crusade. We know also that the outcome of the Third Crusade was indecisive because the German contingent (which together with the forces of Richard I of England and Philip II of France could have swung the balance of power against Saladin) disintegrated before it ever reached Palestine. We know, furthermore, that the German contingent disintegrated because its leader, Frederick Barbarossa, was drowned while bathing in a river in Asia Minor (1190). If the circumstances surrounding his strange death clearly manifested a G-configuration (there is no report that they did), then a case might be made for the claim that the collapse of the crusading movement of the twelfth century is to be explained as a judgement of God upon Western Europe. The point is not to take sides in this issue but simply to outline what would have to be

seen, since the end-fulfilment of world history (the general resurrection) has not yet occurred. But it can be _known_ nonetheless, for it is clearly adumbrated, says Pannenberg, in the promise-fulfilment structure latent within the micro-'event' comprehending the history of Israel and culminating in Christ (his resurrection particularly). See Pannenberg's contributions to W. Pannenberg, ed., _Offenbarung als Geschichte_ (Göttingen, 1961), pp. 91-114, and to Claus Westermann, ed., _Essays on Old Testament Hermeneutics_, English translation edited by James Luther Mays (Richmond, Virginia, 1963), pp. 314-335.

done many times over in order to verify the fully intelligible claim that God causes certain key events in history which in turn shape its whole course. Even if the claim were in practice beyond verification or outrightly falsified (or disverified), it is intelligible nonetheless.

Having suggested an acceptable meaning for the claim that God explains the course of history, the fallacy in the rest of Braithwaite's argument against regarding (some) G-statements as historical explanations should be obvious. He says that we cannot 'interpret theism as an explanation of the course of history, unless it is admitted (which few theists would be willing to admit) that, had the course of history been different in some specific way, God would not have existed'.[1] Here he seems to be arguing, mistakenly, that if q counts for p, then not-q counts against p or (which amounts to the same thing) counts for not-p i.e., if some statements describing events in history (transcribing Braithwaite's talk about 'the course of history') are taken to count for the statement made by 'God exists', then the negation of those statements would count against that statement and for the statement made by 'God does not exist'.

Such an argument involves a misinterpretation of the meaning of 'counts for' and 'counts against'. If q counts for p, it does not follow necessarily (though it might happen) that not-q counts are to be understood as statements made by the sentences listed), if 'He sends her candy and flowers' counts for 'He loves her', it does not follow that 'He does not send her candy and flowers' count against 'He loves her' and for 'He does not love her' the way 'He sends her arsenic and voodoo dolls' does. On the other hand, if 'There are fresh (human) footprints in the mud' counts for 'Someone passed by this way recently', then 'There are no fresh (human) footprints in the mud' does count against p and for not-p. To cite obvious examples (the following against 'Someone passed by this way recently' and for 'It is not the case that someone passed by this way recently'. It depends entirely upon the content of p and q as to whether, assuming that q counts for p, the denial of q counts against p and for not-p.

So, if a certain historical event counts for a certain G-statement, though the negation of the statement of that event removes one reason for believing the G-statement (i.e., the

[1] *Op. cit.*, p. 7.

negation disverifies the G-statement to the extent that the affirmation provided evidence for it), that negation does not necessarily count against the G-statement or for its negation. Whether or not it does depends totally upon the content of the historical statement and the G-statement. The denial of the statement made by 'The tomb of Joseph of Arimathea (in which the corpse of Jesus of Nazareth was interred) was empty on Easter morning', insofar as that denial amounts to an affirmation that the corpse of Jesus still resided in the tomb on Easter morning (there would then be no Easter), would count against and count conclusively against the statement made by 'God raised Jesus of Nazareth from the dead on Easter morning'. Then again, one could imagine the course of history to have been substantially different, with no Exodus, no Christ-event (virgin birth, miracles, ethical teachings and divine claims, crucifixion, resurrection), without any of the historical events which orthodox Christians regard as counting for their theism, and such an altered course of history would in no way count against the statement made by 'God exists' or for the statement made by 'God does not exist'. It would disverify, defeat, and remove the historical grounds for belief in the theistic claim, but it would not falsify that claim.

Furthermore, even if these specific events had not happened, other historical events requiring G-explanations might have happened instead, perhaps in Zanzibar during the early part of the twelfth century. And these events would then reinstate the historical grounds for the theistic claim relinquished by the non-existence of those other events. Braithwaite is quite wrong: Had the course of history been different in some specific way, it in no wise follows that God would not have existed, By and large, then, Braithwaite's argument against the possibility of G-statements being used as historical explanations is unconvincing.

Since Braithwaite's discussion lacks a full account of the method of checking explanatory hypotheses of any sort, we are moved to ask: What kind of historical events require (in the theologian's judgement) G-explanations? Or, what comes to the same, how are G-explanations of historical events to be verified? Three individually necessary and collectively sufficient conditions must be fulfilled for the verification of a G-explanation (or of a regular explanation for that matter) of a historical event:

the explaining event must have occurred and must be known to have occurred; the explaining event must precede the event to be explained and must be contiguous in time and space with it; and it must be proved that if the cause-event had not happened the effect-event also would not have happened. Let us see how these conditions apply to, and whether they are fulfilled by, a sample G-explanation of a historical event: 'Why was the tomb of Joseph of Arimathea (in which the corpse of Jesus of Nazareth had been interred) empty on Easter morning? The tomb of Joseph of Arimathea was empty, because God raised Jesus of Nazareth from the dead.'

In order for this G-explanation to stand as verified, first we must have good reason for believing that the explaining event actually occurred, which is tantamount to saying that we must have good reason for believing that the statement reporting the explaining event is true, as a primary condition for the verification of the explanation. Since the explaining event in the present case is a G-event and the statement reporting it a G-statement, we are here squarely confronted by the important question, 'How are G-statements verified?'.

Because the verification procedures (and attendant problems) will be worked out in detail in Chapter VI for the statement made by 'God raised Jesus of Nazareth from the dead', an abbreviated discussion of those procedures will suffice here. The statement made by 'God raised Jesus of Nazareth from the dead' is an inference from an alleged body of empirical data which (it can be argued) reveal a distinctive pattern or configuration. That alleged body of data includes Jesus' claims to divine sonship and predictions of his death and resurrection as signs corroborating those claims, his death on the cross, and finally his resurrection as evidenced in the empty tomb and post-resurrection appearances. All of these matters are open to empirical investigation and determinable by means of it; whether or not together they constitute a pattern or configuration is, of course, not an empirical matter. But it is the pattern that spells the difference, since none of the data in isolation from the rest signifies the divine act, though the last item of the three mentioned comes much closer than the other two. If a sound case can be made for the claim that the body of pattern-forming data stipulated above counts conclusively for the statement made

by 'God raised Jesus of Nazareth from the dead', then the first
condition for the verification of our G-explanation for what is
stated in 'The tomb of Joseph of Arimathea (in which the corpse
of Jesus of Nazareth was interred) was empty on Easter morning' will have been satisfied.

Even as our first condition is related to what is sometimes
referred to in discussion of explanations as 'the testability
criterion', so also our second condition is substantially the same
as what is referred to in those discussions as 'the relevance
criterion'.[1] In order for an explanation to be verified, the
explaining clause must be testable, tested, and confirmed, and
that clause must be relevant to the clause which states the matter
to be explained. In other words, there must be some justification
for using the explanation indicator 'because' to link up the
clause that states the matter to be explained with the clause that
states the proposed explanation.

To tie this point in with the G-explanation under discussion,
in order to verify the statement made by 'The tomb of Joseph of
Arimathea (in which the corpse of Jesus of Nazareth had been
interred) was empty on Easter morning, because God raised
Jesus of Nazareth from the dead', we must have good reason for
believing not only that the latter event actually occurred but also
that it caused the former event or that the former event happened
as a result of (because of) the latter event. This is as much as to
say that we must have grounds for establishing 'If God raised
Jesus of Nazareth from the dead, then the tomb of Joseph of
Arimathea (in which the corpse of Jesus of Nazareth had been
interred) would have been empty on Easter morning' as a
causal hypothesis, grounds that is for establishing the *relevance*
of the resurrecting of Jesus to the empty tomb.

According to the previous discussion of historical explanation, that which establishes the causal or explanatory relevance
of one historical event to another are the factors of succession

---

[1] See, for instance, Irving M. Copi, *Introduction to Logic*, Second Edition (New
York, 1961), pp. 426-428.

[2] The opportunity must be seized to challenge a piece of philosophical work of
longstanding repute—Hume's analysis of causality. As I see it, Hume's analysis of
causality is not what it attempts to be and not what it is advertised to be, namely a
conceptual analysis. It is not in fact an analysis of the *meaning* of causal expressions
but instead an analysis of the *grounds* for making causal statements or of the *evidence*
required for proving causal statements.

and contiguity in time and space.[2] The explaining event must be prior to yet contiguous in time and space with the event to be explained. The G-explanation of the empty tomb, therefore, satisfies the second condition, for the explaining event (the raising of Jesus) is allegedly prior to and yet contiguous in time and space with the vacancy of the tomb (the event to be explained). The raising of Jesus, due to its temporal and spatial relation to the vacancy of the tomb, is relevant in an explanatory manner to the vacancy of the tomb. The statement made by 'If God raised Jesus of Nazareth from the dead, then the tomb of Joseph of Arimathea (in which the corpse of Jesus of Nazareth had been interred) would have been empty on Easter morning', therefore, is a plausible causal hypothesis.

But the verification of the statement reporting the explaining event together with the establishing of the relevance of the explaining event to the event to be explained, though necessary, are not enough to verify the explanation. For other events might be relevant in an explanatory fashion to the event being explained and other causal hypotheses might be plausible, since other events besides the one already mentioned might satisfy the first and second conditions. An earthquake might have shaken Judea severely just prior to the tomb becoming empty. Would this be enough to explain the empty tomb? Or a magician might have been inside the tomb waving a cape over the body and muttering incantations simultaneously with its disappearance. Would this cover the task of explanation? Each of these events might have actually occurred just prior to and contiguous in time and space with the emptying of the tomb. Plausible causal hypotheses might be formed out of each of them. The grounds of

---

Transposing all of this into terms explained and used throughout this study, Hume is guilty of conflating statements which give the grounds for believing (evidence for asserting) causal statements with statements which give the meaning of causal statements, i.e., he took 'A is prior to B, and B follows A', 'A and B are contiguous in time and space', and 'A and B are constantly conjoined in experience' as *giving the meaning* of 'A causes B' rather than as *giving the evidence required for asserting* 'A causes B', which is their actual use.

Having (for reasons latent within his particular empiricist presuppositions) eliminated from the concept of 'cause' that which in ordinary speech is its full and essential meaning (i.e., the notion of necessary connexion or of power), he was forced to *reduce* the meaning of 'A causes B' to its method of verification—either that or declare it meaningless. And in this reductionist move Hume is seen to anticipate the checkability theory of meaning.

relevance, i.e., succession and contiguity in time and space, therefore, are not sufficient for the verifying of a historical explanation.[1] Something more yet is needed.

The proof that if God had not raised Jesus of Nazareth from the dead then the tomb of Joseph of Arimathea would not have been empty (despite the earthquake and the magician's trick) must resort again to the strength of the pattern in the data upon which the G-explanation rested in the first place. If that pattern is strong, then these other explanation-candidates are ruled out on the grounds that they do not begin to cover the whole pattern of events in which the event to be explained is enmeshed. If that pattern is weak and there are no patterns supporting the other options, then the G-explanation must still be favoured but inconclusively so; if that pattern is weak and there are other weak patterns supporting the other options, then judgement must be suspended altogether. If that pattern is in fact non-existent, then the G-explanation is ruled out on the first as well as the third condition.

What has been said, especially apropos the third condition, is hardly enough. But the idea of the present discussion is to sketch in rough outline (rather than in finished strokes) what it would take to verify historical explanations in general and this G-explanation in particular. If it is possible to give even in rough outline checking procedures for G-explanations of historical events, then Braithwaite is premature in categorically excluding G-statements from his second group, a group which

[1] The same is true of the grounds for relevance in scientific explanation, i.e., constant conjunction (as established by Mill's methods) notably. Establishing that A and B are constantly conjoined is necessary but not sufficient for establishing that there is a causal nexus between A and B. Suppose that every time a ticker-tape operator in Wall Street hiccupped the Stock Market dropped ten points. The first several dozen times this happened people would probably dismiss it as coincidence rather than causality (though big stock holders might demand the man's dismissal just as a safety precaution). But if the coincidence persisted, people would certainly have good reason to demand that investigations be made to determine if there actually was causality at work here. That would have to be determined by setting up tests to see if there were a number of intermediate and subtle causal steps linking the hiccupping with the market plunges (e.g., the sneeze caused his hand to type the wrong figures, which in turn caused misinformation to be written on the boards, which in turn caused people to make sudden and drastic sales, which in turn made the market plunge). If no such intermediate steps could be discovered, I venture to say that people would go on regarding the constant conjunction a happenstance rather than as causality, even though no other plausible cause was advanced in the interim (which is highly unlikely).

includes by his own admission historical explanations.

4. LOGICALLY NECESSARY STATEMENTS

Finally, do G-statements qualify for membership in the same class with the logically necessary statements of logic and mathematics (and their contradictories)? The answer is, as Braithwaite attests, negative. But it is a somewhat uneasy negative and depends for its security on the degree of adherence our definition of 'G-statement' deserves. 'G-statement' has been defined in this study as 'any statement which makes an outright assertion about God, entails an assertion about God, or in any other way presupposes a commitment to God's existence'. Under this definition, the statements made by 'God loves all human beings' and 'Everyone has a need for God' qualify as G-statements, whereas the statement made by 'Everyone professes a need for God' is ruled out. The first makes an assertion about God, the second (while it makes no assertion about God) presupposes the existential commitment about God, but the third neither makes an assertion about God nor presupposes the existential commitment. If such a definition is in all respects acceptable, then and only then will the answer to the present question be an assured negative.

Those statements which make outright assertions about God or in any other way presuppose the existential commitment about God must be excluded from the present category for exactly the reason that Braithwaite gives: No *logically* necessary proposition asserts existence or presupposes an existential commitment.[1] This should be readily agreed to by most post-Kantian philosophers. But what will likely arouse dispute is whether or not a certain group of logically necessary statements are to be recognized as G-statements even though they lack existential import. It is uneasiness over this group of logically necessary statements which introduces a note of uncertainty into the negative answer to the lead question.

Accompanying every system of propositions (the system of G-statements employed in classical Christian theism included) is a set of propositions stating the meanings of words used in the system and stating entailment relations between statements within the system. Such propositions are logically necessary, or,

[1] *Op. cit.*, pp. 8-9.

if one distinguishes between analytic propositions and those which are logically necessary, these propositions are either analytic or logically necessary. (Braithwaite's third category, it seems to me, disregards a distinction between the analytic and the logically necessary, lumping the two together for practical purposes.) Strictly speaking, any such set of propositions, lacking existential import, does not belong to the system to which it is attached. Nevertheless, the attachment is often so strong as to render moot the question of whether or not the terms of membership in the system should be broadened so as to include this set.

Take for example the sentence 'God is the proper object of worship'. This 'G'-sentence has one use in which the statement it makes is indisputably a member of the system of G-statements. When it is so used that it is equivalent in sense to 'God ought to be worshipped', then it makes a statement about God, presupposes the existential commitment (i.e., unless God exists the question of the truth or falsity of this statement fails to arise), and qualifies under our definition of G-statement. But when the sentence is used so as to be equivalent in sense to ' "God" means "proper object of worship" ', then it makes a statement about 'God' rather than about God (in it 'God' is mentioned, not used), which has no existential presupposition and which does not qualify as a G-statement under our definition. The first use of this 'G'-sentence makes a G-statement, but that statement is not logically necessary because of its existential presupposition. The second use of the 'G'-sentence is analytic because its truth is checkable against meanings only. But is it a G-statement? It does not qualify under our definition of 'G-statement', lacking as it does any existential commitment. And yet is exerts some sort of influence which makes us want to group it together with the class of G-statements. There is some temptation to want to reconstitute the class of G-statements by christening this statement and others like it 'G-statements'.[1]

Another example brings out the temptation even more strongly. If the statement made by 'God raised Jesus of

---

[1] Real definitions of God (such as those cited in the preceding chapter taken from various creeds and confessions), in contrast to nominal definitions of 'God', constitute no problem in this regard. Because they are necessary (stating as they do the defining properties of God) but not *logically* necessary, they can and do presuppose the existential commitment and hence clearly belong to the class of G-statements.

Nazareth from the dead at t_2' entails the statement made by 'Jesus of Nazareth was dead at t_1 and alive again at t_3' (as I hope to show in the following chapter), then the statement made by 'If God raised Jesus of Nazareth from the dead at t_2, then Jesus of Nazareth was dead at t_1 and alive again at t_3' must be an analytic statement. Lacking any definite existential commitment, it does not qualify as a G-statement under our definition. It simply lays down an entailment relation between two statements the first of which by itself would qualify under the definition of 'G-statement'. As with the above, there is a strong temptation to want to christen this a 'G-statement' in order to bring out its close association with other G-statements, particularly the G-statement made by '*Since* God raised Jesus of Nazareth from the dead at t_2, then Jesus of Nazareth must have been dead at t_1 and alive again at t_3'. The latter statement, unlike its counterpart, is only quasi-analytic, since its truth depends only partially and not completely upon the meaning of the clause which states its antecedent. Because the latter conditional affirms rather than hypothesizes the truth of its antecedent, its truth depends also upon the truth of that antecedent. And since that antecedent presupposes an existential commitment to God's reality, the whole conditional has existential import and thereby clearly qualifies as a G-statement under the previous definition.

The exclusion of such analytic statements from the class of G-statements, therefore, is a somewhat uneasy exclusion and depends for what security it has upon the reasons for adhering to the definition of 'G-statement' given above. Though those reasons should probably prevail, they do so with some pull in the opposite direction. Philosophical definitions—this one certainly—usually exist in a polar field with inclinations to be drawn in opposite directions.

One other point about Braithwaite's handling of G-statements apropos the category of logically necessary statements needs to be discussed. About the traditional arguments for a Necessary God (the ontological and cosmological) he says: 'The necessity attributed by these arguments to the being of God may perhaps be different from the logical necessity of mathematical truths; but, if so, no method has been provided for testing the truth-value of the statement that God is necessary being, and con-

sequently no way given for assigning meaning to the terms
"necessary being" and "God".'- Disregarding (for fear of being
repetitious) the obvious criticism that could be brought against
the claim made in the latter part of his statement to the effect
that checking procedures are a necessary condition for meaning
or provide a way for assigning meaning (the criteria-evidence
conflation all over again), his incisive suggestion that the
necessity in these arguments may not be the logical necessity of
mathematical truths bears careful scrutiny.

It seems to me clear, in the case of the cosmological argument
at least, that the conclusion 'God necessarily exists' does not
mean 'The proposition "God exists" is logically necessary'.
'Necessary' does not mean the same as 'logically necessary', else
the latter expression would be redundant, which it is not. The
force of modal qualifiers (such as 'necessary', 'probable',
'improbable', 'possible' and 'impossible' and their adverbial
forms, and cognates such as 'cannot', 'must', etc.) in arguments
is to indicate how much credibility the asserter of the conclusion
is willing to invest in that conclusion in view of the strength of
the evidence he has to go on.[2] When a man says that his
conclusion is necessary or follows necessarily, he means that he
is willing to put his full authority behind the conclusion—a
claim about his estimate of the worth of the argument but not
about the grounds for that estimate. When, on the other hand,
a man says that his conclusion is *logically* necessary, he means
the same as the preceding, but in addition he indicates the

[1] *Ibid.*, p. 9. For discussion of Necessary Being and what 'God necessarily
exists' means, see the following: contributions in *New Essays* by J. J. C. Smart
(pp. 38-41), J. N. Findlay (pp. 47-56, 71-75), G. E. Hughes (pp. 56-67), and
A. C. A. Rainer (pp. 67-71); Patterson Brown, 'St Thomas' Doctrine of Necessary
Being', *Philosophical Review*, LXXIII (1964): 76-90; R. L. Franklin, 'Necessary
Being', *Australasian Journal of Philosophy*, XXXV (1957): 97-110; Charles
Hartshorne, *The Logic of Perfection and Other Essays in Neoclassical Metaphysics* (La
Salle, Illinois, 1962), pp. 3-117; Ronald W. Hepburn, *Christianity and Paradox*,
pp. 171-185; John Hick, 'God as Necessary Being', *Journal of Philosophy*, LVII
(1960): 725-734, and 'The Idea of Necessary Being', *The Princeton Seminary
Bulletin*, LIV (1960): 11-21; P. AE. Hutchings, 'Necessary Being', *Australasian
Journal of Philosphy*, XXXV (1957): 201-206, and 'Necessary Being and Some
Types of Tautology', *Philosophy*, XXXIX (1964): 1-17; Terence Penelhum,
'Divine Necessity', *Mind*, N.S. LXIX (1960): 175-186; and Alvin Plantinga,
ed., *The Ontological Argument from St Anselm to Contemporary Philosophers* (Garden
City, New York, 1965).
[2] For a full discussion of this account of the role of modal qualifiers in argument,
see Stephen Toulmin, *The Uses of Argument*, pp. 11-93.

L

grounds for his estimate; he indicates that his conclusion is entailed (formally or materially) by the evidence statements and that in verifying the evidence statements one would have *ipso facto* verified the conclusion.

In the cosmological argument, there is no question that the conclusion is not entailed (in the semantical sense of 'entails')by the evidence statements. To say at the conclusion, 'God necessarily exists' or 'God therefore must exist', is only to say that God does in fact exist and that in view of the strength of the evidence and argumentation (not entailment) one has to go on one is willing to stake one's whole authority on the claim. If an accurate account of the meaning of 'God necessarily exists' has been given here, then neither the meaning nor the evidence for that statement are in doubt. The meaning has just been given, and the checking procedures are exactly the same as those for 'God exists' which have been stipulated in the preceding chapter.

It is, however, one thing to give the meaning and checking procedures for 'God necessarily exists' (or 'God therefore must exist') and another thing to give them for 'God, the Necessary Being, exists', a sentence which is used in theology to make a different claim. Inasmuch as 'necessary being' is a foil for 'contingent being' (i.e., 'causally dependent being'), a necessary being and a causally independent being are one and the same. To say that God is the Necessary Being, therefore, is to say that God is uncaused, or self-caused, or self-existent. It is not, however, to say that God is the first cause (for God could exist uncaused without causing anything else to be), nor is it to say that God is eternal (for God might have sprung into being spontaneously at some point in time, though this would presuppose that something else existed when he did it, since time is a relation of things among themselves). And to say that a Necessary Being exists is to say that there exists one thing which does not owe its existence to some other thing (i.e., which is not caused). Specifying checking procedures for the statement made by 'God, the Necessary Being, exists' is a difficult matter which need not detain us here. The important point to be brought out is that the statement made by 'God, the Necessary Being, exists' has existential import and consequently cannot belong to Braithwaite's third category. He is right in this but wrong in concluding from it that 'God, the Necessary Being, exists' is cognitively meaningless.

5. RESUMÉ AND AGENDA

Two excellent representatives from among the challengers (the metatheological sceptics) have been heard out on the checkability issue. There has been much to learn, constructive as well as negative, from an examination of the metatheological contributions of Flew and Braithwaite. Before moving ahead to the chapters in which my views of the falsifiability and verifiability of G-statements will be brought to completion, a recapitulation of the criticisms and lessons elicited in this chapter and the one preceding, and a preview of the material to be covered in the next two chapters, are in order.

Through an examination of the theses proposed in Flew's essay and in Braithwaite's lecture, a number of recurring fallacies have been brought to light. The root error in both was seen to be the conflation of evidence with criteria, of the grounds for believing a statement to be true or false (the checking conditions) with the conditions which would actually make a statement true or false (the truth-conditions). This error is manifested (for both) in their adherence to some version of the checkability theory of meaning. A natural corollary (for both) of that theory is the view that having empirical checking procedures is a necessary condition for factual meaning (whereas it has been shown in Chapter II that having checking procedures of any sort, empirical or non-empirical, is a sufficient but not a necessary condition of factual meaning). Closely associated with the checkability theory and its corollary is the empiricist dogma (shared by both Flew and Braithwaite) that all and only empirical facts are facts, that factual meaning is to be identified with empirical meaning, and that the only checking procedures relevant to establishing factual assertions are empirical checking procedures. From these presuppositions the approach of Flew to the falsifiability of G-statements and of Braithwaite to their verifiability is easily explainable.

In the process of examining some of the problems in the metatheological contributions of Flew and Braithwaite, a number of points were made which should enhance our grasp of

the logic of G-statements. Verification and falsification procedures were outlines for the statements made by 'God loves all
human beings' and for 'God exists', since Flew pressed the
issue on those G-statements in particular, and it was shown how
and to what extent empirical considerations enter into the
checking procedures for those statements. Even as general
procedures for checking existential claims were sketched in the
course of treating 'God exists' specifically, so also general procedures for checking explanations were worked out in the course
of discussing the verification of certain G-statements which
could be used in appropriate contexts to do the job of historical
explanations. The intricacies of 'direct', 'indirect', and 'know' in
difficult epistemological contexts were explored and applied to
the problem of verifying G-statements. But by far the most
profitable result of the work done in the present and preceding
chapters is the insight into G-statements gained through extensive and detailed comparison and contrast of them with the
paradigm cases of cognitive discourse (i.e., particular empirical
statements, explanations and general empirical statements, and
logically necessary statements) and with certain classes of
statements also rendered problematic by the checkability theory
(i.e., statements about other minds, the past, the external
world, the future, and scientific unobservables). Such comparing
and contrasting is just the sort of philosophical work through
which the location of G-statements on the logical map (to use
a metaphor with some currency in contemporary philosophy)
must be plotted.

Besides the problems exposed and the profit extracted from
the present and preceding chapters, there have also been
promises as yet unfulfilled. These may be summarized briefly in
preparation for their discussion in the following two chapters.
A full defence of the conclusive (in principle) falsifiability and
verifiability of some G-statements on empirical grounds alone
has been promised as the climax of this entire study of the
relation of the cognitive meaning of 'G'-sentences to the
checkability of the corresponding G-statements. Involved in the
proof and also promised beforehand, accounts must be given of
how the checkability is 'conclusive' in the light of the infinite
corrigibility and open texture objections, of how patterns or
configurations in the empirical data provide grounds for G-

statements, and of how the logical type-gap between empirical evidence and theological conclusion can be warranted. These matters are among the most interesting and difficult in philosophy, and their relevance to the main thrust of this entire study is undeniable.

CHAPTER V

FALSIFIABILITY

In Chapter III checking procedures were suggested for the G-statement made by the sentence 'God loves all human beings'. Since the primary evidence statements both for and against this G-statement are themselves G-statements, its principal checking procedures admittedly are non-empirical. Stipulating *non-empirical* checking procedures for some G-statement or class of G-statements, however, might impress but could hardly be expected to convert the metatheological sceptic. His requirement for cognitive significance—checkability *on empirical grounds alone*—has been shown to be unnecessary. But if it could nevertheless be satisfied for some G-statement or class of G-statements, then from the metatheological sceptic's viewpoint a more compelling case for the cognitive significance of the sentences used in making those G-statements is unimaginable. Having already demonstrated the inadequacy of the major premise (the checkability theory of meaning) of the sceptic's prime argument, it remains now to conclude the disproof of its minor premise (that G-statements are in principle uncheckable empirically).

Some G-statements, contrary to the sceptic's conviction, *are* in principle conclusively verifiable and conclusively falsifiable on empirical grounds alone. Those G-statements are the ones having some empirical anchorage,[1] as reflected in their having

[1] I am not referring to the same thing that I. T. Ramsey refers to with his phrase 'the empirical anchorage of theology'. I have in mind the connexion between certain G-statements and statements about the past external world; he has in mind the connexion between each G-statement and some statement or set of statements about present subjective experience. For according to Ramsey, theological language is understood only when it evokes a 'discernment-commitment' response experience, a sudden apprehension of meaning (hinted at by such phrases as 'the penny drops') followed by a typically religious commitment. See his *Religious Language: An Empirical Placing of Theological Phrases*, pp. 11-48 especially; 'Contemporary Empiricism: Its Development and Theological Implications', *The Christian Scholar*, XLIII (1960): 181-184; and *Christian Discourse: Some Logical Explorations*.

some empirical entailments and incompatibles. Being G-statements, not all of their entailments and incompatibles can be empirical (i.e., G-statements are not reducible to empirical statements). But those entailments and incompatibles that are empirical provide the possibility to the related G-statements of conclusive checkability on empirical grounds alone.

Putting aside the verifiability problem for the next chapter, the argument of the present chapter states that G-statements with empirical entailments and incompatibles can be conclusively falsified on empirical grounds alone along one or both of two lines: (1) If a G-statement has a purely empirical entailment, and if that empirical entailment is conclusively falsifiable on empirical grounds alone, then the entailing G-statement is (on analogy with *modus tollens*) *ipso facto* conclusively falsifiable on empirical grounds alone; or if a G-statement has a purely empirical incompatible, and if that empirical incompatible is conclusively verifiable on empirical grounds alone, then the incompatible G-statement is (on analogy with *modus ponendo tollens*[1]) *ipso facto* conclusively falsifiable on empirical grounds alone. (2) If no G-configuration can be seen in the empirical data supporting a G-statement, then that G-statement is disverified; and if a counter G-configuration can be seen in the empirical data supporting a G-statement, then that G-statement is falsified.

A number of separate points must be secured in order for the argument of the present chapter to stand fast. First, examples of G-statements having empirical entailments and incompatibles must be given and their place in the theological system (classical Christian theism) relative to other G-statements explained.

---

[1] *Modus ponendo tollens* is a fallacy in the truth-functional logic *only*, where disjunction is defined inclusively (i.e., where 'p or q' is true if both p and q are true or if either p or q is true). But where disjunction is defined exclusively (i.e., where 'p or q' is not true if both p and q are true), then *modus ponendo tollens* is a valid method of inference. See Ralph M. Eaton, *General Logic: An Introductory Survey*, pp. 184-185.

When the incompatibility of two statements is formulated as a disjunction, i.e., when 'p or q' means either 'p is contrary to q' or 'p contradicts q', then exclusive disjunction is in operation and *modus ponendo tollens* is valid. Consequently, when an empirical statement is incompatible with a G-statement, we are bound to deny the G-statement if there are solid grounds for asserting the empirical statement. The difference between incompatibility and inclusive disjunction must be kept in mind by anyone tempted to regard *modus ponendo tollens* as fallacious under all conditions.

Secondly, it must be proved (against some powerful objections) that these G-statements do in fact have the empirical entailments and incompatibles here imputed to them. Thirdly, it must be proved that the conclusive falsifiability of these G-statements on empirical grounds alone follows from either the conclusive falsifiability on empirical grounds alone of their empirical entailments or the conclusive verifiability on empirical grounds alone of their empirical incompatibles. Fourthly, it must be proved (in the light of the infinite corrigibility and open texture factors) that empirical propositions are both *conclusively* verifiable and *conclusively* falsifiable. And lastly, there must be shown an acceptable procedure for falsifying these G-statements conclusively and on empirical grounds alone when the first line fails, i.e., when the empirical entailments (though in principle falsifiable) are in fact not false and when the empirical incompatibles (though in principle verifiable) are in fact not true. The necessity for this alternative falsification procedure will be explained when we come to it, and its justification will perforce extend over into the following chapter, since it involves an explanation of the role of G-configurations in checking G-statements (one of the major themes of Chapter VI).

1. THE EMPIRICAL BASIS OF CLASSICAL CHRISTIAN THEISM

Three things should be kept in mind as prolegomena to the discussion of the empirical basis of classical Christian theism. First, it bears repeating that the entire present study is hermeneutically selective, addressing itself as it does to a single system of theological understanding while bypassing others including some of the exciting new options. This must be acknowledged once again lest what follows be thought theologically uninformed and out of touch with current developments. There is real upheaval on the contemporary theological scene over how Christians ought rightly to understand their faith. I have consciously skirted some modern hermeneutical issues of great significance by gearing this study to what I take to be still the 'official' interpretation (insofar as it is any longer possible to speak of one) of Christian faith—classical Christian theism. I have defined classical Christian theism as a somewhat loose confederation of theological systems with agreement on the character of God and on the centrality for faith of the mighty acts of God in history, the resurrection of Christ supremely. It has been my intention on the one hand to defend only the intelligibility (the cognitive significance), not the theological superiority or facticity, of my theological premise and on the other hand to keep my programme as close as possible to consensus (albeit a tenuous one) Christian faith, in which the mighty acts of God in history (as witnessed to in the preaching of the early church, in Scripture, in the historic creeds and confessions of Christendom, and in both Catholic and Protestant orthodox theology) play a decisive role.

Secondly, though the empirical base of classical Christian theism is recognized as multifarious, only what I consider to be its core will be brought under examination here. The God of classical Christian theism is conceived of as transcendent but also immanent and evident within the range of human experience. He is a God who is detectable because his existence and actions are thought to make a difference in the world men know experientially. Classical Christian theism locates its empirical base, synoptically, in man's encounters with the physical universe, human history, and the depths of his own soul. Some classical Christian theists have been intent upon discovering God in the sheer contingent existence of nature, or in its patterned regularity, or in such physical processes as motion, causality, the appearance of novel and more complex forms, hydrogen replenishment, or the transformation of field energy into kinetic energy. Others have found evidence of the divine in mystical visions and presentiments, in the sense of divine-human communion and acceptance, in being addressed and commanded by the word of God heard in the voice of preached Scripture, in the irresistibility of the experience of faith itself, in the feeling of absolute dependence (Schleiermacher), and in anxiety over the threat of non-being (Tillich). The empirical potential for classical Christian theism inherent in physical nature and religious experience, however, is bracketed in this study (without judgement one way or another), in order the better to concentrate upon that which more centrally informs Christian preaching, liturgy, theology, and faith—the person of Christ and his unique history. This decision is made in full awareness that modern theological issues are being ignored

—the issue of whether or not the history of Jesus is recoverable, the issue of whether or not that history, if recoverable, is theologically germane, and above all the issue of whether or not that 'history' is really history or in fact mythology.[1]

And thirdly, classical Christian theism is not the only theology with empirical import, not the only theology which is testable (empirically or otherwise), not even the only theology for which the checking procedures herein elaborated have applicability. Even though the following analysis of the checkability of G-statements is worked out for only a select portion of the empirical base of only one of several hermeneutical understandings of the cognitive meaning of 'G'-sentences in the Christian religion, it is hoped that the general approach here developed will have relevance across a broader front. The present approach is to locate the intersections of religious belief with other areas of human experience and thought and to show how facts established in these areas bear upon the truth or falsity of religious belief. It is a matter of tracing out the checkable consequences of G-statements and of showing how G-statements themselves are checkable in terms of them.

Every theological system, I would maintain, has checkable consequences on the basis of which it stands or falls as a candidate for human credence. If, for example, it could be proved that natural things are not ontically contingent (a partially but not entirely empirical matter), several modern options outside classical Christian theism would be deeply affected. Schleiermacher's theology would be disverified, since he predicated his whole system upon the cognitive content to be extracted from an awareness of ontic contingency (he called it 'the feeling of absolute dependence'). Tillich's theology would be trivialized,

[1] The figure of Rudolf Bultmann stands in the midst of these and related controversies in modern theology. Among recent works, the reader might consult: Hans Werner Bartsch, ed., *Kerygma and Myth: A Theological Debate*, tr. by Reginald H. Fuller, Vol. I (New York, 1961) and Vol. II (London, 1962); Carl E. Braaten and Roy A. Harrisville, eds. and trs., *The Historical Jesus and the Kerygmatic Christ: Essays on the New Quest of the Historical Jesus* (New York and Nashville, 1964) and *Kerygma and History: A Symposium on the Theology of Rudolf Bultmann* (New York and Nashville, 1962); Rudolf Bultmann, *Jesus Christ and Mythology* (New York, 1958); Van Austin Harvey, *The Historian and the Believer: The Morality of Historical Knowledge and Christian Belief* (New York, 1966); Schubert M. Ogden, *Christ Without Myth: A Study Based on the Theology of Rudolf Bultmann* (London, 1962); and James M. Robinson, *A New Quest of the Historical Jesus* (Naperville, Illinois, 1959).

for he defined God as the ground of all (contingent) being'
putting such a God forth as the solution from revelation that
correlates with the existential problem of anxiety over the
threat of non-being. There would be no threat of non-being if
natural things were not ontically contingent, and without the
existential problem the revealed answer would be left dangling.[1]
In like manner, the neoclassical theism of Charles Hartshorne is
checkable. In accordance with his dipolar view of God, God's
existence as a contingent factual reality makes an empirical
difference upon the way the world is, but one which is not
readily ascertainable.[2] More importantly, God's existence as a
necessary or essential reality, though it makes no empirical
difference at all, can be established for Hartshorne by the
ontological argument, of which he is the leading modern exponent. God's existence in the latter mode is also falsifiable, since
the logic of perfection can produce negative as well as positive
results: If the notion of perfection were incoherent (if the notion
of a perfect being were inconceivable) then God would necessarily not exist.[3] Surely the analysis of the checkability of
theology can be extended far beyond what I attempt in this study
with classical Christian theism alone in view.

With these introductory points in mind, we may proceed with
the examination of the empirical basis of classical Christian
theism.

There is no strict hierarchy of types among the G-statements
comprising the system of classical Christian theism. An
important difference must be recognized, nevertheless, between
those G-statements which have some empirical entailments and
incompatibles and those which have none. The difference is

---

[1] It is interesting to note that Tillich's God is as ontically dependent upon natural
things as they upon him. Since Tillich *defines* God as the ground of being (*Systematic
Theology*, I, 156), if there were no beings there would be no God. If God is to
survive in thought the hypothetical non-existence or destruction of the natural
world, then his ground-of-being aspect must be, contrary to Tillich, non-essential
to or non-definitive of his nature.

[2] *The Logic of Perfection*, pp. 108-110.

[3] J. N. Findlay has advanced an ontological disproof of God's existence, for
which see *New Essays*, pp. 47-56, and *Language, Mind and Value* (London, 1963),
pp. 96-104. In the preface to the latter volume, however, he credits Hartshorne
with having convinced him that the logic of perfection leads to the inversion of his
argument as well, i.e. that if God's existence is possible (if the notion of a perfect
being is coherent) it is also necessary.

important enough to mark it by referring to members of the first set of G-statements as 'G_1-statements' and to members of the second set as 'G_2-statements'. Examples of the second set would include such G-statements as those made by the sentences 'Hear, O Israel, the Lord thy God, the Lord is one' (the Old Testament monotheistic thesis), 'God is one yet three, a trinity in unity and unity in trinity', 'God the Holy Spirit proceeded from God the Father and from God the Son together, not from God the Father alone', and 'God loves all human beings'. Each of these G_2-statements (as well as their entire class) has for its entailments and incompatibles only other G-statements. And though empirical facts may enter into their checking procedures at some point, the primary and ultimate data for G_2-statements (their direct evidence) will be expressed only by other G-statements (many of them G_1-statements).

G_1-statements differ in both respects, having some empirical entailments and incompatibles and having only empirical evidence as their primary and ultimate data. The prime example of a G_1-statement and the one upon which we shall concentrate our attention in this and the following chapter is the statement made by 'God raised Jesus of Nazareth from the dead near Jerusalem at t_2'. This G_1-statement entails (*prima facie*) the statements made by 'Jesus of Nazareth was dead near Jerusalem at t_1' (where t_1 is a time just prior to t_2) and 'Jesus of Nazareth was alive and in the vicinity of Jerusalem at t_3' (where t_3 is a time just subsequent to t_2), due to its inclusion of time and place indicators and reference to an empirically identifiable person. These features give the statement its empirical anchorage and thereby its character as a G_1-statement. The statements expressed by 'Jesus of Nazareth was not dead near Jerusalem at t_1' and 'Jesus of Nazareth was not alive in the vicinity of Jerusalem at t_3' are (*prima facie*) incompatibles of the statement made by 'God raised Jesus of Nazareth from the dead near Jerusalem at t_2'.

The claim of the present chapter is that the G_1-statement made by the sentence 'God raised Jesus of Nazareth from the dead near Jerusalem at t_2' is conclusively falsifiable on empirical grounds alone either if its empirical entailments (any of them) are conclusively falsifiable or its empirical incompatibles (any of them) conclusively verifiable on empirical grounds alone, or if a counter G-configuration can be picked out in the empirical evidence (the resurrection predictions Jesus made and the context in which they were made, the circumstances of his death, the empty tomb, the post-resurrection appearances) from which the G_1-statement is inferred.[1] This statement links God with a historical event which is reported to have happened to a particular person at a particular time and in a particular place. Since the person, time, place, and event all belong to the empirical order, the G_1-statement has an empirical anchorage which provides the possibility of empirical checkability. Though the type of empirical checks applicable at the time the event occurred (establishing that the person in question was either dead or alive at t_1 and at t_3) differs from the type of empirical checks applicable now (establishing the authenticity, reliability, and credibility of the historical documents which report the event) the checks are in both cases empirical and the implication for our discussion the same.[2]

---

[1] Actually I am somewhat unfaithful to previous declarations by calling these entailments and incompatibles 'empirical'. They are statements about the past, and such statements have been shown to be different in important respects from the paradigm cases of empirical statements, which, like the statement made by 'The cat is on the mat now', are about the *present* external world and make reference to no substances, properties, relations, or events which are not *now* subject to empirical checks. The historical propositions we are considering, while they make reference to no substances, properties, relations, or events which were not subject to empirical checks *at some time in the past*, are in principle not checkable in that fashion *now*. The logical differences between past-tense statements and present-tense statements must be reckoned with, to be sure. But for the purposes of this discussion, we may by-pass the problem of the past tense and deal with these entailments and incompatibles as though they were empirical statements in the full sense. The important thing is that the people, places, and events named in these statements belong (within their own temporal frame of reference) to the empirical order of things.

[2] As additional examples of G_1-statements, one could cite the statements made by 'God delivered the children of Israel from bondage in Egypt at t_2' and 'Jesus Christ was conceived by the Holy Ghost of the Virgin Mary in Nazareth at t_1'. The first of these two G_1-statements entails the statements expressed by 'The children of Israel were in bondage in Egypt at t_1' and 'The children of Israel were not in bondage in Egypt at t_3' and is incompatible with the denials of each of these entailments. The second entails the statement made by 'Jesus of Nazareth had no biological father' and is incompatible with the statement made by 'The Roman soldier Panthera was the biological father of Jesus'. Both of these G_1-statements have empirical anchorage due to their specific mention of empirically identifiable people, places, and times. And both are conclusively falsifiable on empirical grounds alone either if any of their entailments is conclusively falsifiable or any of their incompatibles conclusively verifiable on empirical grounds alone, or if a counter G-configuration is detectable in the empirical evidence from which they are inferred.

Because G_1-statements have empirical anchorage and because they are logically central to the system of classical Christian theism, it may properly be said that that system rests on an empirical basis. This is tantamount to saying that the same system is grounded in empirical fact (or claims to be) and that the primary and ultimate data for classical Christian theism as a system of beliefs is empirical fact. Proving this claim is contingent upon being able to prove both that G_1-statements do in fact have the empirical anchorage here imputed to them and that they enjoy logical priority within the system in question. The next section of this chapter will be devoted to proving the first of these two contingencies. So we may proceed with the proof of the second now.

G_1-statements, as they are actually used in classical Christian theism, record what are referred to in current theological idiom as 'the mighty acts of God in history'. These mighty acts taken together comprise the kerygma of the church, the proclamation of how God has revealed himself and acted in history for man's salvation. The task of theology is to exegete the kerygma and to trace out the implications and ramifications of the mighty acts of God. Taking the mighty acts of the kerygma as starting-point, the classical Christian theist elaborates as system of beliefs each of which must be justified in terms of whether or not it is a legitimate inference from what is stated or implicit in the kerygma. Since the kerygma is filled with references to historical people, places, dates, and events as well as with references to God and his acts, what those people mean who call Christianity a historical religion and what I mean by attributing an empirical basis to classical Christian theism must be fairly evident.

If this brief sketch of the theological methodology for the system in question is accurate, then one would expect two metatheological points to follow: (1) that G_1-statements would be regarded as in some sense foundational to the system, and (2) that G_2-statements would find their justification ultimately in G_1-statements. The first expectation is fulfilled in the fact that it is now a theological common-place to speak of Christian faith as Easter faith. For the claim that God raised Jesus from the dead is at the very heart of the kerygma, and in reflection upon this one mighty act of God much of the structure of New

Testament theology was worked out.[1] And this leads into the next point, that the second expectation is fulfilled in the fact that so many doctrines in classical Christian theism are justified on the grounds of the resurrection claim. For example, the Apostle Paul argued that belief in Jesus Christ as the Son of God is backed (at least in part) by his resurrection from the dead,[2] as is belief in the general, future resurrection of the dead at the end of the age, when Christ promised to come again.[3] The complex patterns of inference and interpretation here involved are not at issue at this juncture, only the fact that in classical Christian theism with salvation-history orientation G_2-statements are backed ultimately by reference to G_1-statements.

If these claims about the relations between G_1-statements and the other G-statements in the system we are inspecting are true, then it is surely anomalous that in all of the recent metatheological literature (to the best of my knowledge) no attempt has been made to subject G_1-statements to careful logical analysis. The controversies have centred around discussion of the more complex and tricky G_2-statements, such as the statements made by 'God loves all human beings', 'God exists necessarily', 'God is omnipotent', and the like. But if a difficult G_2-statement such as the one made by 'God loves all human beings' (in which the God problem is compounded with the other minds problem) is backed in part by the statement expressed by 'God sent his son to die for the sins of the world', which in turn is backed in part by the statement made by 'The Word became flesh in the person of Jesus Christ', which in its turn is backed partly by the statement made by 'God raised Jesus from the dead', then the discussion of the checkability of G-statements should focus on the logical analysis of G_1-statements. The trend apparent in the recent literature ought to be reversed; the analysis should concentrate on the foundation

---

[1] For corroboration of this claim, one might check the sermons of Peter, Stephen, and Paul in *The Acts of the Apostles* and refer to the following prominent American theologians (among others): Floyd V. Filson, *Jesus Christ the Risen Lord* (New York, 1956), pp. 31-57; Van A. Harvey, 'Resurrection of Christ', *A Handbook of Theological Terms* (New York, 1964), pp. 203-206, and Richard R. Niebuhr, *Resurrection and Historical Reason: A Study of Theological Method* (New York, 1957), p. 90.

[2] Romans 1:4.

[3] I Corinthians 15:12-28.

first and later on the superstructure. Our concern in the present chapter and in the one following, therefore, will be with G_1-statements exclusively

2. THE EMPIRICAL ENTAILMENTS AND INCOMPATIBLES OF G_1-STATEMENTS

Given the claim that G_1-statements are to be distinguished from G_2-statements on the basis of empirical anchorage, the all-important questions arise: Do G_1-statements in fact have this empirical anchorage? Are some of their entailments and incompatibles empirical statements? How can a G-statement entail an empirical statement?[1] In answering these questions our previous discussion of the semantical notions of entailment and incompatibility must be kept in mind,[2] for points established there will be invoked constantly.

The position taken here is that a G_1-statement has empirical entailments if there are entailment-rules to that effect, and empirical incompatibles if there are incompatibility-rules to that effect. To put the matter in terms of our central example, the statement made by 'God raised Jesus of Nazareth from the dead near Jerusalem at t_2' entails the statement made by 'Jesus of Nazareth was dead near Jerusalem at t_1 and alive there again in the flesh at t_3' if and only if there is an entailment-rule to the effect that the first statement entails the second. And that G_1-statement is incompatible with the statement made by 'Jesus of Nazareth was alive near Jerusalem at t_1 and/or dead there at t_3' if and only if there is an incompatibility-rule to the effect that the G_1-statement is incompatible with the other statement mentioned.

---

[1] The question of *how* a G-statement can entail an empirical statement is largely a question about the relation of language to reality and does not concern us at this juncture. Our concern is whether or not some G-statements do in fact have empirical entailments. The even more nettling question of *how* a being like God can cause events in the historical order is of no concern here. But we might draw comfort from the parallel question of how mind-events can cause body-events. It might in fact be false that mind-events cause body-events, or it might be the case that we are unable to say how they do. But it does not follow that a sentence such as 'Jones happened to remember that today is Smith's birthday, so he gave Smith a call', a sentence making just such a claim, fails to make literal sense.

[2] Pages 47–64.

Whether or not there are in fact such an entailment-rule and such an incompatibility-rule can be answered only by an empirical study of the linguistic conventions governing the Meaning (Use) of the sentence 'God raised Jesus of Nazareth from the dead near Jerusalem at t_2'. If by linguistic convention that sentence in Use says something about Jesus being dead at one time and alive at a subsequent time, then the entailment-rule in question exists. And if by linguistic convention that sentence in Use denies that Jesus was alive at one time and dead at a subseqent time, then the incompatibility-rule in question also exists. It will be assumed for the purposes of argument (because it is beyond the province of this study to adduce the relevant empirical evidence) that the linguistic conventions in question actually exist and that therefore the entailment-rule and incompatibility-rule in question also in fact exist, since there is a strong presumption in favour of their existing. Then two objections arise, the first of which accepts the assumption but denies that the cognitivist's conclusion follows from it, and the second of which challenges the correctness of the assumption itself.[1]

The first objection posits that the predicate alone of a 'G'-sentence is responsible for whatever empirical entailment it might have and that therefore nothing at all about the cognitive

---

[1] A powerful theological objection to the assumption, since it rests on premises beyond the methodological scope of the present study, can only be mentioned in passing. Some of the foremost Protestant theologians of the day agree that the understanding of Christ's resurrection in classical Christian theism is a corruption of its original meaning; what was meant to be taken as a mythological symbol, they say, has been mistakenly literalized. They maintain accordingly that in the minds of the earliest Christian witnesses the statement made by 'God raised Jesus of Nazareth from the dead' did not entail that the man Jesus whom they saw crucified, dead, and buried was found later to be physically alive in a publicly observable and objectively verifiable way. Demythologizing the resurrection and interpreting it existentially in an effort to recover its original and therefore normative meaning, these theologians conclude that if the resurrection points to any event at all it is not the objective-historical event of Jesus' bodily resuscitation but the subjective-historical event of the upsurge of faith in Jesus that created the believing church. See Rudolf Bultmann, 'New Testament and Mythology', in Bartsch, ed., *Kerygma and Myth*, I, 38-44, and *Theology of the New Testament*, tr. by Kendrick Grobel (New York, 1951), I, 292-306; and Paul Tillich, *Systematic Theology*, II, 154-158.

For criticisms of the bifurcation of theology and objective history, see John Macquarrie, *An Existentialist Theology: A Comparison of Heidegger and Bultmann* (London, 1955), pp. 159-192; and Richard R. Niebuhr, *op. cit.*, 72-104.

M

significance of the 'G'-sentence *as a whole* follows from the fact that its predicate has empirical entailments. According to this view, it is not the 'G'-sentence itself that has the empirical entailments but rather its predicate. To elucidate by example, this view has it that 'God raised Jesus of Nazareth from the dead near Jerusalem at t_2' does not have the empirical entailment imputed to it above; strictly speaking, it is the predicate alone of that sentence which has the empirical entailment. Join the predicate 'raised Jesus of Nazareth from the dead near Jerusalem at t_2' with any subject imaginable, even those which make nonsense of the sentence as a whole, and the same entailment would result. We can see why, according to this view, the cognitive significance of the sentence 'God raised Jesus of Nazareth . . .' does not follow from the fact that its predicate has an empirical entailment, for any nonsense sentence with that predicate would have the same entailment exactly.

The refutation of this objection turns upon a linguistic convention and its corollary.[1] It is a fact about the rules that bind the use of 'entails' when it is used as a semantical relator (the use in force when it is claimed that a G_1-statement entails an empirical statement) that 'entails' can relate only statement to statement. That fact is implicit in calling 'entails' in this particular use a *semantical* relator, for 'statement' is a semantical concept whereas 'predicate' and 'sentence' are grammatical concepts. It follows that 'entails' in the semantical sense cannot relate predicate to predicate, predicate to sentence, or even predicate to statement, since predicates apart from participation in full sentences in actual use have no meaning from which entailments can be drawn.[2] The present objection, formulated

---

[1] Again we must remind ourselves that there is nothing necessarily sacrosanct about linguistic conventions. Some of them ought to be denounced and revised, i.e., those which corrode the basic function of language—clear communication. But that is not to say that all linguistic conventions are arbitrary and that one is as good as another. A convention which protects the basic function of language is on that ground defensible. To rest an argument upon a linguistic convention, therefore, is not necessarily a mark of weakness. It depends upon the defensibility of the particular convention in question. The defensibility of the convention in question at this juncture is strong.

[2] True, we do on occasion meaningfully and properly say such things as ' "Black" entails "dark in colour" '. But the meaningfulness and propriety of such statements do not reverse the fact that they are ellipses which when filled out support the present thesis. ' "Black" entails "dark in colour" ' is an ellipsis for ' "x is black" entails "x is dark in colour" ', which in turn is an ellipsis (since such expressions

on the belief that the predicate 'raised Jesus of Nazareth from the dead near Jerusalem at t_2' alone entails the empirical statement made by 'Jesus of Nazareth was dead near Jerusalem at t_1 and alive again there at t_3'—that objection collapses.

But suppose that the objection was revised to read: The *statement* which the sentence formed by this predicate in conjunction with any subject imaginable is used to make entails the same empirical statements which 'God raised Jesus of Nazareth . . .' has been reputed to entail. This reformulation of the objection takes into account the fact that 'entails' in the semantical sense can relate only statement to statement. But it falls into paradox and collapses in failing to take into account the corollary of that fact, i.e., that a nonsense sentence makes no statement at all and consequently is incapable of entailing sense, nonsense, or even itself. For the very process of semantical entailment presupposes that a significant assertion has been made in the first place. The reformulated objection collapses through paradox, therefore, in that it implies that a nonsense sentence makes a statement. If the sentence is nonsense it makes no statement, and if it makes a statement it is not nonsense. But a sentence cannot both be nonsense and make a statement.

The falsity of the claim that the sentence formed by the predicate 'raised Jesus of Nazareth from the dead near Jerusalem at t_2' combined with any subject imaginable makes a statement which entails the very same empirical statements that the statement made by 'God raised Jesus of Nazareth . . .' entails can be demonstrated through the analysis of a series of examples. 'X raised Jesus of Nazareth . . .' does not have the empirical entailments in question, because it is a formula, and formulae have no sense (and hence make no statements and have no entailments) until interpreted. This formula is interpretable by replacing the variable 'X' with an appropriate expression. But

as 'x is black' are formulae and hence grammatical entities and hence incapable of semantical entailment) for some such assertion as the one made by 'The statement that the Virgin of Chartres is black entails the statement that the Virgin of Chartres is dark in colour'. So it is possible to give a plausible account of what it means to assert that one predicate entails another. But what could possibly be said to render plausible the claim that a predicate entails a complete sentence or (more fat-fetched yet) a statement? What sense could possibly be given to the sentence 'The predicate "black" entails some such sentence as "The Virgin of Chartres is dark in colour"' or to the sentence 'The predicate "black" entails some such statement as that the Virgin of Chartres is dark in colour'?

there are definite limitations on the type of expression which can combine with this particular predicate to form a sensible sentence capable of making statements with entailments, as will emerge in the following examples: The expression must be a nominal expression, it must be self-consistent, and it must clear with certain type-restrictions.

'Downward raised Jesus of Nazareth . . .' and 'The raised Jesus of Nazareth . . .' both fail to make sense through infraction of grammatical rule. The grammatical rules of the English language forbid the use of adverbs and adjectives as sentence subjects. And since grammatical correctness is a precondition of sense and hence of statement and entailment, these sentences cannot make statements which have the same empirical entailments that the statement made by 'God raised Jesus of Nazareth . . .' has, for they cannot make statements at all.

'The round-square cupola on Berkeley College raised Jesus of Nazareth . . .' also falls under the category of nonsense, and this for two reasons. First of all, the subject-expression, though properly nominal (the root problem with the two preceding examples was that their subject-expressions were adverbial and adjectival rather than nominal), is not self-consistent, and self-consistency is another prerequisite of meaningfulness. But, secondly, even if the inconsistent modifying expression 'round-square' were dropped from the sentence, it would still fail to make sense, for it violates certain important type-restrictions.[1]

The notion of type-restrictions, a semantical notion, is the key to the refutation of this entire first objection. The person who raises this objection is not likely to be much concerned with formulae which are not sentences due to the presence of variables in them, or with sentences which contain nonsense words or break grammatical rules, or with sentences containing inconsistent expressions. In attempting to make his point that the subject has nothing to do and the predicate of the sentence in question has everything to do with producing the empirical entailments in question, he is more likely to be concerned with sentences that are grammatically well-formed and logically self-consistent and that combine with the predicate in question subject-expressions such as 'the cupola on Berkeley College',

---

[1] For a clear statement on the subject of semantical type-restrictions, see P. F. Strawson, *Introduction to Logical Theory*, pp. 224-227.

'the number three', 'the bronze Buddha of Nara', or 'Santa Claus'. Any sentence formed from the combination of the predicate in question with any of these subject-expressions (and many others with similar properties) fails to make sense and hence to be of use in making a statement with the empirical entailments in question, due to the violation of type-restrictions.

There are conceptual as well as grammatical limitations on the combining of words into cognitively meaningful sentences. A type-restriction is simply a semantical rule that prescribes which of the grammatically acceptable combinations of words are also conceptually acceptable combinations for literal sense. 'The blonde-haired triangle flirted with the first volume harmonized by the square root of two' is perfectly grammatical (compare it with 'The blonde-haired waitress flirted with the first sailor beached by the shoreboat'). But it breaks a number of type-restrictions: A geometrical figure (triangle) is in concept not the sort of thing which grows hair of a specifiable colour (blonde), inanimate objects (triangle, book) are in concept not the sorts of things that can be related in animate activity (flirtation), and a number (the square root of two) is in concept incapable of causal action (harmonization).

Consider another example: We all know the literal sense of 'right triangle'. But what possible literal sense could 'right-handed triangle' have? We can imagine metaphorical uses for 'left-handed triangle' (an awkwardly shaped triangle perhaps) and 'off-handed triangle' (a carelessly drawn triangle maybe). We might even be able to concoct a metaphorical sense for 'right-handed triangle'—a triangle with an elongated side inclining toward the viewer's right, say. Even if a metaphorical sense could be found for this expression, it would still violate type-restrictions, since type-restrictions govern the limitations on literal but not metaphorical sense.[1] And just as there are type-restrictions on which modifiers can combine with which substantives to make literal sense, so also there are type-

---

[1] It is true that type-restrictions are not permanently fixed and incorrigible rules. What was metaphor yesterday may become literal sense today, or tomorrow. No one today, for example, regards the expressions 'a current of electricity' and 'a flow of electrons' as metaphors, because the words 'current' and 'flow' have become incorporated into the technical vocabulary of electronics. Yet no one would deny, upon reflection, that these expressions have their roots in metaphor.

restrictions on which subject-expressions can combine with which predicate-expressions to make literal sense.

The predicate 'raised Jesus of Nazareth from the dead near Jerusalem at t_2' cannot (due to semantical type-restrictions) combine with any and every grammatically acceptable subject-expression to form a sentence that makes literal sense. There are several type-restrictions on the subjects combinable with this predicate to form a sentence with literal sense. Most importantly, 'to raise' is a causal verb requiring by semantical rule a subject which names an efficient-causal agent.[1] 'The cupola on Berkeley College raised Jesus of Nazareth . . .', 'The number three raised Jesus of Nazareth . . .', and 'The bronze Buddha of Nara raised Jesus of Nazareth . . .' all fail to meet this requirement for literal sense. 'Santa Claus' names a causal agent, but since the predicate in question calls for a non-fictional causal agent, 'Santa Claus raised Jesus of Nazareth . . .' also fails to make literal sense.

'Zeus raised Jesus of Nazareth . . .' and 'Allah raised Jesus of Nazareth . . .', on the other hand, clear with the type-restrictions placed on the causal verb 'to raise'. These sentences make literal sense, and they can be used to make statements with the empirical entailments in question. (The same could be said of sentences employing such subject-expressions as 'Gabriel', 'Satan', 'the Apostle Peter', and 'Pontius Pilate'.) Granted, there may not be or ever have been a Zeus or an Allah (or a Jahweh for that matter), but falsity is not to be confused with fiction nor an entity which does not in fact exist with one which in concept is imaginary. It still makes literal sense to say that Zeus or Allah raised Jesus of Nazareth from the dead at t_2. And granted, there are powerful theological objections to making these assertions even if there were in fact a Zeus or an Allah,

---

[1] The stress here belongs on the word 'agent'. The cupola on Berkeley College, the number three, and the bronze Buddha of Nara are capable of causal *efficacy* (for which point as well as for other helpful criticisms of this section especially I am indebted to Professor George I. Mavrodes of the University of Michigan) though not of causal *agency;* they are capable of producing a causal effect but not expressly through the medium of themselves taking action. If it were said 'The cupola on Berkeley College created a furore among the alumni', 'The number three fascinated Pythagoras', or 'The bronze Buddha of Nara attracts many visitors', causal efficacy but not causal agency or action is attributed to the respective sentence subjects. It is literally impossible to conceive of such things as these taking an action of any sort, unless their present natures were altered (which is conceivable).

i.e., there are doctrines within the theological systems in which 'Zeus' and 'Allah' play a part which would come into sharp logical conflict with the assertion that either Zeus or Allah raised Jesus of Nazareth from the dead near Jerusalem at t_2.[1] But this fact does not argue against the literal meaningfulness of those assertions.

What can be concluded from the discussion of this first objection? It can be concluded that the claim upon which that objection is predicated is false, the claim that the sentence formed by the predicate 'raised Jesus of Nazareth from the dead near Jerusalem at t_2' in combination with any subject-expression imaginable can be used to make a statement which entails the very same empirical statements that the statement made by 'God raised Jesus of Nazareth . . .' entails. The claim is false, because only statements entail statements, and because a nonsense sentence cannot be used to make a statement which entails, and because certain grammatical and semantical restrictions render nonsensical the sentences formed by the predicate in question in combination with many imaginable subject-expressions. 'God raised Jesus of Nazareth from the dead near Jerusalem at t_2' is not the only sentence with that predicate which can be used to make a statement with the empirical entailments in question, but many sentences with that predicate fail to have the sense from which those entailments can be drawn.

This 'G'-sentence makes a statement with no distinctive empirical entailment, it is true. That is to say, the corresponding G-statement has no empirical entailment that is lacking to the statements made by 'Zeus raised Jesus of Nazareth . . .', 'Something raised Jesus of Nazareth . . .', or any other cognitively significant sentence with the predicate in question. But it does not follow that therefore 'God raised Jesus of Nazareth . . .' has no distinctive G-significance at all, for the statement that sentence makes will have other (non-empirical) entailments that no other statement with the same predicate has.

The point of all this, of course, is that if any sentence is used to make a statement having the entailments in question, this

---

[1] It is, for example, orthodox Muslim belief that the prophet Jesus did not die on the cross, having been replaced by a facsimile (who did die on the cross) and translated directly into heaven. This belief is, of course, radically incompatible with the resurrection claim.

alone says something about the cognitive significance of that sentence. For only an actual statement has entailments, and only a cognitively significant sentence can be used to make an actual statement.

The second objection grows out of the theory about language-strata.[1] This theory posits that language is stratified into layers each of which is characterizable on the basis of 'the texture of the concepts which occur in a given stratum, the logic of its propositions, the meaning of truth, the web of verification, the senses in which a description (in that stratum) may be complete or incomplete'.[2] Examples of discrete strata would be scientific laws, material-object statements, sense-data statements, and other-minds statements, to mention only a few. The theory also posits that each stratum is logically independent of all others, that is to say that entailment- and incompatibility-relations are always intra-stratal and never inter-stratal.[3] After several decades of attempts to prove the opposite, it must now be admitted that a material-object statement, to cite one example, is not entailed by and does not entail a set (however large) of sense-data statements. And the same must be said for statements about minds over against statements about bodies, and for scientific laws over against statements recording particular observations. The reductive analyses are now defunct. That is the language-strata theory.

If one were to view the thesis of the present chapter—that G_1-statements have empirical entailments—within the context of the language-strata theory, one might be prompted to come up with this objection: Statements such as that made by 'God raised Jesus of Nazareth from the dead near Jerusalem at t_2' and statements such as that made by 'Jesus of Nazareth was dead near Jerusalem at t_1 but alive there at t_3' must be placed in different language strata (since they differ in concept-texture, verification web, etc.), any two language strata are logically independent, and therefore the first statement cannot entail the

---

[1] See F. Waismann, 'Language Strata', in *LL*-II, pp. 11-31, and 'Verifiability' in *LL*-I, pp. 128-129.

[2] Waismann, 'Language Strata', in *LL*-II, p. 30.

[3] Waismann, 'Verifiability', in *LL*-I, p. 128: 'We may say that the known relations of logic can only hold between statements which belong to a *homogeneous* domain; or that the deductive nexus never extends beyond the limits of such a domain.'

second. This objection, though cogent on the face of it, can be turned back by accepting the major but rejecting the minor, or by rejecting the major. But the former method of refutation is preferable.

It *could* (but will not here) be argued in reply to the objection that, since empirical investigation shows that there is an entailment-rule joining the first statement to the second, i.e., that people do in fact take the meaning of the first to include the meaning of the second, it follows that these two statements belong to the same language stratum. The major premise of the objection, in other words, is false. But this refutative move would presuppose that logical independence is the defining characteristic of a language stratum and that the other criteria for differentiating language strata are only secondary. It would seem, however, from the way the language-strata theory is constructed that just the opposite is the case—that concept-texture, verification-web, etc., are the defining characteristics of a language stratum and that logical independence is an empirical generalization (rather than a defining characteristic) drawn from the study of many independently established language strata.[1] Out of respect for what seems to be the proper interpretation of the theory, therefore, denying the major will not be pressed as a method of refuting the objection.

The objection is still disposable by rejecting the minor. There is some point to insisting that the two statements in question belong to different language strata; certainly an application of such criteria as concept-texture, verification-web, etc., would support that placement.[2] Granting the major premise of the

[1] It is very difficult to say one way or the other just from a reading of Waismann's two articles. It is perhaps only fair to say also that in an editorial note prefacing the 'Language Strata' article in *LL*-II, the reader is informed that some of Waismann's views in the article have changed since its original presentation to the Jowett Society at Oxford in 1946. But which views and the direction of their change is not indicated.

[2] At the same time, there is also some point in placing both in the same language stratum: Beside the fact (already noted) of their entailment relations, both are statements about the past, a language stratum with a significant style all its own. Perhaps the greatest deficiency of the language-strata theory is that it inclines toward a deceptively simple picture of language in which each statement has one and only one placement. Actually, any given statement has several placements, e.g., the statement made by 'God loved Jacob but hated Esau' is a G-statement, an other-minds statement, and a statement about the past (with some unique differences due to the time-eternity problem in theology) all at the same time. And for any

objection, however, does not oblige us to concede the conclusion. If logical independence is not a criterion for differentiating one language stratum from another, then the minor premise stands or falls with the observed lack or presence of entailment and incompatibility relations between language strata. If logical independence is not part of the meaning of 'language stratum', then there is no theoretical objection to the thesis that a statement of one language stratum entails statements of another stratum. And whether or not that entailment-relation holds is a question to be decided by investigating the meaning of the sentences used in making the particular statements involved, not by applying a definition or even an empirical generalization about other language strata. Without impugning in the slightest the contention that the deductive nexus does not extend between scientific laws and particular observation statements, between material-object statements and sense-data statements, between other-minds statements and statements about bodily behaviour, etc., therefore, we are free to assert that G_1-statements have empirical entailments if the relevant entailment-rules can be backed by an empirical investigation of how people actually do use and understand the statements involved.

3. THE FALSIFIABILITY INFERENCE-PATTERN

Having refuted objections to the claim that some G-statements have empirical entailments and incompatibles, the next step is to prove the following: If those entailments are conclusively falsifiable or those incompatibles conclusively verifiable on empirical grounds alone, then the entailing or incompatible G-statement is also conclusively falsifiable on empirical grounds alone. In order to make fast the falsifiability inference-pattern

---

one placement a statement may find itself in the company of other statements from which it is separated in another placement. Statements p and q may be placed together on the statements-about-the-past, -present, -future differential, but placed separately on the statements-about-minds and -about-bodies differential. And in certain respects a past material-object statement and a past sense-datum statement are more similar in style than a past material-object statement and a present material-object statement, while in other respects the converse is true. Generally speaking, any picture of or theory about language which obscures significant similarities and differences between specific statements through placement in a system of hard and fast categories is to be criticized. And the language-strata theory is surely not immune to this criticism.

for G-statements as just described, we must argue from analogy. Surely we can count on *modus tollens* and *modus ponendo tollens* (for exlusive disjunction only) being fully accredited argument forms in the eyes of the metatheological sceptic, and they will serve as the analogues in this justification of the falsifiability inference-pattern for G-statements.

The justification itself is simple, self-contained, and perspicuous. It may be summarized as follows: If 'p entails q' and 'q is false' together entail 'p is false' (which they do, under the rubric of *modus tollens*), then by virtue of the analogy between 'false' and falsifiable' 'p entails q' together with 'q is conclusively falsifiable on empirical grounds alone' entail 'p is conclusively falsifiable on empirical grounds alone'; and if 'p is incompatible with q' and 'q is true' together entail 'p is false' (which they do, under the rubric of *modus ponendo tollens* applied to exclusive disjunction), then by virtue of the analogies between 'true' and 'verifiable' and between 'false' and 'falsifiable' 'p is incompatible with q' together with 'q is conclusively verifiable on empirical grounds alone' entail 'p is conclusively falsifiable on empirical grounds alone'.

I can anticipate only one strong objection that could be brought against this inference-pattern leading to the falsifiability of those G-statements that have empirical entailments and incompatibles. There are also at least two weak objections that might come up, which shall be disposed of first.

To begin with, it might be pointed out that any G-statement, regardless of how many *empirical* entailments and incompatibles it may have, has at least some non-empirical entailments and incompatibles, for no G-statement is reducible to empirical statements. How then, it might be asked, can we speak of any given G-statement being *conclusively* falsifiable without showing that *all* of its entailments are conclusively falsifiable and *all* its incompatibles conclusively verifiable? And how can we speak of any G-statement being conclusively falsifiable *on empirical grounds alone* when some of the entailments which must be shown to be conclusively falsifiable and some of the incompatibles which must be shown to be conclusively verifiable are *non-empirical?*

The answer to these questions is straightforward. For a start, it must not be assumed that the non-empirical entailments of any given G-statement could not themselves be conclusively falsifiable on empirical grounds alone just because they are non-empirical.[1] This is a mistaken assumption, for it just might be that all of the non-empirical as well as the empirical entailments of that G-statement are conclusively falsifiable on empirical grounds alone. The same holds for the non-empirical incompatibles of any given G-statement. But this is a secondary point. The main point here is that it is not necessary that all of the entailments of a G-statement be conclusively falsifiable on empirical grounds alone or all of its incompatibles conclusively verifiable on those grounds in order for the G-statement itself to be conclusively falsifiable on empirical grounds alone. The conclusive falsifiability of only one entailment or the conclusive verifiability of only one incompatible on empirical grounds alone is sufficient to establish the conclusive falsifiability on empirical grounds alone of the original G-statement. An understanding of *modus tollens* and *modus ponendo tollens* will confirm this claim.

In the second place, it might be reasoned that if p entails q, the conclusive falsifiability of q on empirical grounds alone is evidence for the conclusive falsifiability of p on empirical grounds alone, but the former does not establish the latter deductively. The query here pertains to the reputed certainty with which the conclusive falsifiability of p can be known from the conclusive falsifiability of q.

The answer to this query is subtle but compelling. It must be granted that if it is known that q (an entailment of p) is inconclusively falsifiable, then p can be no more than inconclusively falsifiable (unless, of course, some other entailment of p is known to be conclusively falsifiable). It must also be granted that if it is not known that q is conclusively falsifiable (q again being an entailment of p), then it cannot be said that p is known to be conclusively falsifiable (with the same proviso as above). Whatever evidence counts for the conclusive falsifiability of q, however, counts *ipso facto* for the conclusive falsifiability of p, and we can *know* that p is conclusively falsifiable if we *know* that q is conclusively falsifiable *and* that p entails q. What the query brings to light is the present hypothetical nature of the inference-

---

[1] It is difficult to know whether statements with some empirical and some non-empirical entailments should be called 'empirical', 'non-empirical', 'quasi-empirical', or what. I solve the problem by stipulation and call them 'non-empirical'.

pattern leading to the conclusive falsifiability of p. All that has been said in this section is that *if* q is entailed by p and is conclusively falsifiable, *then* p is *ipso facto* by a deductive process also conclusively falsifiable. This query is guilty of anticipation and will be silenced once it is shown (in the following section) that the entailments of G_1-statements are in fact conclusively falsifiable on empirical grounds alone and their incompatibles conclusively verifiable on the same type of grounds.

The one major objection that could be posed against the falsifiability inference-pattern presently under consideration is predicted on the observation that *modus tollens*, upon which that inference-pattern depends, seems to break down in certain cases including the present one. When p entails q and p is a spurious statement (having at least one unfulfilled existential commitment) but q a genuine statement (having no unfulfilled existential commitments), in Strawson's senses of 'spurious' and 'genuine' again, then neither the falsity nor even the falsifiability of q can be conferred by *modus tollens* upon p. If p is spurious, *ex hypothesi* it can be neither true nor false and hence neither verifiable nor falsifiable, regardless of the truth value or checkability status of its entailments. For example, the statement that the present king of France is bald (a spurious statement since there is at present no king in France) entails the statement that someone is bald (a genuine statement).[1] Suppose it is the case that no one happens to be bald and hence that the statement made by 'Someone is bald' is false. It would not follow that any statement, spurious or genuine, which entails that somebody is bald (e.g., the statement that the present king of France is bald) must like its entailment be false or even falsifiable. This example demonstrates that and under what conditions *modus tollens* is exceptionable.

To anyone for whom the existence of God is questionable, the falsifiability inference-pattern I have been expounding will surely seem on these terms suspect. The statement made by 'God raised Jesus of Nazareth from the dead near Jerusalem at

---

[1] A statement need not be genuine in order to have entailments. A spurious statement can entail, and even entail a genuine statement. For a statement to be able to entail, it need only be an actual statement in contrast to a merely putative statement. The statement that the present king of France is bald is actual rather than putative and its corresponding sentence 'The present king of France is bald' a cognitively significant sentence.

t_2', for example, may well entail the statement made by 'Jesus of Nazareth was dead near Jerusalem at t_1 but alive again at t_3', as I have argued. But, it could be urged, the falsifiability of the entailing G_1-statement is not necessarily deducible by *modus tollens* from the entailment relation plus the falsifiability of the empirical entailment. If it were, it would seem that the entailing G_1-statement would have to be genuine and hence that God would have to exist. But it would be preposterous to posit that God's existence was proved by proving that some G_1-statement entails an empirical statement which happens upon examination to be genuine and false. According to the present objection, therefore, nothing about the falsifiability of a G_1-statement p can be concluded from the facts that p entails q and q happens to be falsifiable (and hence genuine).

This objection can be turned back by means of a distinction and a qualification. First, it must be recognized that even a spurious statement is perfectly falsifiable *in principle* though not in practice. We know precisely how to falsify in principle the spurious statement made by 'The present king of France is bald': Go to France, look up the king, and see that he has a fine head of his own hair. This is feasible, because falsifiability in principle depends only upon the actuality and not the genuineness of the statement in question, i.e., only upon the cognitive meaning of the sentence used in making the statement in question. Falsifiability in practice, on the other hand, depends upon a number of contingent, empirical matters, including the genuineness of the statement in question; proving that all the existential presuppositions of a statement are fulfilled is, of course, a contingent, empirical matter. Even though genuineness is a precondition of falsifiability in practice and even though the question of falsifiability in practice does not arise for spurious statements, the falsifiability inference-pattern for G_1-statements presently under discussion is not threatened so long as falsifiability in principle alone is considered. That is to say, even if a given G_1-statement were spurious, as long as it was actual in contrast to merely putative and as long as it had clearly falsifiable entailments, its falsifiability in principle could be deduced from the entailment relation plus the falsifiability of its entailment.

What now of the falsifiability *in practice* of G_1-statements under the present scheme? Must that facet be abandoned? No, for it can be argued that they are indeed falsifiable in practice also, though only provisionally or conditionally. The condition they must fulfil is that they be genuine or that their genuineness at least be open to discussion. The glaring difference between the statement made by 'The present king of France is bald' and any such G_1-statement as that made by 'God raised Jesus of Nazareth from the dead near Jerusalem at t_2' is that the first is *known* to be spurious whereas the second is not. So, while we must say that the first is not false, falsified, or falsifiable in practice (the very question of its falsifiability in practice fails to arise), we are permitted to say of the second that nothing prohibits the question of its falsifiability in practice from arising and even that it is falsifiable in practice provided it is genuine and God exists. As long as the question of God's existence is at least open to discussion, the provisional falsifiability of G_1-statements in practice under the present scheme (via *modus tollens*) remains intact.

Nor is it possible for this situation to worsen with further inquiry into the existence of God. Since the transcendent existence of God (though disverifiable) is not falsifiable, G_1-statements can never be known to be spurious. Hence their falsifiability in practice must always remain at least provisionally open. Were God's existence to be verified, on the other hand, it would then follow that any given G_1-statement was as completely falsifiable in practice (unconditionally, unprovisionally) as in principle.

How damaging is the acknowledgement of this one qualification (falsifiable in practice only *provisionally*) upon the falsifiability scheme for G_1-statements presently under consideration? It does no damage at all. In the first place, for the purposes of this study falsifiability in principle is sufficient to establish the cognitive significance of 'G'-sentences. We have seen that the cognitive significance of a given 'G'-sentence follows from the falsifiability in principle of an entailment of its corresponding G_1-statement, even if that statement were spurious by having a false existential presupposition. The cognitive significance of 'G'-sentences, therefore, is not endangered by contingent, empirical matters such as whether their corresponding G-statements are genuine or spurious and whether or not God exists.

Furthermore, while God's existence is open to discussion, it seems reasonable to assume for the sake of argument that G_1-statements are in fact genuine rather than the opposite and falsifiable in practice rather than not, in order to keep the checking enterprise viable. If we assumed the opposite, we would quit checking out prospective G_1-statements and the investigation of whether or not G_1-statements are falsifiable in practice would be prejudiced. There is, consequently, no decisive reason for regarding the present scheme for establishing the falsifiability of G_1-statements via *modus tollens* as suspect even when falsifiability *in practice* is under consideration.

4. STRONG VERSUS WEAK CHECKABILITY

It remains to establish that the empirical entailments of G_1-statements are *conclusively* falsifiable and their empirical incompatibles *conclusively* verifiable on empirical grounds alone. In order to do this, satisfactory answers must be found and presented against the claim that the infinite corrigibility and open texture factors render all empirical statements *in principle* inconclusively verifiable and falsifiable. For it would follow from this claim that all G_1-statements are *ipso facto* at best inconclusively falsifiable. Inconclusive falsifiability might satisfy the metatheological sceptic's qualifications for cognitive meaningfulness. But the risk that it would not is unnecessary, since it is possible to complete the argument for the conclusive falsifiability of some G-statements.

Waismann's arguments with respect to the theoretical inconclusiveness of the verifiability and falsifiability of all empirical statements are typical,[1] and so the rebuttal can be developed from a consideration of them alone. For Waismann, empirical statements are in principle inconclusively verifiable because they are infinitely corrigible and because the empirical concepts contained in them have the quality of open texture. To say that an empirical statement is infinitely corrigible is simply to say that, since there are always more tests of already known types that could be performed relative to the verification of that statement, its verification is essentially incomplete at any given

[1] 'Verifiability', in *LL*-I, pp. 118-124.

moment and consequently our judgement on it perennially subject to revision in the light of some future test. And to say that the empirical concepts contained in an empirical statement have the quality of open texture is to say that, since these concepts are not bound by rigid rules covering every imaginable situation in which the concepts might be applied, brand new situations might eventually arise which would create new types of tests, call for new linguistic decisions, and change the present boundaries of those concepts.

If the infinite corrigibility and open texture arguments hold against the possibility of conclusive verifiability, they must hold also against the possibility of conclusive falsifiability.[1] For if p, an empirical proposition, is in principle not conclusively verifiable, then not-p (also an empirical proposition per force the meaning of negation) must also be in principle not conclusively falsifiable.[2] The question is whether the infinite corrigibility and open texture arguments hold against either conclusive verifiability or conclusive falsifiability. It will be contended here that they hold against neither.

Those who deny conclusive or strong verifiability (or falsifiability) often resort instead to inconclusive or weak verifiability (or falsifiability).[3] The move is natural, but in it their undoing comes to light. It has been pointed out, and I believe correctly, that the way the sceptic draws the line between conclusive and inconclusive verifiability (or falsifiability) makes

[1] *Ibid.*, pp. 125-126.

[2] Popper maintains that this is not true for scientific laws, the checking procedures for which, he says, are asymmetrical, i.e., laws are conclusively falsifiable but not conclusively verifiable. See *The Logic of Scientific Discovery*, pp. 40-44, 84-92. I myself believe that Popper's proposed asymmetry is a delusion springing from the same sources as the infinite corrigibility doubt. Besides, Popper overlooks the fact that the conclusive falsification of any law-statement, L, depends upon the conclusive verification (and hence verifiability) of some singular negative empirical proposition, not-p. For L is conclusively falsified only if L entails p and not-p is conclusively verified. And if it makes sense to speak of the conclusive verifiability of not-p in the face of the infinite corrigibility factor, then I maintain it makes sense to speak also of the conclusive verifiability of L in the face of its universal reference, even though at no time can we have canvassed all the cases to which L applies. In both cases, not-p and L, we would then be using 'conclusively verifiable' in its ordinary sense, i.e., even when there are unchecked possibilities in view and entailment of the conclusion by the evidence is out of the question.

[3] See Waismann, 'Verifiability', in *LL*-I, p. 125: 'I propose to say that the evidences $s_1, s_2 \ldots s_n$, *speak for* or *against* the proposition p, that they *strengthen* or *weaken* it, which does not mean that they prove or disprove it strictly.' (Italics his.)

of it a pseudo-distinction and that therefore the withholding of the expression 'conclusively verifiable' (or 'conclusively falsifiable') from empirical statements is based on a confusion.[1] It is not that 'conclusive verifiability' (or 'conclusive falsifiability') and 'inconclusive verifiability' (or 'inconclusive falsifiability') mean the same thing, but rather that as used they have no clear meaning at all. The proof of this point is the crux of my refutation of the infinite corrigibility and open texture arguments against the conclusive verifiability and falsifiability of empirical statements.

The argument goes something like this: If all empirical propositions are inconclusively verifiable (or inconclusively falsifiable), then 'conclusively verifiable' (or 'conclusively falsifiable') would have to be a literally significant expression. But if 'conclusively verifiable' (or 'conclusively falsifiable') is a literally significant expression, then it would have to *make sense to say* that there were some conclusively verifiable (or conclusively falsifiable) statements, even though it might in fact be false that there were any. But the people who speak of inconclusive verifiability (or inconclusive falsifiability) deny that it even makes sense to say of any statement that it is conclusively verifiable (or conclusively falsifiable). And those who tried to save the significance of 'conclusively verifiable' (or 'conclusively falsifiable') by allowing that it made sense to say that sense-data statements were conclusively verifiable (or conclusively falsifiable) failed to achieve their purpose, because sense-data statements are not verified (or falsified) in the requisite sense. One does not *verify* sense-data; one simply *has them*. So, it emerges that 'conclusively verifiable' (or 'conclusively falsifiable') is not a literally significant expression for these people, because it does not make sense for them to say either truly or falsely that any statement is conclusively verifiable (or conclusively falsifiable). And if 'conclusively verifiable' (or 'conclusively falsifiable') is not for them a literally significant expression, then neither can the contrary expression, 'inconclusively verifiable' (or 'inconclusively falsifiable') be literally significant.[2]

---

[1] Morris Lazerowitz, 'Strong and Weak Verification I' and 'Strong and Weak Verification II', *The Structure of Metaphysics* (London, 1955), pp. 117-143. Strawson's *Introduction to Logical Theory*, pp. 238-241, is also relevant.

[2] Lazerowitz, *op. cit.*, pp. 122, 138ff.

This argument is basically sound. Those who reject conclusively verifiability (or conclusive falsifiability) encounter
difficulties contingent upon their departure from the ordinary
use of 'conclusively verifiable' (or 'conclusively falsifiable').
They suppose, mistakenly, that this expression is applicable
only to statements about which it is *logically impossible* to be
wrong, a class void of empirical statements. It is not here denied
that empirical statements one and all have the factors of infinite
corrigibility and open texture. They have them. What is here
denied is that, having them, empirical statements are thereby
not conclusively verifiable (or conclusively falsifiable).

With respect to any given p, the infinite corrigibility and
open texture factors raise 'shadow doubts'; that is to say, there
might not be any actual negative evidence against p on the
scene at any given moment, but it is logically possible that there
could be. We are aware of what would count against p (although
it has not occurred, say), and we are aware that we are unaware
of completely novel situations which might someday arise to
count against p (although we cannot for the life of us imagine at
the moment what they might be, say). And somehow we give
equal weight, or perhaps even *more* weight, to these shadow
doubts than we would give to some actual counter-evidence
against p, were some available. We take the shadow doubts and
convert them into counter-evidence. We say, in effect, that the
logical possibility of counter-evidence against p, either of the now
known (the infinite corrigibility factor) or of the now unknown
(the open texture factor) types, arising in the future *is itself
counter-evidence against* the conclusive verifiability (or conclusive
falsifiability of p. And this is ridiculous.

Shadow doubts do not warrant withholding the verdict of
'conclusively verifiable' (or 'conclusively falsifiable'). The
logical possibility of new evidence arising in the future is not
itself new evidence, either pro or con. Only a genuine doubt
warrants withholding the verdict of 'conclusively verifiable' (or
'conclusively falsifiable'). A genuine doubt arises when we have
no evidence at all, or when we have some positive evidence
mixed with some negative evidence, or when we have in the
absence of negative evidence some but not enough positive
evidence, or when we have enough of one type of positive
evidence but none or not enough of other known types of

positive evidence, etc. Surely it is in principle possible to have enough of all the known types of positive evidence in the absence of any negative evidence. *But this is all that 'conclusively verifiable' means.* Surely, therefore, there is no giant obstacle blocking the argument for the thesis that the conclusive falsifiability on empirical grounds alone of their empirical entailments or the conclusive verifiability on empirical grounds alone of their empirical incompatibles entails the conclusive falsifiability on empirical grounds alone of G_1-statements.[1]

Now to get down to cases. Agreement is assumed that the statement made by 'God raised Jesus of Nazareth from the dead near Jerusalem at t_2' entails the statements made by 'Jesus of Nazareth was dead near Jerusalem at t_1' and 'Jesus of Nazareth was alive again in the flesh near Jerusalem at t_3', and that the denials of these two entailments are incompatible with the original G-statement. If either one of the entailments is conclusively falsifiable on empirical grounds alone, then so is the entailing G-statement. And if either one of the incompatibles is conclusively verifiable on empirical grounds alone, then the G-statement is conclusively falsifiable on empirical grounds alone. Actually, showing that the entailments are conclusively falsifiable and showing that the incompatibles are conclusively verifiable are one and the same process, since the incompatibles in this case are merely the denials of the entailments. So for simplicity's sake, we shall focus only on the entailments, but for the sake of breadth we shall attempt to show that those entailments are both conclusively verifiable and conclusively falsifiable on empirical grounds alone.

Prior to embarking upon this venture, it is necessary to have an understanding with the historian and one with the philosopher. The historian must be made to see that no encroachment upon his territory is taking place. We are not here trying to

[1] Lazerowitz had the early writings of A. J. Ayer in view when he criticized the weak-verifiability position. It is interesting to observe how Ayer's thinking has changed over the years. On the verifiability score he now says: 'There are a great many statements the truth of which we rightly do not doubt; and it is perfectly correct to say that they are certain. We should not be bullied by the sceptic into renouncing an expression for which we have a legitimate use. Not that the sceptic's argument is fallacious; as usual his logic is impeccable. But his victory is empty. He robs us of certainty only by so defining it as to make it certain that it cannot be obtained.' *The Problem of Knowledge*, p. 68.

determine whether or not in fact Jesus was dead at t_1 and alive at t_3. That is his business, not ours. We are simply trying to establish prescriptions for checking the truth or falsity of these entailments, i.e., we are trying to state clearly what would in principle count conclusively for and conclusively against these statements. As for the philosopher, he must be informed that for the purposes of brevity something important is to be deliberately left out. The statements in question are trans-categorical, that is, they belong both to the category of statements about the past and to the category of statements about the external world. The fact that they have membership in both categories compounds the factors involved in outlining verification and falsification prescriptions. So, to simplify matters, the factors relating to checking statements about the past will be dismissed, and we shall regard the statements for which verification and falsification prescriptions are to be outlined as statements about the present external world. In other words, we shall transpose ourselves backward in time and view the verification and falsification prescriptions for these statements from the standpoint of their own temporal context.

What would it take to falsify conclusively on empirical grounds alone the statement made by 'Jesus of Nazareth was dead near Jerusalem at t_1'? We would have to be able to show either that the person in question was not Jesus of Nazareth, or that this person was not dead, or that the time in question was not t_1, or that the place in question was not the environs of Jerusalem. Let us discount the time and place problems to begin with, supposing that we are there on the scene, that accurate chronometers show that it is now t_1, and that maps, charts, sextants demonstrate that we are in the environs of Jerusalem. Let us proceed from there. If the person in question had in his clothing an authentic birth certificate with photograph, fingerprints, and descriptions of bodily characteristics (height, weight, eyes, hair, scars, etc.), all of which identified him as someone *other* than Jesus of Nazareth, and if the parents of the person in question likewise identified him as someone else, and if a person in the crowd could establish that he himself (through birth certificate, parental testimony, etc.) was Jesus of Nazareth, we would have no other choice than to admit that the statement with which we began was conclusively falsified.

But let us suppose, on the other hand, that the birth certificate on the dead man, parental testimony, etc., all identified him as Jesus of Nazareth, then the statement in question could still be conclusively falsified by proving that the man was not really dead. If there were present a board of six eminent physicians, each of whom in turn (and without comparing diagnoses until the very end) took the pulse, listened to the heart-beat through the stethoscope, tested respiration, checked the electro-encephalogram for brainwaves, and performed all the known tests for establishing biological (in contrast to clinical, from which people have known to resuscitate) death; and if all six unanimously concurred in the judgement that the person in question was *still living:* and if we were given the opportunity to run through the same tests, check their instruments and reputations, and all of this confirmed their judgement, then we would have to concede that the statement in question was conclusively falsified.

From what has just been worked out, it is not difficult to write up a prescription for the conclusive verification of the statement made by 'Jesus of Nazareth was dead near Jerusalem at t_1'. Ways of conclusively checking on the identity of the corpse have already been suggested, and if in addition through the physicians' testimony and our own observations we found that the pulse had stopped, that the heart was not beating, that there were no respiration and no brainwaves, that the body had become bluish and rigid, and perhaps that the tissues were beginning to decompose and to putrify, and that over 40 per cent of the cerebral cortex had disintegrated, then what else could be possibly said other than that the lead statement was conclusively verified?

Prescriptions for the conclusive verification and falsification of the statement made by 'Jesus of Nazareth was alive again in the flesh near Jerusalem at t_3' would follow the same pattern, only the chronometers would give a different reading. If at t_3 we were present at the tomb of Joseph of Arimathea (making sure through sufficient checks that we had the right location), and if the corpse of Jesus of Nazareth (similar tests being used to establish the identity of the corpse) were in that tomb, stiff, blue, putrified, decomposing, and with no pulse, heartbeat, respiration, brainwaves, Babinski reflex, etc., then the lead statement would be conclusively falsified. If, on the other hand, at t_3 we find the tomb of Joseph of Arimathea vacant, and then we encounter a living man (using all the relevant tests to establish that he was really alive) whom we could identify as Jesus of Nazareth (applying the aforementioned tests for this), then obviously the appropriate thing to say would be that the lead statement was conclusively verified.

These prescriptions for the conclusive verification and falsification of the two empirical entailments of the statement made by 'God raised Jesus of Nazareth from the dead near Jerusalem at t_2' are more rigorous in their demands than they really need be. Some appropriate subset of tests in each relevant area would actually suffice in proving the same points beyond the shadow of reasonable doubt. But since such expressions as 'sufficient evidence' and 'beyond a reasonable doubt' are vague in logical discussions of this variety, it was thought wise to make the prescriptions so complete that none but the shadow-doubt sceptic could possibly dissent.

If anyone demands that more evidence be provided before the verdict of 'conclusively falsifiable' or 'conclusively verifiable' is pronounced, then the onus is upon him to show through cogent argumentation why the prescriptions suggested are really insufficient and how much more evidence and of what types would be needed in order to be able to come to a verdict. If he cannot so stipulate and in his stipulations show a significant difference between his prescriptions and those suggested here, or if in his stipulations he falls back on the infinite corrigibility and open texture factors, then either he is simply intransigent or he has somewhere in the course of the discussion transformed the meanings of its controlling expression 'conclusively verifiable' and 'conclusively falsifiable'.

For if by 'conclusive' he means 'enough evidence to render a mistake in the verdict *logically impossible*', then either his meaning is intelligible but his victory completely hollow or else his meaning is unintelligible and his argument therefore hopelessly confused. In either case, we are entitled to ignore him altogether. For if he can render intelligible the expressions 'conclusively verifiable empirical statement' and 'conclusively falsifiable empirical statement' (remembering that empirical statements are never secure from the logical possibility of error), then he is absolutely right and has won a complete victory on the ground marked out by his definition of 'conclusive'. The problem is that this ground is not the ground marked out for discussion, since we are interested in determining whether or not empirical statements are conclusively verifiable and falsifiable in the *ordinary* sense of 'conclusive', which has nothing to do whatsoever with the *logical* impossibility of error. If, on the other hand, he cannot render intelligible his understanding of the expressions 'conclusively verifiable empirical statement' and 'conclusively falsifiable empirical statement', then his whole point sinks into a quagmire of conceptual confusion.

In the face of such argumentation, nothing finally seems to forbid our granting that the empirical entailments and incompatibles of G_1-statements are conclusively verifiable and falsifiable on empirical grounds alone.

5. G-CONFIGURATIONS AND FALSIFIABILITY

The theory of falsifiability for G_1-statements is, however, still incomplete and needs to be augmented in order to include methods for falsifying two types of claims: claims in which God's actions are falsely attributed to some other causal agent and claims which falsely attribute some action to God as causal agent. That the falsifiability scheme already explicated (via *modus tollens*) is inapplicable to such cases will be shown in what follows.

Involved in the falsification procedure for both types of claims is the employment of G-configurations as the standard for establishing falsity. By 'G-configuration' I mean a pattern which is either present in the evidence, absent from the evidence, or contradicted by the pattern which is present in the evidence bearing upon the G-statement in question. As the term 'G-configuration' itself suggests, the pattern in question is the pattern one would expect (under some specific definition of God) to find in experienced data if that experience were indeed an experience of that God. For every definition or concept of God (set of prescriptions for identifying God in thought) there can be derived a corresponding set of prescriptions for identifying God in experience or for identifying any experience as an experience of that God. Such a set of prescriptions for identifying God in experience can be called a 'model G-configuration' and can be used for spotting actual G-configurations in experienced data. The justification of the role I am imputing to G-configurations in the checking procedures for G-statements will be deferred until the next chapter, in which it can be presented more expeditiously. The urgency here is just to give completeness to the theory of falsifiability for G_1-statements.

Suppose for the sake of argument that we knew with certainty that Jesus of Nazareth was in fact dead near Jerusalem at t_1 and alive again in the flesh in the same locale at t_3. Suppose further that of three men in possession of this information one says 'Jahweh raised Jesus of Nazareth . . .', another says 'Baal raised Jesus of Nazareth . . .', and the last claims 'Zeus raised Jesus of Nazareth . . .'. All three of these causal hypotheses are meaningful from the standpoint of the type-restrictions governing what subject-expressions can be meaningfully combined with that particular predicate-expression, and so all three of these G-statements entail the statements made by 'Jesus of Nazareth was dead near Jerusalem at t_1' and 'Jesus of Nazareth was alive again in the flesh near Jerusalem at t_3'. All three would be falsified if their empirical entailments were known to be false (or if their empirical incompatibles were known to be true). But according to the present supposition, the empirical entailments of all three are in fact true, and so falsification is not possible along the lines of the inference-pattern outlined in the preceding three sections of this chapter. And yet the three G-explanations seem, on the surface at least, to come into sharp logical conflict with one another. The situation described points up the necessity for a falsification procedure for G_1-statements which applies when their empirical entailments are in fact true and when their empirical incompatibles are in fact false.

The notion of 'G-configuration' is the key to the needed falsification procedure completing the theory of falsifiability for G_1-statements. If the G-configuration conceptually related to the subject-expression of a G-statement cannot be seen in the empirical data supporting that G-statement, then that G-statement is disverified; and if a configuration counter to the one conceptually related to the subject-expression of a G-statement can be seen in the empirical data, then that G-statement is falsified. So much for the over-view of the falsification procedure; now let us see how it applies to the situation described above.

All of the concepts and articles of faith essential to a given theological system provide the raw material from which the G-configuration for that system is abstracted (although I shall not venture here a precise refinement of how this is accomplished). Given as data the facts that Jesus of Nazareth was dead near Jerusalem at t_1 and alive again in the flesh there at t_3, how are these facts to be explained, and how are we to know when proposed explanations are true or false? In accordance with the falsification procedure outlined above, we have only to ask and answer this question: Is the G-configuration for theological system X present or absent from the empirical data requiring explanation? If the G-configurations for the theological systems incorporating Jahweh, Baal, and Zeus are all absent from the data requiring explanation, then all three of the G-explanations proposed within these three theological systems must be pronounced disverified (though not known to be false). If the G-configuration for any one of the three is present, then the relevant G-explanation must be pronounced true and the others false, since the remaining two come into sharp logical conflict with it. No two G-configurations will be exactly alike, for the theological systems from which they are abstracted will have significant conceptual and creedal differences. In cases where G-configurations overlap appreciably we may not be able to make an intelligent decision about the truth or falsity of the two pertinent G-explanations. But such a limitation does not render the falsification procedure employed here null and void, though it does point up its limitation. Where two G-configurations are sharply differentiable (e.g., those for Jahweh and for Zeus), then we should expect to encounter no difficulty in coming to a certain verdict. So much for the case where God's (i.e., the God of classical Christian theism) actions are falsely imputed to some other causal agent.

Now what about those cases where some action is falsely attributed to God as the causal agent? How could we go about falsifying the statement made by 'God made Jones drive his golfball into the rough' when its empirical entailment (the statement made by 'Jones drove his golfball into the rough') is in fact true, or how could we successfully deny the statement made by 'God prompted Mr X. to kill his wife and children with a hatchet' (such stories are occasionally reported in newspapers) when its empirical entailment (the statement made by 'Mr X. killed his wife and children with a hatchet') is unfortunately true to fact? The process is much the same. We have only to ask and answer the telling question: Is the G-configuration for the God in question (in these cases, presumably, the God of classical Christian theism) present, absent, or contradicted by the configuration which actually is present? If the G-configuration in question is present, then the causal statement with 'God' as subject-expression must be pronounced true. If that G-configuration is simply absent, then the causal statement is disverified (but not in the full sense falsified). And if some configuration counter to the G-configuration in question can be seen in the data requiring explanation (the schizophrenia configuration, say, if we have in view the examples above), then the causal statement can be said to be fully falsified.

It must be admitted that this process at times yields only disverification and not falsification in the full and proper sense. This should evoke no lamentation. There are numerous comparable situations outside the theological realm when the best we can do is disverification and when the course of rational moderation is to say that in the light of the evidence available, though the proposition in question cannot be said to be true nor false, at least it can be said that it is without support and hence lays no claim to our belief. With these points the discussion of the cognitive significance of 'G'-sentences relative to the falsifiability criterion is terminated.

CHAPTER VI

VERIFIABILITY

Whatever ground may have been gained in the chapter just concluded will hopefully be fortified and made more secure by the argument of the present chapter. For it the metatheological sceptic credits empirically based falsifiability as a sufficient condition for cognitive meaningfulness, presumably he can be counted upon to pay the same respect to empirically based verifiability. The thrust of this chapter, therefore, is continuous with that of the one preceding, namely to try to show the metatheological sceptic that G_1-statements are on his own terms cognitively significant from yet another vantage point—conclusive empirical verifiability. To put the matter in alternative phrases, the present chapter sets itself the task of rendering the logic of G_1-statements perspicacious by making explicit the data from which the conclusion is drawn (in an inference to a G_1-conclusion), the warrant authorizing the inference, and the backing used in support of the warrant.[1]

[1] 'Data', 'conclusion', 'warrant', and 'backing' are (along with 'qualifier' and 'rebuttal') the key terms employed in Stephen Toulmin's general layout of arguments See *The Uses of Argument*, pp. 94-107. It will be convenient to borrow his apt terminology for the present analysis, for it provides a powerful theoretical framework for the sort of logical analysis we shall need to do in this chapter. The customary terminology leaves implicit too much of importance and is therefore prone to hampering obscurity. To speak of a statement and the evidence which verifies it leaves unanswered (and unasked) the question of what gives us the right in any particular case to call the evidence *evidence* and the question of what kind of step is taken in any particular case from the evidence to the statement to be verified. Referring to this step in every case as 'verification' might mislead us into believing that the step is in every case the same, which it is not. Employing the alternative terminology of 'data', 'conclusion', 'warrant', and 'backing' brings these matters out into the open and provides a more powerful instrument for the analysis of verification procedures. The concept of 'warrant' reminds us that an inference takes place from the evidence to the statement being verified and that, since warrants vary, the step is not always the same. And the concept of 'backing' reminds us that any set of data is logically neutral until it has been constituted as evidence by due process of backing. For the function of the warrant-backing process is essentially just this—to constitute the data as *evidence* from which an inference can be drawn.

1. DATA AND WARRANT: ARGUING FROM CLUSTERS OF SIGNS

In accord with the principle that every sort of statement has its own sort of logic, we might expect to find a variety of inference-routes employed in theological reasoning. It has already been explained that G-statements are a heterogeneous lot displaying logically significant differences. 'God so loved the world . . .' makes an other-minds claim which, though expressed in the past tense, is understood to apply not only to time past; '. . . that he gave his only son . . .' states something about God's historical action that is understood to refer to a specific time in the past. The statement made by 'God will judge the quick and the dead' differs in logic from that made by 'God raised Jesus of Nazareth from the dead near Jerusalem at t_2', not only in the respects that predictions (which can also, and in this case do, function as promises or threats) differ from resports (which can also, and in this case do, function as instruments of persuasion and rein-forcement of belief), but also in the respects that legal actions such as pronouncing the verdict of guilty or innocent differ from causal actions such as raising a dead man to life again. It is only natural, therefore, that reason in deriving these logically heterogeneous G-conclusions should draw upon different orders of primary information (data), employ a variety of inference-rules (warrants) and justify those rules on divergent grounds (backing).

The moral of all this is plainly that we would do well to approach the analysis of religious language with an eye to discriminating the logically significant features of each indivi-dual G-statement. Such an approach would present a salutary contrast to the one often encountered—analysis through place-ment in a classifactory scheme containing a few (*too* few) gross and insufficiently discriminative categories.

Cognizant of this very moral, it is possible nevertheless to see broad similarities in the inference-routes leading to a large number of fundamental G-conclusions, including G_1-conclusions, the objects of our special interest in this study. The general inference-route in question takes as its data a cluster of signs, moves from there to the G-conclusion by means of an inference-rule or warrant that might be stated with deceptive simplicity as

'D (a cluster of signs) signifies C (some G-conclusion)', and backs this warrant by drawing attention to the way the individual signs in the cluster hang together in a pattern or configuration.

Sign reasoning, i.e., taking a step in thought from a sign (something which stands for or points to something else) or signs to that which the signs indicate or signify, has wide applicability in daily life. By means of it we forecast tomorrow's weather as rainy or fair, diagnose the baby's ailment as roseola, discern Mary's true feelings toward John, and try to anticipate the Russians' next move at the disarmament conference table. This needs to be said in order to remove at the outset any suspicion that the inference-route just described belongs to some logical limbo rather than to the order of rationality. The type of backing required by the warrant in sign reasoning may vary from argument to argument, as will emerge later. The point here is that the common acceptance and great utility of this kind of reasoning testify to its freedom from inherent stigma.

The importance of the data being constituted by a *cluster* of signs also needs to be stressed at the out-set. Individual signs indicate very little in isolation from their natural clusters due to the fact that most individual signs are polyvalent. A man scratching the tip of his nose, for example, may in the context of one cluster of signs indicate that he has an itch at that location, in another context indicate that he suffers from a nervous affliction, and in yet another context indicate that he wants his bridge partner to follow up his no-trump lead in the bidding. But in isolation that sign is ambiguous and means none of these things specifically, precisely because in the relevant cluster it may mean any one of them. The same is true of such facial signs as the grimace: In the context of a certain cluster it indicates physical pain, in another severe disappointment, in yet another a reaction to a poor joke, etc. Snapping of the fingers may be indicative of an eager response to the rhythm of a piece of music, or of a command to the dog to heel, or of an attempt to get the waitress' attention, etc., again depending upon the context of the cluster of other signs in which it occurs. It is, therefore, clusters of signs rather than individual signs that serve as the data in sign reasoning. Or, if you prefer, the cluster itself *is the sign*.

It was said that sign reasoning figures prominently as an inference-route leading to G-conclusions, and this needs to be illustrated. Here we might once again invoke the parable of the gardener, in the same positive context in which Wisdom introduced it rather than the pejorative use Flew made of it. As was remarked in Chapter III where Flew's treatment of the parable was criticized, the strength of the inference that an invisible, intangible, eternally elusive gardener tends the plot increases in proportion to the vividness with which the garden-pattern stands out in the plot itself (together with the failure of tests to locate an empirical gardener). A few scattered flowers growing among the weeds hardly warrants the inference. But neat, artfully arranged rows of healthy flowers which rotate perfectly with the seasons, a faultlessly functioning irrigation system, a perennially trimmed hedge, a white picket fence that never needs painting, a sign saying 'Keep on the footpath', absence of weeds—such a phenomenon together with failure to detect a normal, empirical gardener would be a very different matter for any rational mind to try to cope with and understand. For such a pattern in the plot would constitute a garden, and a garden is a sign signifying the presence and effort of a gardener. These observations on the gardener parable should illuminate the logical contour of the teleological argument for God's existence, though the question of whether the mind-pattern is actually to be found in nature is, to be sure, another matter. The vividness with which it may be found is the measure of the cogency of that argument, for if such a mind-pattern exists it signifies the presence and industry of a transcendent mind.

For the sake of variety, let us look at another example, one with less philosophical but perhaps more popular religious appeal. The statement made by 'God has transformed Jones's life during the past ten years' may be cited as another (albeit hypothetical) G-conclusion based on sign reasoning. It has to do, let us imagine, with a causal explanation for a striking change in Jones's will as manifested in a cluster of behavioural signs implicit in a story which might read as follows: For thirty solid years, Jones was in inveterate criminal, a habitual alcoholic, and a cruel, irresponsible husband and father. The combined efforts of several outstanding psychiatrists, Alcoholics Anonymous, the best methods of penal correction, and a patient, loving family netted only negative results. Jones's own persistent and sincere efforts at self-reformation changed nothing. He was pronounced hopeless by every authority who interviewed him. Then one night ten years ago, in a drunken stupor he opened the Bible at random and read a passage that electrified him: 'But he said to me [Paul], "My grace is sufficient for you, for my power is made perfect in weakness." I will all the more gladly boast of my weaknesses, that the power of Christ may rest upon me.' (II Corinthians 12:9, RSV.). Immediately his head cleared, he later testified, and he prayed with great urgency for God's grace. A very real sense of peace followed the prayer, according to his own story, and an inward strength which has never left him. And for the past ten years he has been an exemplary husband and father, employee, churchman, and citizen.

The details of the story have been exaggerated for illustrative purposes. I do not say that this argument from story to G-conclusion is unassailable; its *style* alone is of present interest. The point of the example is that, as with the garden-gardener inference, the G-conclusion is derived from a cluster of signs by means of an implicit warrant 'D signifies C'. If an inquirer presses for the backing for this inference from data to conclusion, he who professes the truth of the conclusion has no other recourse than to try to point up how the parts of the story fit together into a coherent pattern or configuration signifying divine agency. He might stress the experimental failure of all the other means, or the religious context in which the trans-formation occurred, or the striking correspondence between the scripture verse and Jones's religious experiences immediately following the prayer for God's grace, or the qualities of awe and wonder which pervade the sudden and radical transformation out of a hopelessly entrenched pattern of behaviour, or any number of other features about the sign cluster. Controlling all of his efforts to back his inference, however, would be the necessity of showing his interlocutor that the data were more than a random collection of bits of information and in fact displayed a certain pattern which has been referred to before in this study as a 'G-configuration'—that pattern which marks data as G-significant and by means of which God is to be identified in experience.

The success of the backing process depends entirely upon the degree of emergence or non-emergence of the G-configuration. If a G-configuration stands out vividly in the data, then the warrant 'D signifies C' has to be regarded as backed and validated and the conclusion of the inference (supposing, of course, that all the details of the data are also known to be true) established conclusively. Obscurity or vagueness in the G-configuration would require modification of the qualifier in the conclusion to read 'Probably C' or 'Possibly C' rather than 'Certainly C'. If, on the other hand, a G-configuration fails altogether to emerge from the data, then the backing process has aborted, and the warrant has to be regarded as invalidated and the inference (even though we might know that all of the data are true) as nullified. This is not to say, of course, that the conclusion of the inference has been disproved or its negation proved, but only that the conclusion is disverified and its truth-value for the time being suspended. The conclusion may in fact be true, but the argument advanced in its behalf has not established that fact. And finally, if a configuration does emerge from the data which to some degree conflicts with the model (i.e., normative) G-configuration, then we must say of the G-conclusion that it is probably false or certainly false, depending upon the extent and seriousness of the conflict.

That is to say, if there stood out vividly in the data a Zeus-configuration or a Gabriel-configuration or a Satan-configuration or (more possibly) some sort of human agent or natural process configuration, let us say, instead of a configuration matching the model (normative) G-configuration for classical Christian theism (prescription for identifying God in experience, derived from the definition of God or prescription for identifying God in thought formulated within that particular theological system), then the G-conclusion would be falsified to the extent the conflicting configuration stood out in the data. This point about falsification was stressed in the last section of the preceding chapter. But our main concern presently is with verification. Apropos verification it need be emphasized that in theological sign reasoning, it is the warrant-backing operation—use of the model (normative) G-configuration for detecting a G-configuration in the data—which if successful constitutes the data a sign signifying some G-conclusion. In sign reasoning generally, the essential function of the warrant-backing process (let me

o

repeat) is to instate the data as *evidence* from which an inference is reasonably drawn.

These are the general outlines of and methods for testing the inference-route from sign clusters to G-conclusions. The varieties of data from which the sign clusters are formed as well as some of the logical idiosyncracies of the conclusions drawn from those clusters matter very little to the validity of this sort of sign reasoning. The logical style of the inference will be the same in all cases, and so a single set of standards for criticism will apply. The inference may move from a sign cluster rooted in mystical or religious experience to some such conclusion as the statement made by 'God has transformed my life'.[1] It may

---

[1] Three remarks need to be made apropos of G-inferences in which the sign cluster is rooted in religious or mystical experience. In the first place, those who claim to have had such experiences often describe them as direct encounters with God. Such a description is apt and need not conflict with the claim that sign reasoning is involved. For a discussion of how knowledge can be direct and inferred at the same time—for that is the issue here—see pages 135-138. Secondly, inferences from the experiences themselves can be drawn only by those who have had them. The second party to the fact can make inferences only from the *manifestations* of those experiences in the bodily behaviour of the first party. In other words, Smith cannot make inferences from Jones's religious experiences but only from the behavioural manifestations of those experiences. And thirdly, some but not every affirmation that a Christian *qua* Christian is called upon to make can be derived from what is commonly called religious or mystical experience. There is no set of religious experiences that I or anyone else can have in 1969, for example, from which I or anybody else can by sign or any other reasoning conclude that God raised Jesus of Nazareth from the dead near Jerusalem in the first half of the first century A.D. In other words, religious experience alone provides far too slim a foundation for the total super-structure of Christian belief.

For some recent discussions of the argument from religious experience see the following: John Baillie, *The Sense of the Presence of God*, pp. 64ff.; Frederick Copleston, 'The Philosophical Relevance of Religious Experience', *Philosophy*, XXXI (1956): 229-243; A. C. Ewing, 'Awareness of God', *Philosophy*, XL (1965): 1-17; John Findlay, 'The Logic of Mysticism', *Religious Studies*, II (1967): 145-162; W. D. Glasgow, 'Knowledge of God', *Philosophy*, XXXII (1957): 229-240; Ronald W. Hepburn, *Christianity and Paradox*, pp. 24-59; H. J. N. Horsburgh, 'The Claims of Religious Experience', *Australasian Journal of Philosophy*, XXXV (1957): 186-200; H. D. Lewis, *Our Experience of God*, pp. 104-145 especially; H. D. Lewis and C. H. Whitely, 'Symposium: The Cognitive Factor in Religious Experience', *Proceedings of the Aristotelian Society*, Supplementary Volume XXIX (1955): 59-92; Alasdair MacIntyre, 'Visions', in *New Essays*, pp. 254-260; C. B. Martin, 'A Religious Way of Knowing', in *New Essays*, pp. 76-95; H. H. Price, 'Faith and Belief', in John Hick, ed., *Faith and the Philosophers*, pp. 3-25; Huston Smith, 'Do Drugs Have Religious Import?', *Journal of Philosophy*, LXI (1964): 517-530; Paul Weiss, 'Religious Experience', *Review of Metaphysics*, XVII (1963): 3-17; and John Wilson, *Language and Christian Belief*, pp. 16-31, and *Philosophy and Religion: The Logic of Religious Belief*, pp. 60-95.

move from observations of design and order in the physical universe to a categorical conclusion such as the statement made by 'The ruler of the universe abhors disorder' or (more cautiously) to a hypothetical conclusion such as the statement made by 'If there is a divine ruler of the universe, he abhors disorder'.[1] Or again, it may proceed from a cluster of historical events to some such G-conclusion as the statement made by 'God raised Jesus of Nazareth from the dead near Jerusalem at t_2'.[2] If arguments within any of these three types of theological sign reasoning are to be judged valid, they must meet the standards laid down above. And if any are judged invalid, it will be because they have failed to meet those standards. For the sake of economy and specificity alike, the remainder of the discussion will focus upon the third type of theological sign reasoning illustrated above, i.e., the type which moves from a sign cluster of historical events to a G-conclusion recording one of the mighty acts of God in history (our G_1-statements).

Now that a programme for verifying G_1-statements conclusively on empirical grounds alone has been mapped out, the supreme challenge is sure to sound from some quarter to the effect that the inference-route from sign cluster to G-conclusion is fallacious *in principle* and that therefore the criteria for separating those that are valid from those that are invalid are null and void. It is anticipated that this challenge will be predicated upon four objections. Objection number one will claim that it is logically impossible to bridge the *type-gap* between the sign and the thing signified and that hence the sign is not really a sign and signifies nothing. Objection number two will maintain that, even if it were possible in theory to bridge the type-gap, it is ridiculous to speak of backing the warrant that would bridge it with a *G-configuration*. The third objection will assert that,

---

[1] Recent discussions of the argument from design include: A. C. Ewing, 'Two "Proofs" of God's Existence', *Religious Studies*, I (1965): 29–45; Ronald W. Hepburn, *Christianity and Paradox*, pp. 155-186; J. J. C. Smart, 'The Existence of God', in *New Essays*, pp. 41-45; and Richard Taylor, *Metaphysics* (Englewood Cliffs, New Jersey, 1963), pp. 94-102.

[2] The argument from history has been treated by Ronald W. Hepburn, *Christianity and Paradox*, pp. 91–127; A. C. MacIntyre, 'The Logical Status of Religious Belief', in *Metaphysical Beliefs*, pp. 206-211; T. R. Miles, *Religion and the Scientific Outlook*, pp. 189-214; Patrick Nowell-Smith, 'Miracles', in *New Essays*, pp. 243-253; and Ian T. Ramsey, *Miracles: An Exercise in Logical Mapwork* (Oxford, 1952).

even if a warrant backed by a G-configuration would bridge the type-gap, verification of the G_1-statement would thereby not be on *empirical grounds alone*, since seeing a G-configuration in the sign cluster is not seeing in the empirical sense. And the last objection will hold that, even if the verification procedure were based on empirical grounds alone, the G-conclusion could never be regarded as *conclusively* verified for at least two reasons—the infinite corrigibility and open texture factors and the lack of entailment between data and conclusion.

If these four objections can be met successfully, the thesis of the present chapter will have passed its crucial test. They will be considered in reverse order, so that the less complex may be dealt with first.

2. 'CONCLUSIVELY' AND 'ON EMPIRICAL GROUNDS ALONE'

The fourth objection is the easiest of the lot to answer and in large measure has already been answered in the previous chapter. The claim being objected to is the claim that it is possible in theory at least for a G_1-statement to be conclusively verified, or, to put the matter in the alternative phrases introduced in this chapter, it is possible in theory at least for the G-conclusion of a sign argument to read 'Certainly C, therefore'. The objection posits that this state of affairs is even in theory impossible, because we can never be certain of the data due to the infinite corrigibility and open texture factors and, even if we were certain of the data, the data do not entail the conclusion. In other words, this objection finds lesions in the certainty of the conclusion both at the point of the data and at the point of the inference from the data.

As far as the theoretical uncertainty of the data is concerned, we need not review the arguments establishing (hopefully) that under the best of conditions the empirical statements which record the data are conclusively verifiable despite the infinite corrigibility and open texture factors. In brief, it was argued in the preceding chapter that if it makes sense to speak of an inconclusively verified empirical statement, the sense of 'conclusively verified' can be determined from that, and so it is not true that a conclusively verified empirical statement is a logical impossibility or that 'conclusively verified empirical statement' is nonsense. Shadow doubts arising from the indubitable facts of infinite corrigibility and open texture must not be allowed to metamorphose into what are taken for rational doubts. There is here, therefore, no valid opposition to the claim that the data can in theory be certain or that the empirical statements which record the data can in principle be conclusively verified.

But what about this other matter? What about the reputed lesion in the certainty of the conclusion due to the nature of the inference by which we obtain that conclusion? It cannot be disputed (nor need it be) that the inference in question is not an entailment. If it were, it would not involve sign reasoning, for entailment and sign reasoning are two entirely different types of inference. Everyone would gladly admit that certainty is a concomitant of entailment. One of the attractive features of the argument for the conclusive falsifiability of G_1-statements presented in the previous chapter was that it rests on entailment: The entailment by p (a G_1-statement) of q (an empirical statement) together with the conclusive falsifiability of q *entails* the conclusive falsifiability of p. But is certainty in logic a concomitant of entailment *only*? This is what we must determine.

It is not our concern in this study to make a brief for the *actual* certainty of any G_1-conclusions. It is for others—the theologians together with the historians perhaps—to decide which, if any, of them are in practice actually certain. Our concern is to determine under what conditions, if any, *in theory* any of them would have to be acknowledged as certain. This reminder may silence the opposition of those who believe that *in fact* no G_1-conclusion is known for certain. They may be right, or they may be wrong. But what must be understood is that the position being advanced here is not incompatible with their being right, nor does it entail that they are wrong. It may just be that G_1-statements are in principle conclusively verifiable but in practice not so. It may just be that sign reasoning of the type under discussion can in principle yield conclusions which are certain but in practice somehow always falls short of this theoretical perfection. The assignment here is simply to show that certainty is a concomitant of sign reasoning in theory, not necessarily in practice.

The view that the inference from sign cluster to G-conclusion is inherently less than certain is itself the result of shadow doubting. It is true that the warrant for the inference is not a truth-table tautology, or what would count in mathematical logic as a universally valid inference-rule, or an analytic rule of language. It is true also that whether or not the data are sufficient in such arguments, whether or not the data (even if sufficient) fit together into a G-configuration, and even what the necessary and sufficient components of the model (normative) G-configuration for classical Christian theism are—these are questions which fallible human judgement must settle without the guarantee of *logical* certitude to guide it. In other words, it is *logically* possible for any inference from sign cluster to G-conclusion to be wrong with respect to the constitution of the model G-configuration, with respect to the presence or absence of the G-configuration in the data, and with respect to the sufficiency of the quantity of data in which to look for a G-configuration. But these concessions are innocuous from the standpoint of the present objection and do not add up to the conclusion that inferences from sign clusters to G-conclusions are inherently less than certain. For certainty need not be *logical* certainty, and the absence of logical certainty from this type of sign reasoning foists shadow doubts exclusively. The logical possibility of error in judging the validity of arguments based on sign reasoning is not grounds for a reasonable doubt.

Since we are able to specify under what conditions a reasonable doubt would exist and under what conditions it would not, there is no valid objection left to the thesis that theological sign reasoning may in theory yield certainty. If theologians were in serious doubt as to what the components of the model (normative) G-configuration in classical Christian theism are, or if in any specific case they were in doubt about the sufficiency of the data (and could specify how much more evidence would be necessary to remove doubt, and that amount were significant) or about the presence or absence of a G-configuration in the data (and could specify what in the data was lacking of the G-configuration), then and only then would their doubt about the certainty of the inference be rational doubt. If, on the other hand, there were adequate data for a specific inference, the G-configuration in that data stood out with crystal clarity, and theologians knew for sure just what the components of the model

G-configuration for classical Christian theism were, then there would be no room for rational doubt relative to that specific inference. So, in review, the theoretical certainty of G-conclusions (their conclusive verifiability) can be impugned neither on the grounds of the infinite corrigibility and open texture of the statements recording the data nor on the grounds of the non-entailment nature of the inference which leads from sign clusters to those conclusions. This answers the fourth objection, the one centring on the word 'conclusively'.

The third objection centres on the expression 'on empirical grounds alone'. It argues that verification of a G_1-statement is not verification on empirical grounds alone, because seeing a G-configuration in the sign cluster is not seeing in the empirical sense. The premise of this argument is absolutely correct, that seeing a G-configuration in the data is not seeing in the empirical sense[1] and that there is therefore an *a priori* element

---

[1] Wittgenstein used the diagram of the duck-rabbit to illustrate two distinct uses of 'see': the straightforward empirical sense of 'see' and the somewhat subtle notion of 'seeing an aspect of'. *Philosophical Investigations*, pp. 193e-214e. I am not sure that Wittgenstein's 'seeing an aspect of' is exactly the same as my 'seeing a configuration in', but the similarity is surely worthy of note.

Some remarks of John Wisdom's in his article 'Gods' (*Philosophy and Psycho-Analysis*, pp. 149-168) also tie in nicely at this juncture. Wisdom speaks of the employment of 'models with which to "get the hang of" the patterns in the flux of experience' (p. 151). This is as close as two notions could be to my notion of using the model or normative G-configuration to detect a G-configuration in the data. Wisdom also says, 'It is possible to have before one's eyes all the items of a pattern and still to miss the pattern' (p. 153), and there is implicit in this statement the two senses of 'see'. Wisdom goes on to draw the illuminating (though limited) analogy between G-statements and aesthetic judgements: Just as beauty is not something one sees in a picture in the same sense of 'see' as one sees the various colours, contrasts, textures, and shapes, so also God is not seen in historical events in the same sense of 'see' as Moses saw the burning bush (say). And yet, even as beauty is something to be seen in some sense of 'see' and is not seen in the picture apart from seeing the colours, shapes, contrasts, textures, etc., so also God is something to be seen in some sense of 'see' and is not seen apart from the seeing of a burning bush, a risen Christ, a community of faith in its worship, sacramental life, preaching of the word, social concern, etc. For further remarks in the same vein, refer to Wisdom's *Paradox and Discovery*, pp. 1-22. Other theorists also make use of the notion of using a model to detect a key pattern in the evidence: Frederick Ferré, *Basic Modern Philosophy of Religion*, pp. 371-407, *Exploring the Logic of Faith: A Dialogue on the Relation of Modern Philosophy to Christian Faith* (with Kent Bendall), pp. 163-181, and 'Mapping the Logic of Models in Science and Theology', *The Christian Scholar*, XLVI (1963): 9-39; and I. T. Ramsey, *Religious Language: An Empirical Placing of Theological Phrases*, pp. 49-89.

When Jesus is made to say, 'He who has seen me has seen the Father' (John 14: 9, RSV), 'see' is being used in two distinct senses. 'See' in 'He who has seen me' is

somewhere in theological sign reasoning.[1] But the conclusion that verification of G_1-statements is thereby not verification on empirical grounds alone does not follow from this premise. For the *a priori* element in theological sign reasoning is not located in the grounds but rather in the backing operation. Since the data from which G-conclusions are inferred by a process of sign reasoning are empirical data entirely, and since the data in this inference and the grounds for the verification of G_1-statements are one and the same, it follows that the grounds in question are empirical and only empirical after all.

It might be added to strengthen the point that if an *a priori* element in the backing operation somehow disturbed the 'verification on empirical grounds alone' claim, then many (perhaps all) statements which we all believe have a right to that claim would have to surrender it. This requires some explanation. Suppose we are driving down the highway with Jones and he says, 'This car will run out of petrol before we have gone another five miles.' We ask him why he thinks so, and he says, 'Because the fuel gauge registers empty'. Here we have a statement and the evidence that is supposed to verify it, or, to put the matter in alternative and preferable phrases, here we have a conclusion and the data from which it has been inferred. If we pressed him and asked what possible bearing the fuel gauge reading has or should have upon his prediction that the car will soon run out of petrol, he would no doubt respond that whenever the fuel gauge registers empty the car is about to run out of petrol (warrant for his inference) and that we know this through a rather constant correlation in past experience between fuel gauges registering empty and cars running out of patrol (backing for his warrant).

It is the backing for this warrant that we must inquire about, for surely everyone would agree that the prediction about the car running out of petrol soon was verified in this case on empiri-

empirical sight plain and simple; 'see' in 'has seen the Father' is what I am calling 'seeing a configuration in', for in the first sense of 'see' no one has or can see the Father (John 1:18, RSV: 'No one has ever seen God'). The exegesis of this verse suggests the possibility of explicating religious talk about the reception of revelation entirely in terms of the notion of 'seeing a G-configuration in the data'. Perhaps a warrant for such an explication could be found in the fact that the Christian Church has always understood its concept of revelation largely in terms of perceptual (visual, auditory) models.

[1] John Wisdom acknowledges this very point in 'Gods', *op. cit.*, p. 157.

cal grounds alone. The backing in question would be labelled by most people accordingly as an empirical correlation. But the correlation is empirical only in the sense that it is a correlation between two sets of empirical data (observing fuel gauges in many instances and cars running out of petrol in many instances); the correlation process itself is an *a priori* operation, a matter of matching one pair of observations (in which one member belongs to the set of fuel gauge readings and the other member belongs to the set of out-of-petrol cars) against a second pair and against a third pair and against a fourth pair, and on and on. Taking fuel gauge readings is an empirical operation and determining that cars are out of petrol is another, but correlating the one set of findings with the other is an *a priori* operation of matching. So, if an *a priori* element in the warrant-backing process queers the claim of a statement to verification on empirical grounds alone, then few if any statements have a right to that claim. Such *reductio ad absurdum* reasoning is meant only to strengthen the contention that it is on the basis of data and not backing that we determine whether or not a statement is verified on empirical grounds alone.

An illuminating corollary of the above *reductio* argument might well be brought out before moving ahead because of the insight it adds to our understanding of theological sign reasoning. There is a striking parallelism between the warrant backing operation which involves the correlating or matching of two sets of empirical data and the warrant backing process in theological sign reading. For the latter also involves correlation or matching, but between a cluster of empirical data on the one hand and a model G-configuration (which is non-empirical) on the other. The difficult notion of seeing a G-configuration in the data, therefore, may with illuminating results be explicated in terms of a correlating or matching process: In these terms seeing a G-configuration in the data amounts simply to being able to match or correlate the configuration in the data with the model G-configuration.

3. BACKING THE WARRANT:
THE ROLE OF G-CONFIGURATIONS

Examination of the fourth and third objections have brought to light some features of the verification procedure for G_1-statements which make possible a more explicit and precise formulation of that procedure. In theological sign reasoning, to wit, we are entitled to the inference 'D, therefore C' if and only if we can upon request produce a warrant covering that inference which states 'D is a sign cluster signifying C'. It now becomes evident that the validity of the whole verification procedure rests squarely upon the warrantability of this warrant, upon the legitimacy of this inference-rule. And the warrant is warrantable if and only if it can be satisfactorily backed. So the question of the warrantability of the warrant (as well as the question of the validity of the verification procedure for G_1-statements, or, what amounts to the same thing, the validity of the inference from data to G_1-conclusion) reverts to the questions, 'What is the backing for this warrant?' and 'Is the backing really backing?'.

Putting the second question aside temporarily, we have seen that the question 'What is the backing for this warrant?' has to be answered in terms of G-configurations. Backing the warrant is tantamount to proving that the data is what the warrant proclaims it to be—a sign cluster. (For if the data are in fact a sign cluster, then as a matter of course the conclusion signified by that sign follows from the data as the inference asserts.) And proving that the data constitute a sign cluster is a matter of seeing or detecting a G-configuration in the data, which in turn is a matter of matching or correlating the pattern in the data (if any) with the model (normative) G-configuration. Backing the warrant in theological sign reasoning, therefore, is achieved by establishing that there is a pattern in the data which correlates with the model G-configuration, for such a correlation constitutes the data as a sign cluster. And since a sign is by definition something which signifies something else, the fact that the data are a sign underwrites the inference to the G-conclusion.[1]

Herein lies a solution to the problem of identifying God in

---

[1] Since correlation is always a matter of degree, the correlation between the pattern in the data and the model G-configuration can range from perfect correspondence to vague resemblance. The degree of correlation should be reflected by the appropriate qualifier in the conclusion. If the correlation is optimal, then the conclusion should read 'Certainly C'; if strong but somewhat less than optimal, 'Probably C'; if weak, 'Possibly C'; etc.

experience, raised on pages 108-109. From the definition of God in classical Christian theism (the way that system formulates its prescription for identifying God in thought) we infer what any experience would have to be like if it were indeed an experience of God. We infer, in other words, a prescription for identifying God (as that system defines God) in experience. This prescription is formulated as a model (normative) G-configuration and employed in theological sign reasoning as outlined above.

To bring the discussion down to cases, suppose that the verification of the statement made by 'God raised Jesus of Nazareth from the dead near Jerusalem at t_2' were the subject of inquiry. The biblical record states that on several occasions Jesus of Nazareth predicted his resurrection[1] (sometimes quite explicitly as a retroactive sign of his divine authority), that he was crucified and biologically dead at t_1, and that at t_3 the tomb in which his body had been laid was no longer occupied and the early witnesses encountered alive a man whom they identified as Jesus of Nazareth. These are the data from which our G_1-statement is inferred as conclusion.[2]

The inference, if justifiable at all, must be justified by reference to a warrant which states that the data are a sign cluster indicating that God raised Jesus of Nazareth from the dead. But how do we know that the data constitute the requisite sign cluster? Why should we take the data as something more than a random collection of odd historical events? Why should we take the data as indicative of divine agency? These are all questions about the warrantability of the warrant and requests for the backing necessary in making the warrant functional. The contention here is that if upon inspection of the data we detect in it a pattern which correlates with the model G-configuration

[1] Some modern scholars of biblical history regard the passages recording these predictions as *vaticinia ex eventu*. Whether they are or not is not an issue for this study, for we are not trying to determine the actual truth-value of the resurrection claim. It is a legitimate concern of this study, however, to determine what *would* be the result *if* they *were*. And in this regard, it would have to be admitted that if these predictions were *vaticinia ex eventu*, the data for the conclusion that it was *God* who raised Jesus of Nazareth from the dead would be weakened (but not vitiated) and the G-configuration in the remaining data would be less definite (though it would not disappear altogether).

[2] Perhaps it would be more accurate to say that these are the *primary* data, for in a larger sense the total 'Christ-event' (the circumstances surrounding his birth, life, and death, the details of his words and deeds, etc.) constitute the data in which we are to look for the G-configuration.

(i.e., if we see a G-configuration in the data), then the warrant is backed and the inference valid. And if no such G-configuration can be detected in the data on the basis of the model G-configuration, then the warrant is not backed and the inference invalid (which differs from saying that the conclusion is false, it must be remembered).

Just as it is irrelevant to the purposes of this study to try to pass judgement upon the factuality or non-factuality of the data from which 'God raised Jesus of Nazareth . . .' is inferred, so also it is irrelevant to the purposes of this study to pronounce upon the presence or absence of a G-configuration in these data. But it is not irrelevant to our purposes to take a stand on the characteristics these data would have to manifest if a G-configuration is there to be seen in them. In order to be able to speak for or against the presence of a G-configuration in the resurrection data or any other data purportedly implying a G-conclusion, something more must be known about the model (i.e., normative) G-configuration—its composition and origin. For, as was said before, seeing a G-configuration in the data is simply a matter of matching the pattern (if any) in the data against the model G-configuration.

The model G-configuration for classical Christian theism evolves from the concept of God in that system and is composed of a family of characteristics some subset of which the data must manifest to support the claim that a G-configuration can be seen in those data and that they (the data) constitute a sign cluster signifying the appropriate G-conclusion. No single characteristic in the family of characteristics is in every case either necessary or sufficient for establishing the presence or absence of the G-configuration in the data, but any one characteristic may be for some particular case either necessary or sufficient. With no pretence at completeness, we can enumerate at least the core characteristics in the family by means of which a body of historical data can be identified as the result of divine activity or on the basis of which we can say that the hand of God is evident in those data. In short, what would we expect a G-event to be like in experience if God is defined in thought as '. . . a Spirit, infinite, eternal, and unchangeable in his being, wisdom, power, holiness, justice, goodness, and truth' (to invoke the Westminster shorter Catechism of 1647 once more)?

First of all, if God is thought of as infinite power the data among other things ought to display tremendous force or energy at work and hence pose a stubborn demand for causal explanation. In other words, the data cannot appear unimpressive in effects or fortuitous. The sheer power, according to the biblical narratives, manifest in the parting of the waters of the Red Sea (or whatever body of water it was) for the children of Israel in their exodus from Egypt and manifest in the resurrection of Jesus of Nazareth from the dead (no brief is here held for the historicity of the biblical records reporting these 'events', it must be remembered) would figure prominently in the G-configuration (if any) present in the data supporting the G-statements made by 'God delivered the children of Israel from bondage in Egypt' and 'God raised Jesus of Nazareth . . .' respectively.

But tremendous power is displayed daily at Boulder Dam and in the A-bomb explosions over the Nevada desert without prompting anyone to affirm 'God is generating electricity at Boulder Dam' or 'God is blasting huge craters in the Nevada desert'. So, in the second place and in addition to displaying great power, the data in most cases would need to be preternatural, i.e., out of the ordinary course of nature. If God is an invisible, intangible Spirit, then we would expect the power-source behind the phenomenon in question to be transcendent and empirically undiscoverable and the phenomenon itself scientifically unexplainable. Not everyone has seen hydro-electric power in the making; fewer still have witnessed an atomic explosion first-hand. Probably only the on-site engineers and scientists come to regard such phenomena as just another part of the working day. Yet there is nothing preternatural about the generation of hydro-electric power or nuclear fission, the power-source in each case is empirically discoverable, we understand the laws governing both, and hence neither is to be identified with the power of God (except in the extended and semi-inscrutable sense in which theology imputes all phenomena in the last analysis to God). It is on the basis of this very characteristic, in fact, that the exodus of the Israelites from Egypt distinguishes itself, purportedly, from an occurrence such as the evacuation of the BEF at Dunkirk during World War II. If the narratives about the water standing back in walls for the Israelites to pass through on dry ground but descending with devastation upon Pharaoh's army are literal narratives and historically true, the exodus was attended by preternatural phenomena. But the evacuation of the BEF was not. The covering of fog allowed the small boats to do their work unhindered by air attack, true, but there is nothing unusual about fog over the British Channel.

Preternaturalness alone, however, is not enough. For the parthenogenesis of a mouse or the resurrection of a beetle or even the periodic reconstitution from ashes of the beautiful and long-lived Phoenix—preternatural as each of these phenomena would be if it actually occurred—would not provoke hypotheses about the divinity of the creatures involved or about the transcendent source of the process to which they had been subject. Curiosities they would be, but they would lack what Rudolf Otto in *The Idea of the Holy* calls the quality of the numinous. Since the God of classical Christian theism is eminently holy, a third and very important characteristic in the G-configuration is numinousness: The data ought to be of such a nature as to suggest a transcendent cause of great mystery and majesty. The virgin birth or resurrection of a Jesus or a Socrates or a Gandhi would suggest such a cause; the same phenomenon worked upon a weasel or a fruit fly would not. Certainly the phenomenon of Jones hitting his golfball into the rough would not provide data in which the numinous was to be found.

The first three characteristics group together in a mutually complementary fashion, and so do the next three. The evidence of a mind-like quality in the data would argue for the presence of a G-configuration there: If the data suggest purposefulness, order, the activity of a conscious and supremely intelligent being (one who lays and executes plans or employs means to gain ends), all of this is associated with the model G-configuration, for God is understood by classical Christian theism as infinitely wise and mind-like.

God is also understood by that theological system as redemptive; the great purpose of an infinitely good God in history according to that theology, is redemption. If the data manifest redemptive activity, this too would argue for the presence of a G-configuration in those data. It is on the grounds of this characteristic that some are moved to acclaim 'God delivered the BEF at Dunkirk', for the Dunkirk evacuation was a rescue mission and in this respect parallels the exodus of Old Testament fame. Were this characteristic alone sufficient to establish the presence of a G-configuration in the data, then Dunkirk might perhaps be added to the strand of sacred, redemptive history. But since several of the family of characteristics that compose the model G-configuration are usually required to establish that point, at best we would have to declare Dunkirk an indeterminate borderline case.

The third characteristic of the second set of three is morality, for God is thought of as infinitely just. Actually this characteristic provides more of a negative than a positive test for the G-configuration, for nothing very definite follows from its presence in the data. But if the actions which the data record were unethical, then, as was pointed out in the last section of the preceding chapter, a counter G-configuration would exist in the data which falsifies any G-conclusion that may be asserted to follow from them. If Mr X killed his wife and children with a hatchet, and if they were innocent of any grievance against him so that his act could not be justified on the basis of provocation, self-protection, retribution, etc., and if they were not dying of some gruesome disease or trapped in a burning building, etc., so that his act could not be rationalized on the grounds of mercy killings, in other words if his killing of them was *murder* (a term connoting moral condemnation), then the G-statement made by 'God made Mr X kill his wife and children with a hatchet' is not only disverified (due to the absence of the G-configuration) but positively falsified (due to the presence of a counter G-configuration).[1]

---

[1] The case of God commanding Abraham to offer his only son Isaac as a human sacrifice (Genesis 22) comes to mind here as a possible parallel. But the two cases are not really parallel, for in the biblical story God does not permit the unethical act to come to pass. He stops the action dramatically at the point where his ethical character is more firmly established than before. The command to slay Isaac *seems* unethical, to be sure, but there is something to Kierkegaard's claim (in *Fear and Trembling*) that instead the command constitutes a teleological suspension of the ethical. In issuing the command God suspends his ethical character in order to reinstate it forcefully. If the purpose of the incident was to teach Abraham the immorality of human sacrifice in an age rife with it (as some say) or to give him a lesson in justification by faith (as others say—see Hebrews 11:17-19), either way the purpose was to reveal to man God's moral concern for his well-being. The upshot of the whole incident, therefore, is the dramatic reaffirmation of the morality of God.

A seventh characteristic—perhaps the least important of those considered here—has to do with contextual cues. We might be more prone to find the hand of God in an abrupt disappearance of an inoperable cancer if the afflicted person had prayed and been prayed over, if he had receved the ministration of faith healing, if he had taken to heart some promises for wholeness communicated to him through sermons and/or scripture, than if there was a total absence of such contextual cues in the case. But at best such considerations could only support and reinforce other characteristics representative of the model G-configuration. They could hardly stand on their own.

The enumeration (and explanation) of these seven characteristics (tremendous power, preternaturalness, numinousness, mind-likeness, redemptive activity, morality, and contextual cues), though tallying nicely with the Westminster Shorter Catechism definition of God, is suggestive rather than exhaustive of the family of characteristics composing the model G-configuration against which the presence or absence of a G-configuration in the data is judged. In actuality everything which the system of classical Christian theism affirms about God enters into the model G-configuration and might figure in determining the presence or absence of a G-configuration in any set of real data. And this disclosure marks the transition between the question of the composition of the model G-configuration and the question of its origin.

'Where does the model G-configuration come from?', someone might ask suggesting the possibility of circularity in the inferential process involved in theological sign reasoning: The model G-configuration as an instrument for identifying God in experience is drawn from the total theological system and then is employed in proving certain affirmations within that system. This might look like circularity, but it is not. An argument is circular if and only if the truth of the premises is dependent upon the truth of the conclusion. This unfortunately would create a reciprocal dependence, for by virtue of its status as an argument the truth of the conclusion must be dependent upon the truth of the premises. In theological sign reasoning, the model G-configuration is drawn from everything the theological system affirms about God, but only part of that G-configuration will be relevant to the logical process of any particular

G-argument, and in no case are we forced to pit the truth of those affirmations relevant to the G-configuration for that case upon the truth of the conclusion of that G-argument. For example, the numinousness of God plays a part in backing the inference from the resurrection data to the G-conclusion stated by 'God raised Jesus of Nazareth . . .', but the truth of the claim that God is numinous does not rely part and parcel upon the truth of that G-conclusion. Furthermore, circularity is a matter of the interdependence of truth-values between data and conclusions, whereas the model G-configuration and the theological affirmations from which it is drawn enter into the argument not as data but as backing for the warrant. So there is no actual threat of circularity in theological sign reasoning, and the question of the origin of the model G-configuration is raised here only to dispel a qualm.

We would probably all accept the suggestion that the origin of the methods for backing syllogistic inferences was irrelevant to the question of the validity of those inferences. The same obtains for theological sign reasoning. Furthermore, no one upon reflection would credit Aristotle with the creation of the laws of contradition, excluded middle, and identity. He codified and expanded upon the logic embodying those logical laws—an achievement not to be minimized—but he did not originate that logic. It is true, nonetheless, that practically everyone who has practiced syllogistic logic in the generations since Aristotle has learned this science from Aristotle. We often look to the codifiers for things we could have (with talent and effort) perhaps figured out for ourselves from existing practice. Similarly, no one would credit Augustine, Aquinas, Calvin or any of the other theological fathers of the Christian church with the origination of the G-configuration. They have functioned as discoverers perhaps and certainly as codifiers but not as creators in this regard. And yet the church has always looked to her theological fathers for an elaboration of the *model* G-configuration and hence have learned it from them.

Perhaps a more illuminating illustration can be found in the work of the Curies with radioactivity. Today the high school physics student studies about radioactivity by reading textbooks which draw upon the work of the Curies. The Curies coined the term 'radioactivity' and devised the tests for estab-

P

lishing its presence in any substance. The student most likely has never worked with radioactivity in a laboratory experiment. But if he ever came across the phenomenon of radioactivity in his laboratory work, (supposing he has done his lessons thoroughly) he could identify that phenomenon as radioactivity by matching it against the description (the model radioactivity configuration) derived from the work of the Curies. And yet the Curies did not create or invent radioactivity; they happened across a phenomenon for which no existing physical terminology was adequate, created the name 'radioactivity' for that phenomenon, and devised methods of testing for it.

The application should be clear. We today are dependent upon our theological predecessors for the model G-configuration we apply in determining the presence or absence of a G-configuration in any set of actual data present or past. We test the inference from resurrection data to the G-conclusion stated by 'God raised Jesus of Nazareth . . .' by matching the pattern (if any) in the data against the model G-configuration they have in effect bequeathed to us. They did not invent God, nor did they create the G-configuration in the data they studied. Rather, they in their own religious experience (and that of others for which information was accessible to them) happened across phenomena for which no existing terminology was adequate. They systematized religious belief about these preternatural, numinous, etc., experiences, in many cases created the terminology in which the reality behind these experiences was referred to, and devised methods of testing for the presence of this reality.

It is true that they discovered the G-configuration in the data they studied without matching that pattern against some pre-existing model (for no such model existed for them). But then neither did the Curies discover the radioactivity configuration in the phenomena they studied by matching that pattern against some pre-existing model the way the physics student does today. The benefits to the masses in religion no less than in physics depend upon the insight of a few innovators who see in phenomena patterns which the common man can see only by having them pointed out to him. The model G-configuration, then, does find its origin in the codified beliefs of the community of faith. Those who codified it did (like the Curies) function as discoverers who had to perform their work without the benefit of a pre-existing standard of judgement. But these facts in no way militate against the validity of theological sign reasoning as practised by those who employ in the warrant-backing process the model G-configuration bequeathed to them by the theological fathers of the church.

Mention of the creation of new theological terminology in response to certain preternatural, numinous, etc., experiences counsels the insertion at this juncture of an important distinction in order to block a possible error—mistaking theological sign reasoning for the process of redescribing the data in different terms. The distinction I have in mind is that between applying a new name to the data and imputing a cause to the data, or between an inference from criteria to designation and an inference from sign to thing signified.

Consider the following inference: 'There are two teams of eleven men apiece playing upon a grassy field one-hundred yards long. They are playing with an oval leather ball. The ball is carried, passed, caught, kicked, and each team has four downs to gain ten yards in order to maintain possession of the ball. A team scores by moving the ball across the goal-line and is credited with six points for such a manoeuvre. Therefore, the game they are playing is American football.' This inference moves from the criteria for applying a designation to the assertion of the designation; it applied the appropriate name to a phenomenon manifesting the criteria for that name.

Contrast the argument from criteria to designation with these specimens of inference: 'Jones appears withdrawn and depressed, says on some days that he has half a head and on other days that he is Paul Revere, and manifests delusions of persecution through decided homicidal and suicidal tendencies. Therefore, Jones is a paranoiac schizophrenic.' 'The substance glows in the dark, exposes a photographic plate, diminishes by half its mass in such-and-such a period of time. Therefore, the substance is radioactive.' In both of these inferences, the conclusion functions not as a redescription of the phenomena described in the premises. The conclusion functions rather as an explanation of the phenomena described in the premises, and the explanation is predicated upon a sign cluster which manifests itself in the phenomena. The expression 'paranoiac schizophrenia' names the cause (a mental disorder) behind the symptoms and not the

symptoms themselves; to say that Jones is a paranoiac schizophrenic is to put Jones into a category, not for the sake of
describing him (he has already been described in the process of
listing his symptoms), but for the sake of explaining his malady
(though that cause is understood but dimly). 'Schizophrenia'
names something mental (not something physical) even though
we are not able to identify that mental something precisely.
And 'radioactivity' names the cause (a physical process) behind
the observable phenomena and not the phenomena themselves.
There is, therefore, a significant difference between the football
inference (a case of redescription) and the schizophrenia and
radioactivity inferences (cases of causal explanation on the basis
of sign reasoning).

Someone might think that the inference from the resurrection
data to the G-conclusion stated by 'God raised Jesus of Nazareth . . .' belongs with the football inference rather than with the
schizophrenia and radioactivity inferences, not at this point
because 'God' names something non-empirical (for the same is
true of schizophrenia and radioactivity), but because we have
spoken of the creation of new theological terminology being
involved in the codification of the model G-configuration. This
person might think that the function of the model G-configuration in theological sign reasoning was therefore simply to give
a new description in the conclusion to phenomena which were
given another description in the data. But such is not the case.
The function of the model G-configuration in theological sign
reasoning is to back the warrant by constituting the data as that
which the warrant asserts it to be—a sign cluster signifying a
causal explanation of the phenomena reported in the data. This
is an inference-process entirely different from that of redescription.

Having approached the question 'What constitutes the backing for the warrant in theological sign reasoning?' from several
significant angles and having confronted the attendant difficulties, it is time to move on to the other question mentioned at the
beginning of this section—'Is that backing really backing?'. The
latter question has a menacing veneer only. For of three
constructions that can be put on the question the first is beyond
the scope of the present study methodologically, the second
renders it unanswerable (either affirmatively or negatively) and

hence nugatory, and the third yields a negative answer but through a process which shows that the question was misguided to begin with. These three interpretations of the question might read: 'Is the model G-configuration specifically for classical Christian theism valid, that is, is it the *right* model?', 'Is the method of backing a warrant (in theological sign argument) by means of a G-configuration of any sort a valid method in the last analysis?', and 'Does the warrant-backing operation in theological sign reasoning conform to the corresponding operation in some *accredited* type of sign reasoning?'. We may deal with the first two interpretations rapidly, but it will prove instructive to develop an answer to the third in greater detail.

The question 'Is the model G-configuration specifically for classical Christian theism valid, that is, is it the *right* model?' is a legitimate and important question but beyond the reach of this study. Every system of theological understanding, Christian or otherwise, enshrines its own unique definition of God (prescription for identifying God in thought) and concommitant model G-configuration (prescription for identifying God in experience). That model G-configuration must be judged best (and in that sense 'valid' or 'right') which in its structure is most sensitive to the whole gamut of human experience and knowledge and which in its operation (as an instrument for identifying God in experience) most accurately facilitates the picking out of what G-configurations (if any) are actually there in the data to be seen. Whether or not the model G-configuration for classical Christian theism, the broad outlines of which were set forth above, is in this sense 'valid' and 'the right model' is beyond the province of the present study to decide.[1] That is a

[1] If I might allow myself to venture an opinion on the matter I would begin by saying that theology in the past has been an evolving science, and I see no reason to believe it has yet attained perfection. Man's understanding of God on the one hand and of himself and his world on the other are of a piece, such that growth on the one front creates a need for adjustments on the other. Classical Christian theism, as I see it, has not responded nearly as fully as need be to the modern scientific revolution, the changes in human nature brought about by immersion in technological society, and the whole new face of human sensibility as manifested in the arts. I am favourably disposed toward some of the newer theologies occasionally alluded to precisely because I believe they are making more valiant efforts in these directions. We live in a time when classical Christian theism may well be supplanted as the theological consensus on how Christians ought to understand their faith. Surely there is upheaval all along the theological front today on the very question

theological problem proper, whereas this study is conceived as an investigation only of certain logical and semantical problems issuing from theology.

I hope to have made clear in Chapter I my reasons for selecting classical Christian theism as the hermeneutical premise for this study. I repeat that I hold no special brief for that particular system of theological understanding. If its model G-configuration (and hence its concept of God) is not fully accurate in the face of all we know today, not fully effective as an instrument for identifying God in experience, if it is imperfect or not the very best presently available, then the truth-status of G-conclusions in the derivation of which it operates cannot but be affected. But this possibility detracts nothing from the validity of my general analysis of theological sign reasoning, which in type all systems of theological understanding must per force the nature of their subject matter employ. We could replace the model G-configuration of classical Christian theism with a better one (or a worse) and the *style* of theological sign reasoning as a genre of argument would remain unchanged. It is for the acceptability of that style alone—not for any specific model G-configuration— that I plead. My general purposes in this study require no more.

To ask, therefore, whether the model G-configuration for classical Christian theism is the right model of the several alternatives devised by theologians resembles in some respects asking whether the two-valued logic, the three-valued logic, or some many-valued logic is the right one. The latter (like the former) is not a question *of* logic; it is a metaphysical question about the correspondence between various logics and reality. It asks which of several alternative logics best transposes into logical operations everything in reality which logic ought to cope with to be fully adequate to its tasks. Within any given system of logic the rules function efficiently to give one the derivations one wants; the question of the adequacy of the system *qua* system to reality, however, is another matter. So also with theological sign reasoning: Within classical Christian theism, say, the model G-configuration for that system plays its

---

of God, his reality and character. But since the consensus theology of the future is at present far from apparent, it would have been precipitious to have focused this study on some different theological premise.

role with dispatch, but the question of the adequacy of the entire system to reality is not a logical question and hence beyond our scope.

Suppose now we take the question 'Is the backing in theological sign reasoning really backing?' to mean 'Is the method of backing a warrant (in theological sign reasoning) by means of a G-configuration of any sort—that for classical Christian theism or some other—a valid method in the last analysis?'. This question is unanswerable and hence nugatory by reason of the fact it presupposes (what is impossible) that the warrant-backing procedures for any line of argument are themselves subject to criticism and appraisal, whereas those procedures themselves *define* the canons of criticism and appraisal for their respective inference-routes. Contrary to this presupposition, there is no one and absolute meta-logic within which these inference-routes *qua* inference-routes can be judged, and there is no single and final set of meta-criteria for passing judgement upon the criteria which define validity for any inference-route and against which individual arguments within that inference-route are judged.[1] When any question about the general propriety of a warrant-backing procedure arises the Wittgensteinian response comes to mind, 'This is simply what we do'.[2] Such a response does not dignify the question by attempting to satisfy its request; it is rather a rejection of the question as improper. After all, a question which can be shown to be beyond the reach of any possible answer should not detain or disturb us.

Suppose, thirdly that we take the question 'Is the backing in theological sign reasoning really backing?' to mean 'Does the warrant-backing operation in theological sign reasoning conform to the corresponding operation in some *accredited* type of sign reasoning?'. The assumption here is that the warrant-backing process for theological sign reasoning can pass inspection only if (rather than being unique and standing on its own merits) it can be assimilated to the warrant-backing process for some other type of sign reasoning which happens to be regarded

---

[1] Strawson employs a similar line of reasoning in grappling with the so-called problem of the 'justification' of induction. See *Introduction to Logical Theory*, pp. 248-263.

[2] *Philosophical Investigations*, p. 85e: 'If I have exhausted the justifications I have reached bedrock, and my spade is turned. Then I am inclined to say: "This is simply what I do." '

as unproblematic.[1] Putting this construction on the question, its answer is negative; the warrant-backing process for theological sign reasoning, even though there are large areas of similarity between it and the warrant-backing process for other types of sign reasoning, is in the last analysis *sui generis*.

But that admission in and of itself should stir up no scandal. For the assumption behind the question—that the warrant-backing process for theological sign reasoning is sound only if it can be assimilated to the corresponding process for some other sort of sign reasoning—is false. Its falsity can be demonstrated by making a survey of the warrant-backing processes for various sorts of sign reasoning, each process of which has its own idiosyncrasies and all of which when put in a certain light can be made to seem as problematic and dubious as that for theological sign reasoning. The fact that all of them can, when put in a certain light, be made to seem problematic should, moreover, rouse suspicion not about the processes but about that light. The suspicion will emerge, hopefully, as we move through the survey.

The basic cleavage in warrant-backing processes for various sorts of sign arguments is the cleavage between the process of empirical correlation and the process of discovering a configuration in the data. The warrant-backing process of empirical correlation is a matter of correlating two sets of empirical data in such a way that a first pair made up of one member from each set correlates with a second pair similarly constituted and with a third pair, and on and on. The warrant-backing process of seeing a configuration in the data, on the other hand, is a matter of correlating the pattern (if any) in the data which serves as the ground for the argument with a model configuration. Since both types of warrant-backing process employ the operation of correlating or matching this with that, the warrant-backing processes for all sorts of sign arguments have at least one feature in common. But within this unity there is considerable diversity, as we shall see. Let us start with those sign arguments which

---

[1] It is interesting (and saddening) how often in philosophy we are told that if A is not conformable to some accepted B, then A is unacceptable or at least in serious trouble. For example, the problem of induction (so-called) reduces to this sort of thing: If induction is not deduction (which has the approval of all men), then induction requires special justification.

are backed by empirical correlation. Among these, sometimes the correlation is causal and sometimes non-causal. Where the correlation is causal, sometimes effects are correlated against causes in order to establish the backing, sometimes causes against effects, sometimes effects against effects, and sometimes a mixture of the three. These differences where empirical correlation is used will now be illustrated.

Consider this argument: 'The baby is very feverish, wakeful, has red spots on its stomach, and so the baby has roseola'. The warrant for this argument would read 'Whenever a baby is very feverish, wakeful, and has red spots on its stomach, the baby has roseola'. The warrant in turn is backed by the causal type of empirical correlation in which the effect is matched with the cause. The symptoms or signs which form the data for the argument are regarded as effects for which the conclusion states the causal explanation. The warrant simply generalizes the causal hypothesis which is particular in the individual argument. And the backing for the warrant appeals to numerous past cases in which the symptoms reported in the data correlated positively with other data which conclusively corroborated the conclusion drawn. The inference about the baby having roseola would be backed only if there were a consistent correlation in past cases between the manifestation of the symptoms mentioned and the presence of the measles virus in the bloodstream (as revealed by blood tests) which caused those symptoms.

Sometimes the backing process correlates cause with effect rather than the other way round as we had it illustrated in the example above. An argument illustrating this type of warrant-backing process is: 'Atmospheric pressure is dropping and temperature rising in this area, a large gathering of nimbus clouds is blowing in from the west, and so it will rain tomorrow.' This argument pertains to weather conditions in one particular area, and the warrant for the argument again simply generalizes the situation and might read: 'Whenever atmospheric pressure drops and temperature rises and there is a large gathering of moisture-laden clouds in the area, rain is to be expected.' The backing again would have to be a consistent correlation in a sizeable set of past cases, a correlation between the signs mentioned and the actual occurrence of rain. The only significant difference between this argument and its backing and the preceding argument and its backing is that in the present argument the inference is from cause to effect rather than from effect to cause and the backing correlates past causes against past effects rather than the other way round.

But in the warrant-backing process the correlation need not be between causes and effects in order to be a causal correlation; it may be between two sets of effects with a common cause. We have an example of such a warrant-backing process by working a simple transformation upon the sample argument used to illustrate the point immediately above. The argument 'The barometer indicates a drop in atmospheric pressure, the thermometer indicates a rise in temperature, the weather station reports a large gathering of nimbus clouds blowing in from the west, and therefore it will rain tomorrow' would have to be backed by a correlation between two sets of effects with a common cause. That backing would have to consist of a large number of past cases in which the symptoms or signs mentioned consistently correlated with rain. But by no stretch of the imagination would anybody impute the causality for the rain to the barometer, the thermometer, weather station reports, rings around the moon, etc. These things do not cause rain, nor are they the effects of rain. They are, however, caused by the same conditions which cause the rain.

Then again sometimes sign arguments are backed by a mixture of causal correlations, i.e., causes with effects, effects with causes, or effects with effects. Take for example the argument 'The traffic signal at the intersection facing us is green, the cars at the intersection on the cross-street are stopped, and therefore those cars are facing a red traffic signal'. The warrant 'Whenever our signal is green and the cars at the crossroad are stopped, then the signal facing them is red' would have to be backed by a mixture of causal correlations. For there is in past experience a (fairly) consistent correlation of an effect-to-cause nature between stopped cars and red signals, permitting us to say that the red signal is the cause and their being stopped the effect. And the green signal facing us, though neither the cause nor the effect of the red signal facing them, is together with the red signal and effect of a common cause i.e., the electronic device controlling the signal unit. The copiously supported correlation between past instances of signal units with green signals pointing in opposite directions and red signals perpendicular to the green, therefore, is an effect-to-effect correlation.

And finally, the correlation in the backing process need not be a causal correlation at all in order to do its job. In fact, the causal nature of the correlation (when it is in fact causal) is actually irrelevant to the effectiveness of the warrant-backing process. 'Causal connection' is not part of the meaning of 'empirical correlation', nor is a causal correlation a necessary part of effective sign-functioning. The only vital thing is that there be an empirical correlation of some sort, regardless of whether the observations being correlated relate causes and effects. We may speak, therefore, of coincidental empirical correlations as well as of causal empirical correlations, and both may serve as the backing for sign arguments.

As an example of a sign argument backed by a coincidental empirical correlation, consider the following: 'Brown hiccupped in London, and therefore the stock market will drop tomorrow in New York.' The argument is highly unlikely, granted, but not impossible. The warrant for it would have to read 'Whenever Brown hiccups (in London or elsewhere), the New York stock market drops'. Such a warrant is only as warrantable as the backing behind it. Let us suppose that Brown has hiccupped numerous times during his lifetime, that every time he has the New York stock market has dropped, that during this same period that market has never dropped without his hiccupping at the same time, and that all attempts to discover some causal connexion between these two sets of phenomena have ended in frustration. (There may be a causal connexion, but one too subtle to detect. Or there may be an epistemological connexion; Browns's hiccupping may be a queer manifestation of a secret extra-sensory perception he has about New York stock market plunges.) If such a highly improbable set of circumstances did actually obtain, then we would have adequate grounds for predicting a New York stock market drop whenever we got word of Brown hiccupping, even though we had to admit that the backing correlation was purely coincidental. For sign arguments such as these operate on the strength of empirical correlation alone, not on the basis of causal connection. And whenever the warrant-backing for a sign argument is a causal correlation, that is only because every causal correlation is also an empirical correlation, though the converse is not true.

So much for those sign arguments which have for their warrant-backing process an empirical correlation of any of the sorts we have illustrated. Every instance of this type of warrant-backing process could be put in a bad light simply by introducing some now-familiar considerations. It could be said of each instance that the warrant was infinitely corrigible and as a general (not necessarily universal) statement went beyond the backing for it, that the backing did not entail the warrant, and that the process of correlating two sets of empirical observations was by definition of 'correlation' an *a priori* process, and all three of these 'charges' would have to be acknowledged as true. But we have been over this ground before and have seen that these 'charges' are not damaging, or that they are pseudo-charges, or that they do not amount to what would be a damaging charge, namely, that the warrant-backing process of empirical correlation is not after all a sound and acceptable method of backing. The shadow doubts which they insinuate are not rational doubts and should not be listened to. If the doubts thereby insinuated were in fact rational, then it would be irrational to predict the weather, diagnose a disease, or venture forth into traffic.

The second principal warrant-backing method employed in sign reasoning is the method of correlating a model configuration with the pattern (if any) in the data which forms the basis of the argument. Since theological sign arguments fit in here, much has already been said about this warrant-backing process. It might well be pointed out, however, that the link between all of the sign arguments in this category is the fact that in each case the conclusion contains an expression ('God', 'Jones's pain', etc.) naming a referent which is in theory inaccessible to direct empirical observation (keeping in mind, of course, the discussion in Chapter IV of the puzzles arising over the use of 'direct' in epistemological contexts). In the straightforward, empirical sense of 'see' there is no such thing as seeing God, nor can we experience Jones's pain in the same way as he experiences it. Conclusions to the sign arguments in the first category discussed, on the other hand, refer only to things which are in theory empirically indicatable. We can get out into the rain tomorrow, laboratory analysis of a blood specimen can reveal the presence of the pneumonia virus, etc.

One other thing that might well be pointed out in advance of the examination of examples has to do with the different type of warrant employed in the second category of sign arguments over against those used in the first category. For sign arguments in the category presently under discussion, the warrant is a particular statement asserting that a sign relation obtains between the data and the conclusion of that particular argument and reads 'D is a sign cluster signifying C'. This explains why the warrant-backing for this category of sign arguments takes the form that it does, i.e., using a model configuration to show that a pattern exists in the data or, what amounts to the same, to show that the data really constitute a sign cluster.

Contrast this with the type of warrant used in the first category of sign arguments. There the warrants were general statements such as 'Whenever barometric pressure drops and the temperature rises and nimbus clouds blow in from the west, it usually rains the next day'. This in turn explains why the warrant-backing process there has a recourse, not to the data for the inference all over again (as in the second category of sign arguments), but rather to two sets of correlated data taken from the past which confirm the general statement serving as warrant.

In short, these two categories of sign arguments differ in respect to conclusion, warrant, and backing. The first category has conclusions mentioning only empirical referents, uses general hypotheticals as warrants, and backs those warrants by establishing an empirical correlation between two sets of past data. The second category, in contrast, has conclusions which mention non-empirical referents, uses particular and categorical sign assertions as warrants, and backs those warrants by proving that the data constitute a sign cluster, which involves showing that there is a pattern in the data and that the pattern correlates with a model. So much for the features which unify the second category and differentiate it from the first category. There is also diversity in the second category worthy of note, because description of the several sub-varieties and their differentiation from the sub-variety used in theological sign reasoning will assist us to understand the uniqueness and individual merits of the latter.

Some sign arguments of the second category—notably those having to do with what goes on in the minds of other people—

employ in their warrant-backing process models which can be confirmed in direct personal experience, although such confirmation is not required for the valid functioning of the model. Take for example the inference 'Jones screams, perspires, grimaces, says "I am in pain", clutches the dagger in his chest, and therefore Jones is in pain'. The warrant for this inference might read: 'Jones's screams, perspiration, facial expressions, protestations of pain, visible physical wound, etc., form a sign cluster signifying that Jones is in pain.' This warrant is backed if the data manifest the pain-configuration of bodily symptoms, and we test for the presence of that configuration by applying a model which we have been taught.

Similarly, we can reason that Jones has an itch if we can identify in his bodily behaviour the itch-pattern, that he is in love if we can detect the love-pattern, and that he is happy if we can see the happiness-pattern. We learn these patterns in the process of learning how to use the words 'pain', 'itch', 'love', 'happy', etc., but at the same time we learn that these words refer to something mental or psychological and not to the patterns of symptoms evidencing the mental experience. In other words, we learn in the process of learning how to use these words that to say 'Jones is in pain' is not just another way of saying 'Jones screams, perspires, grimaces, says he is in pain, etc.', that 'Jones is in pain' is not just a redescription of those symptoms.

These model patterns which we learn in the process of learning how to use psychological terms, however, can receive confirmation through direct, personal experience. In experiencing pain ourselves, we can confirm what we have been taught, namely that 'pain' does not refer to a set of bodily behaviour patterns. And the same can be done for 'itch', 'love', 'happiness', etc. In experiencing pain ourselves, we also learn that a certain configuration of bodily symptoms goes along with the experience of pain, and the same lesson is learned for itches, love, happiness, etc., by experiencing ourselves what those words refer to.

But the valid functioning of these models in inferences leading to other-minds statements is not dependent upon such first-hand experiences, and a person can correctly identify a pain-pattern or a love-pattern in the behaviour of another person without having had the experience of pain or love himself. Knowing the meaning of a word ('pain', 'love', 'God', etc.) is not necessarily a matter of having experienced that to which the word refers; it is more a matter of knowing how to apply the word oneself in discourse and knowing how to understand the word when it is applied in discourse by others. When John burns his little black book, starts making down-payments on a diamond ring, calls Mary twice a day, visits her every evening, presses her hand, watches her every movement adoringly, and tries to steal a kiss occasionally, even the five-year-old observer who has been taught the use of the word 'love' can knowingly and appropriately say 'John loves Mary'. And if having the experience a psychological term refers to were necessary in the process of identifying a pattern in a set of data, then psychiatrists themselves would have to be or have been schizophrenic in order to do their work, which involves identifying the schizophrenia syndrome in the bodily behaviour of patients and applying the term 'schizophrenic' to them.

Having been in love (adult love), therefore, is not a prerequisite for being able to identify love when one encounters it in others or even in one's self; the only prerequisite for being able to identify love is control of the model pattern of love behaviour which one learns in the process of learning the use of 'love'. Nor need one have experienced war personally or seen war films or read war stories or even played at war in order to identify war when one encounters it; in fact, even playing at war presupposes a prior knowledge of the war-configuration plus the ability and desire to simulate it. Nor need the psychiatrist have been through a schizophrenic interlude himself in order to be able to identify the schizophrenia syndrome in the behaviour of one of his patients.[1] Having been in love or having had a schizophrenic

---

[1] Having experienced schizophrenia is not a prerequisite for being able to identify the schizophrenia syndrome, it is true, but a certain amount of expertness in abnormal psychology is. Without a thorough training in abnormal psychology one would very likely miss that syndrome altogether when one encountered schizophrenic behaviour, or else have only a vague awareness that something was abnormal without being able to specify what. This is due to the infrequency with which schizophrenic behaviour is encountered by the layman and also to the fact that the schizophrenia syndrome itself is vague and loosely constructed, in contrast (say) to the electricity syndrome (sparks flying, lights lighting, buzzers sounding, etc.), any one of the members of which is sufficient for establishing the presence of an electric current in a wire.

Parallels to theological sign reasoning here are pronounced. Data manifesting

interlude helps one to confirm the model love-pattern or the model schizophrenia-pattern, as the case may be. But if such confirmation takes place at all, it usually takes place after and need not take place before one has already learned how to identify love or schizophrenia on the basis of model patterns. After all, the man in love or the man in pain is usually too preoccupied with his love or his pain to take note of his behavioural manifestations and the correlations between them and the mental realities they reveal.

We have here a differentia between psychological sign reasoning and theological sign reasoning, for there is nothing comparable in the latter to confirming the model through direct personal experience. People do have religious experiences which they have a right to call 'direct experiences of God' in one legitimate sense of 'direct'. And such experiences do constitute data from which G-conclusions may be inferred—under the aegis of the criteria determining validity and invalidity for such inferences, of course. But such experiences do not constitute confirmation for the G-configuration, because they are not direct in the requisite sense. Experiencing pain first-hand can confirm the pain-model for an individual, because that experience affords the individual who has it a unique opportunity of correlating (provided he is detached enough to perform the correlation) the reality called pain with the bodily symptoms which reveal that reality to others. If I have experienced pain and if during that experience I have taken note of what bodily behaviour pain causes me to manifest, then I am in a position to confirm the model pain-pattern that I apply in identifying pain in Jones. My experience of pain is not evidence for Jones being in pain, but it does serve to confirm the model employed in backing my inference to Jones's pain.

There is nothing like this, however, in theological sign reasoning, nor need there be. If I have experienced what religious people refer to as an encounter with God, my experience does not provide a vantage point for confirming the

the G-configuration is also a rarity, and the G-configuration is also loosely constructed in such a way (as was already stated) that it is composed of a *family* of characteristics none of which is either necessary or sufficient for determining its presence in a set of data. We might expect, therefore, that special learning is required for competence in identifying the G-configuration in data.

G-configuration as being a sign-pattern which truly signifies God. The experience itself, if veridical, is another manifestation or revelation of God and is not *identical* with God in the way that the experience of pain is identical with pain. As a manifestation or revelation of God, such a religious experience is something to which I apply the model G-configuration in order to draw inferences from it; it is not something I can use to confirm the correlation between God and such experiences. The experience of pain affords me a side-on view, so to speak, of pain and the pattern of bodily symptoms manifested during the pain experience. But the encounter with God affords no such side-on view; in fact, in order to be able to refer to the experience as an *encounter with God* I must first apply the G-configuration to it.

Even though no such model-confirming experience is possible in theological sign reasoning, however, we must remind ourselves that none is necessary. The model G-configuration can be taught and learned and function validly in theological sign reasoning without any such confirmation, as we have seen in parallel cases, i.e., the schizophrenia case and others. The model configurations that are used in sign reasoning require neither justification nor confirmation, and when they enjoy confirmation of the sort just described it is a luxury-item rather than a necessity.

Another sub-variety of this second category of sign arguments, i.e., the category for which matching models against the pattern in the data constitutes the warrant-backing process, is distinguished from the theological sign arguments of that second category on experimental grounds. The conclusions to these arguments suggest tests that could be performed which if fulfilled (though the results would not directly and independently establish the conclusion, nor would they confirm the warrant-backing model) would contribute something more to the data from which the conclusions were drawn and in that way broaden the basis of data in which the pattern was to be sought.

Suppose we came across a mineral substance which glowed in the dark, exposed a photographic plate, and was regularly diminishing in mass. Since the radioactivity-pattern would be evident in these data, we would conclude that the mineral substance was radioactive. This conclusion would in turn suggest that we apply the tests of the Geiger Counter and the

Q

neutron monitor. But since taking the readings on these two instruments is not tantamount to seeing radioactivity in the empirical sense of 'seeing', the readings would contribute to the data and broaden the base in which we search for the radio-activity-pattern without directly and independently establishing the conclusion or confirming the warrant-backing model.[1] The contribution to the argument made by the experimental results can be significant, however. For if the data upon which the conclusion was first based are slender and the sign-pattern only vaguely visible in it, then the broadening of the data through the addition of the experimental findings ought to provide a much firmer foundation for the presence of the pattern.

The conclusions to theological sign arguments, however, are not experimental in this sense, not when those conclusions are G_1-statements anyway. They do not suggest tests which if fulfilled would strengthen the data in which the G-configuration is either present or absent. The statement made by 'God raised Jesus of Nazareth . . .', for example, does not imply any test which people today could perform in order to broaden the basis of data undergirding the inference to that conclusion.

Someone might propose that it suggests that God can give a person new life today in answer to the prayer of religious commitment. But any existential changes that a person might experience as a result of such a prayer is a datum undergirding the G-conclusion stated by 'God regenerates the heart of the man who puts his trust in him' and not the G-conclusion stated by 'God raised Jesus of Nazareth . . .'.[2] Manuscript evidence broadening the data upon which the G-conclusion stated by 'God raised Jesus of Nazareth . . .' might indeed come to light to-morrow. If archaeologists discovered authentic Jewish and

[1] Contrast this with such an argument as 'The engine will not turn over, the fuel gauge registers empty, the dipstick comes up out of the tank dry, and there-fore the car is out of petrol', in which the test suggested by the conclusion (i.e., looking into the petrol tank with a flashlight), rather than strengthening the data, directly and independently establishes the conclusion.

[2] Theism, then, contrary to John Wisdom (who denies that theism is an experi-mental issue in 'Gods', *op. cit.*, p. 149), is partially an experimental issue and partially not. Those G-conclusions which are G_1-statements recording the mighty acts of God in history do not suggest experiments which would strengthen or weaken the data undergirding them. But those G-conclusions which are rooted in religious experience do suggest experiments. Wisdom's error stems from not taking into account the heterogeneity among G-statements.

Roman sources older than the Gospels which bore reluctant witness to the resurrection (i.e., reporting that Jesus of Nazareth was known to have been dead at one time and known to have been alive again at a later time), then of course the data for the resurrection inference would be strengthened. The point is that this data-strengthening evidence would not have been procured by means of experiments suggested by the G-conclusion itself.

As with the sign arguments backed by the several varieties of empirical correlation discussed, so also all the sign arguments backed by model patterns can be put into a bad light by spurious reasoning. Here again, it may be truly stated that the warrants are infinitely corrigible and that the backing does not entail the warrants. These claims are perfectly true but as we have seen before do not introduce a margin of rational doubt, so we need not falter over them. Besides these considerations, the question of non-empirical referents is sure to come up. As was pointed out above, one of the distinctive marks of the second category of sign arguments is the use in their conclusions of expressions referring to non-empiricals: expressions such as 'God', 'radioactivity', 'schizophrenia', 'Jones's pain', etc. The empiricist bias would dictate the reduction of all sign arguments employing such referring-expressions to arguments from criteria to designation by reconstruing the meaning of these terms as redescriptions for what under our interpretation of the matter have been called the symptoms evidencing the non-empiricals named by those terms.

But the empiricist's ban upon sign reasoning about non-empiricals is surely question-begging: If these arguments (any of them) are valid then there are non-empiricals, and so a simple bias against non-empiricals is not sufficient alone to discredit this type of sign reasoning. Besides, if an empiricist felt that he could be faithful to his philosophical commitments while surrendering the empiricist theory of meaning (which involves reducing all non-empiricals to empiricals) but still preserving the empiricist theory of verification (which states that every non-analytic statement of which it makes sense to say that it is true or false must either be directly verifiable and falsifiable on empirical grounds alone or depend ultimately upon some statement which is), then he should have no difficulty over sign reasoning of the second category at all. For the data grounding inferences to conclusions in this type of sign reasoning are empirical data exclusively. There seems to be, therefore, as much reason for challenging one type of sign reasoning as for challenging another and no good reason for challenging any of it.

In conclusion, our survey of the various types of warrant-backing processes employed in sign reasoning should have taught us the uniqueness and the merits of theological sign reasoning. Though it is *sui generis* and its warrant-backing process is not identical with that of some other type of sign reasoning, that in and of itself is not ground for rational doubt extending over the whole species of argument. If anyone charged, therefore, that no answer really has been given to the question 'Is the backing for theological sign arguments really backing?', the reply would be that the answer to the first interpretation of the question is beyond the reach of this study; that no answer to the second interpretation has been given because under that construction no intelligible question is asked; and that a negative answer to the third interpretation has been given, but the question under this construction is really misguided. Under any of these three interpretations, then, the question is nugatory from the standpoint of this study. But in the process of showing that it is, the soundness of sign reasoning as a genus of argument has (hopefully) been demonstrated.

4. THE TYPE-GAP IN THEOLOGICAL SIGN REASONING

In the course of working through the fourth, third, and second objections (in that order) to the central thesis of this chapter, a thorough groundwork has been laid for dealing with the first objection—good reason for reserving the discussion of it until last. Since most of the arguments to be used against it have already been employed in contexts preceding, a protracted rebuttal is unnecessary.

The present objection is fashioned around the valid observation that there is a significant difference in logical type—a type-gap—between the data and the conclusion in theological sign arguments. The data are couched in empirical language, while a G-statement is used to report the conclusion. The statements recording the data mention nothing that is not accessible to sensory experience, while the conclusion mentions something (God) which is inaccessible to that kind of experience. This much is agreed upon. But the objection proceeds to make false capital out of the type-gap, charging that it presents an unconquerable barrier to reason. The objection, in effect, avers that it is logically impossible to bridge such a type-gap between the sign and the thing signified and that hence the sign is not really a sign and signifies nothing beyond itself.

The presupposition underlying this objection is that reason is monolithic, that there is one and only one acceptable method of logic—entailment, either syntactical or semantical. Any inference, according to this view, which is not effected by entailment is invalid. It has often been noted that G_1-statements have empirical entailments. When the argument runs from G-statement to empirical conclusion, therefore, there are cases in which entailment operates. But there is no likelihood of reversing the process, of setting forth any set of empirical statements which entail a G-statement. So there is no question of the absence of entailment, both syntactical and semantical, between the data and the conclusion in theological sign reasoning. If entailment were possible in these inferences, there would be no need to employ sign reasoning. But even to say this is to suggest that entailment deserves some sort of priority and that sign reasoning is at best a second-rate substitute for entailment, suggestions to be counteracted as we progress.

The objection can now be set down candidly in logical form: There is a type-gap in theological sign reasoning, that type-gap is not and cannot be spanned by entailment, entailment is the only acceptable method of logic, and so theological sign reasoning in principle and as a species of argument is invalid. The first two premises have already been granted, and there is nothing wrong with the logic used in spelling out this objection. So the conclusion would demand that we bow before it, if the third premise also commands agreement. The third premise can be shown to be false, however, partly by *reductio ad absurdum* and partly by a debunking process. The objection, therefore, does not require consent.

First, let us consider what would follow if it were true that the only valid method of logic were entailment. It would follow that all of the sciences (in the root sense of that word) employing methodologies predicated upon inference-routes other than entailment are spurious sciences. Here surely is material for a *reductio ad absurdum*. Clinical psychologists reason from bodily states to mental states, a trans-type inference-route which is unquestionably not entailment. If entailment were the only valid method of logic, then clinical psychology would be a spurious science. Historians reason from written documents we possess in the present to facts which supposedly happened in the past. Entailment does not cover their type-gap inferences, and so the truth of the supposition that entailment is the only valid inference-route would render the historical science spurious and wipe out the whole historical enterprise. Physical scientists reason from particular observations to general laws and hypotheses with predictive import and experimental possibilities (though the pattern used may not live up to the pattern of classical induction as set forth by Bacon and others). True, they are interested in the experimental entailments predicted by those laws and hypotheses. But entailment certainly is not used in the original formulation of those laws and hypotheses, nor is the logical relationship between the truth of the experimental entailments and the truth of the entailing hypotheses one of entailment. Scientists prefer to call that logical relationship 'confirmation' or 'verification' or something of the sort.

There is no need to continue the catalogue of legitimate sciences which would be rendered spurious if the monolithic-logic supposition about entailment were true. What has been argued about clinical psychology, history, and the physical sciences could be extended to all of the social sciences, the life sciences, the normative sciences (law, aesthetics, ethics)—everything in fact short of pure mathematics. All of them have a methodological type-gap to contend with, and none of them can lay claim to entailment as the basic rational tool involved in their professional toil. This puts all of the sciences in the same camp with theology *vis-à-vis* the supposition about the logical monopoly of entailment. But few thinkers have been courageous enough to take a stand upon such an attenuated view of knowledge, few staunch enough to withstand the storm of counter-objections from men who take a broader view of reason and of the multiplicity of valid inference-routes. The supposition, therefore, that entailment is the only valid method of logic is absurd.

But a *reductio* refutation, even a good one, is seldom conclusive. This one surely is not. In all honesty, we must acknowledge (what *seems* absurd) the possibility that the supposition is after all correct and that its unsavoury consequences simply have to be faced up to. So the *reductio* must be supplemented by more direct methods of disproof. And along that line the next thing that needs to be said is that 'rational methodology' does not in ordinary discourse *mean* 'entailment'. The objector may want to redefine the expression 'rational methodology' by stipulation to mean 'entailment'. If he does so, then his case is iron-clad but one world removed from the origination point of the discussion, which presumably started out to determine which methodologies are rational in any ordinary sense of 'rational'.

Once this is seen, then the question is reopened as to whether any inference-routes or methods of logic besides entailment are in fact rational in some ordinary sense of 'rational'. This move affords the opportunity of pointing out that in its ordinary sense 'rational' (the same is true of 'valid') does not refer to species of argument but rather to individual arguments within species. The proper answer to the question 'Are type-gap arguments as a category valid or invalid?', therefore, is that some of the individual arguments within this category are valid and some of them are invalid. Those with backed warrants are valid, and those with unbacked warrants are invalid.

More specifically, the proper answer to the question 'Are theological sign arguments as a category valid or invalid?' is that those theological sign arguments for which the warrant is backed by a correlation between the configuration in the data and the model G-configuration are valid, and the others are not. This should be a complete and wholly satisfactory answer to the question of how these inferences are justified and which of them are rational or valid. As to the further question regarding whether or not the warrant-backing process for theological sign reasoning is itself justifiable, rational, and valid, the answer (as we have stated before) is that this question cannot legitimately arise—which is not so much an answer as a rejection of the question. For the criteria for backing a warrant in theological sign reasoning *define* what rational or valid inference within this field actually is. By what other standards, therefore, could these criteria in turn be judged? To require that they be judged by or measured against the criteria that apply to entailment, to require that all inference in the last analysis be deductive inference (entailment), is only to invite paradox.

The argument in behalf of the thesis that G_1-statements are in principle conclusively verifiable on empirical grounds alone is now complete, and the case rests. With the four major objections out of the way, it is difficult to see what further obstacle remains to block the ratification of that thesis. And if its ratification does succeed, then hopefully the metatheological sceptic will accept it as additional evidence in favour of the cognitive significance of those 'G'-sentences which are used in the making of G_1-statements.

CHAPTER VII

COGNITIVE MEANING

1. THE COGNITIVE AFFINITIES OF 'G'-SENTENCES

'Are "G"-sentences as understood by classical Christian theism cognitively significant in the requisite G-statement making use we have been testing for?' The posing again of the pilot question gives indication that it is time to take a stand. In behalf of an affirmative answer, the affinities between G-statements and empirical statements (the paradigm cases—along with analytic statements—of cognitive discourse) must be stressed. Three striking affinities more than compensate for the major disparity between empirical statements and G-statements (i.e., the fact that 'God' in G-statements names a non-empirical referent) and argue for grouping them together under the common rubric of cognitive discourse. Most of what needs to be said in corroboration of these affinities is by way of review and can be stated tersely without elaboration or illustration.

In the first place, some G-statements (namely G_1-statements) are in principle conclusively checkable on empirical grounds alone, and the rest are in principle conclusively checkable with reference to the G_1-statements. G-statements taken as a group, then, form a system with an empirical basis, a system within which each G-statement is ultimately accountable either directly or indirectly to empirical facts. Priority is given here to this consideration, because of the three it ought to have the most telling effect upon the thinking of the metatheological sceptic. On his own terms the cognitive significance of 'G'-sentences ought to be granted, for he takes conclusive checkability on empirical grounds as a sufficient condition for cognitive meaningfulness. The empirical accountability of G-statements as a system, therefore, is one good reason for grouping G-statements together with empirical statements under the general rubric of cognitive discourse.

A second reason takes its cue from the entailments and incompatibles of G-statements. Merely having entailments and incompatibles is one indication (a necessary and sufficient one, by the way) that the sentence in question is used to make a statement, that the sentence is governed by linguistic rules that dictate cognitive meaning. The very fact that G-statements have entailments and incompatibles, therefore, speaks for their participation in cognitive discourse. But the matter does not terminate there, for the entailments and incompatibles of any statement also serve to display the meaning of the sentence used in making that statement. Since some G-statements (the G_1-statements again) have *empirical* statements among their entailments and incompatibles, i.e., since the entailments and incompatibles of those statements demonstrate that the sentences used in making the statements have some empirical meaning, a special case can be made for the logical proximity of G_1-statements and empirical statements and for their common inclusion under the general rubric of cognitive discourse.

The third but weakest (since it establishes only a strong presumption of cognitive meaningfulness) affinity between the sentences used in making G-statements and the sentences used in making empirical statements is their common intelligibility within what might be called 'cognitive frames'. Some linguistic frames for effecting indirect discourse are of special relevance in determining which sentences are cognitively significant and which are not. Because of the conceptual connexion between truth, fact, and knowledge on the one hand and cognition on the other, it stands to reason that whatever sentences in their conventional uses make sense rather than nonsense within the cognitive frames 'It is true that . . .', 'It is false that . . .', 'It is a fact that . . .', 'It is not a fact that . . .', 'We know that . . .', and 'We do not know that . . .'—those sentences most probably are cognitively meaningful. (I leave open the possibility that convention might mistakenly support the use in cognitive frames of sentences which on the surface appear to have cognitive meaning but on deeper inspection lack it.) Since nonsense results from filling in any of these cognitive frames with imperatives or exclamations, we have good grounds for holding that imperatives and exclamations have some meaning other than cognitive meaning. Any indicative 'G'-sentence, on the other hand, would most likely strike one as making sense in the cognitive frames. The statements made by 'We know that God created the heavens and the earth', 'It is true that God is love', and 'It is a fact that God raised Jesus of Nazareth from the dead near Jerusalem at t_2' might be false or even in practice undecidable, but the sentences used in stating them seem to make perfectly good sense. Even to deem it serious business to reason to the falsity or undecidability of these statements is a tacit acknowledgement of the cognitive meaningfulness of the sentences which make them.

Here then are three good reasons for maintaining that 'G'-sentences are cognitively meaningful: the checkability of G-statements (sometimes on empirical grounds alone), that fact that they have entailments and incompatibles (sometimes empirical), and the intelligibility of 'G'-sentences within cognitive frames. The metatheological cognitivist rests his case on these three points.

2. THE NON-COGNITIVE FUNCTIONS OF 'G'-SENTENCES

'Are "G"-sentences as understood by classical Christian theism cognitively significant in the requisite G-statement making use we have been testing for?' We have just reviewed the points upon which the metatheological cognitivist rests his case. We know also that it is not possible for the metatheological sceptic to rest his case (as has almost invariably been attempted by metatheological sceptics) upon the claim that 'G'-sentences do not make statements which are at least in principle if not in practice verifiable or falsifiable, for we know from what has gone before that this claim does not hold up under scrutiny. One move only seems open to the metatheological sceptic yet unwilling to surrender his position: to invoke the now-popular principle that the meaning is given by the use and to argue that 'G'-sentences have non-cognitive meaning because they have non-cognitive uses.

The metatheological sceptic by definition contests the cognitive significance of 'G'-sentences in the requisite G-statement making use (though some of them—Miles, Munz, and van Buren, for instance—allow that 'G'-sentences make statements about the meaning of human existence without reference to a transcendent God). But few of them couple with this denial the claim that 'G'-sentences are bereft of any and every sort of meaning. The usual pattern is to deny 'G'-sentences cognitive meaning on the grounds of the checkability criterion of cognitive meaning and then to go on to give some alternative and non-cognitive account of their meaning on the grounds of the use principle.[1] And in the application of the principle, one encounters the attempt on the part of the metatheological sceptic to assimilate 'G'-sentences to other language forms on

---

[1] R. B. Braithwaite in his Eddington Memorial Lecture entitled *An Empiricist's View of the Nature of Religious Belief* exemplifies this pattern perfectly. Braithwaite's allies on the meaning of 'G'-sentences include Ronald W. Hepburn in *Christianity and Paradox* and Paul F. Schmidt in *Religious Knowledge*, and in certain respects also Gerald F. Downing in *Has Christianity A Revelation?*. One can find critical discussion of Braithwaite's viewpoint in the following: A. C. Ewing, 'Religious Assertions in the Light of Contemporary Philosophy', *Philosophy*, XXXII (1957): 206-218; Frederick Ferré, *Basic Modern Philosophy of Religion*, pp. 353-361; John Hick, *Philosophy of Religion*, pp. 90-93; H. J. N. Horsburgh, 'Professor Braithwaite and Billy Brown', *Australasian Journal of Philosophy*, XXXVI (1958): 201-207; E. L. Mascall, *Words and Images*, pp. 49-62; and John Wisdom, *Paradox and Discovery*, pp. 43-56.

My own views of the Braithwaite thesis, attributable in part to what I have learned from the above articles but especially to personal dicussions I have enjoyed with Professor George E. Hughes on the subject, are as follows: (1) Braithwaite fails to give a consistent account of the single function he imputes to both moral and religious assertions (a bewildering use of 'assertion', by the way, in light of its cognitive connotations in everyday speech). In successive contexts he refers to it as the guiding of conduct (p. 10), the expressing of attitudes (pp. 11-12), the expressing of intentions (p. 12), the declaring of intentions (pp. 12-13), and the subscribing to policies of action (p. 13). These five linguistic functions, though similar, are surely also quite discrete. (2) Though various 'G'-sentences might perform any or all of these functions (plus others not named by Braithwaite) in suitable contexts, the knowledge of these functions would not be equivalent to knowledge of their meaning due to the difference between contextual and conventional meaning (more on this later). Besides, in order to perform any of these functions as indicative sentences, they must have the very type of meaning by convention that Braithwaite denies them—cognitive meaning (more later on this too). (3) Braithwaite's analysis of moral assertions (and hence also of religious assertions, since he assimilates the latter to the former) is dubious in detail if not also in type. One might challenge the pro-attitude analysis of moral assertions in general. But even if one accepted that, he would still have to criticize Braithwaite for an unfortunate fixation upon the role that intention-declaring plays in the meaning of moral assertion. Since 'x is right, but I do not intend to perform x' is not a logical contradiction (unless one follows Braithwaite's linguistic recommendation—for that ultimately is what his theory amounts to—to make it a logcal contradiction by stipulative definition), Braithwaite is wrong in analysing the meaning of 'x is right' as 'I intend to perform x'. And (4) Braithwaite presents a grossly over-simplified view of the nature and function of religious assertions by assimilating them in every case to moral assertions. Some religious assertions in suitable contexts and as only part of their functioning in those contexts can do the same work that moral assertions perform. But that is a far cry from identifying the meaning of religious assertions and moral assertions.

the basis of linguistic functions which 'G'-sentences may share in common with those other forms. In particular, attempts have been made to assimilate indicative 'G'-sentences to exclamations because of the emotive functions that the latter frequently take on, and to imperatives due to the functions of prescription and activation or motivation which 'G'-sentences often perform. Three things need to be made quite clear apropos all non-cognitive accounts of the meaning of 'G'-sentences.

In the first place, though we must acquiesce to the metatheological sceptic's suggestion that 'G'-sentences in suitable contexts have non-cognitive functions or uses, this in no way amounts to capitulation.[1] It can be freely admitted that indicative 'G'-

[1] For a balanced and perceptive analysis of the non-cognitive uses of religious discourse in relation to its fundamental cognitive uses, see Frederick Ferré, *Language, Logic and God*, pp. 121-166; and Kent Bendall and Frederick Ferré, *Exploring the Logic of Faith: A Dialogue on the Relation of Modern Philosophy to Christian Faith*, pp. 43-99.

Exponents of an emotive theory of religious language include: Kai Nielsen, 'On Talk About God', *Journal of Philosophy*, LV (1958): 888-890; C. K. Ogden and I. A. Richards, *The Meaning of Meaning: A Study of the Influence of Language Upon Thought and of the Science of Symbolism*, pp. 158-159; Paul F. Schmidt, 'Is There Religious Knowledge?', *Journal of Philosophy*, LV (1958): 529-538. For a negative viewpoint on the emotive theory of religious language, see Ronald W. Hepburn, 'Poetry and Religious Belief', in MacIntyre ed., *Metaphysical Beliefs*, pp. 85–166.

The assimilation of indicative 'G'-sentences to imperatives in a prescription and/or motivation (activation) theory of religious language has also had its exponents. Kenneth Burke, in his *The Philosophy of Literary Form: Studies in Symbolic Action*, Revised and Abridged (New York, 1957), pp. 5-8, sees 'G'-sentences as covert commands and religious language as verbal coercion and as part of the strategy of inducement. He has enlarged this theory into a book under the title of *The Rhetoric of Religion: Studies in Logology* (Boston, 1961). Charles Morris, in *Signs, Language and Behaviour* (New York, 1955), pp. 146-148, presents a modified version of the imperative theory, declaring that the primary function of religious discourse is 'prescriptive-incitive' but not denying its informative and valuative functions (though relegating them to a place of secondary importance). Stephen E. Toulmin, without necessarily extracting all of the cognitive implications of religious discourse, offers in effect an amalgam of the emotive and imperative theories; for him, the function of religious language is to reassure us in the face of the unknown and to put heart into the discharge of our moral duties. See *An Examination of the Place of Reason in Ethics* (Cambridge, 1953), pp. 212-221.

Other dicussions (besides those already mentioned in connection with Braithwaite's essay) of the non-cognitive functions of 'G'-sentences worthy of note include: the exchange between Raphael Demos and C. J. Ducasse, 'Symposium: Are Religious Dogmas Cognitive and Meaningful?', in Morton White, ed., *Academic Freedom, Logic and Religion* (Philadelphia, 1953), II, 71-97; R. M. Hare, 'Religion and Morals', in Mitchell, ed., *Faith and Logic*, pp. 176-193; T. R. Miles, *Religion and the Scientific Outlook*, pp. 157-179, 215-220; and John H. Randall, Jr., *The Role of Knowledge in Western Religion* (Boston, 1958).

sentences upon occasion evince and/or evoke feelings or attitudes (the conventional use of exclamations), prescribe action and motivate or incite people to belief or action (the conventional uses of imperatives), or perform any of a number of other non-cognitive linguistic jobs, without doing any damage to the thesis that the conventional uses of indicative 'G'-sentences are cognitive uses.[1] One method of corroborating this claim is (as was suggested above) the method of inserting sentences into cognitive frames to see if the indirect discourse thereby produced makes sense or nonsense. Since, as we have already seen, indicative 'G'-sentences do seem to make sense whereas exclamations and imperatives do not make sense within cognitive frames, it is impossible to assimilate the conventional meaning of indicative 'G'-sentences to the conventional meaning of either exclamations or imperatives. Here then is one good reason why the admission that indicative 'G'-sentences in suitable contexts do the work of exclamations or imperatives does not endanger the cognitivist's thesis or lapse into an exclamation or imperative theory of religious language.

Another reason springs from the distinction implicit in the first, i.e., the distinction between contextual meaning (*m*eaning or *u*se) and conventional meaning (*M*eaning or *U*se).[2] The contextual *m*eaning (*u*se) is the function that a sentence performs in any particular context and reflects the speaker's purpose or intention on that particular occasion. The conventional *M*eaning (*U*se), on the other hand, has nothing to do with specific contexts, particular occasions, or speaker's purposes; it

[1] We must not lose sight of the phenomenon of multiple functioning; it is entirely possible for 'G'-sentences to perform cognitive and non-cognitive functions simultaneously, although where multiple functioning occurs one function might be primary and the other secondary. Also it may be intimated here, in anticipation of the ensuing discussion of the matter, that even when the cognitive function is forced into the background by the non-cognitive function, the latter is still functionally dependent upon the former and could not operate in its absence.

[2] Professor Daniel C. Bennett introduced me to this distinction. For remarks involving these two different senses of 'meaning' and 'use', see Wittgenstein's *Philosophical Investigations*, pp. e3, e10, e20, e53, e55, e77, e80–e82, e108, e113, e128, e168, e175–e176, e215, e216, e220; and *The Blue and Brown Books*, pp. 27–28, 67–69. Although Wittgenstein is ultimately responsible for the identification of meaning with use and its implications for modern Anglo-Saxon philosophy, this writer at least does not always find him clear on the difference between contextual *m*eaning (*u*se) and conventional *M*eaning (*U*se). See also P. F. Strawson, 'On Referring', in Flew, ed., *Essays in Conceptual Analysis*, pp. 27–33.

has to do with the rules, habits, and conventions which govern the correct Use of that expression on all occasions and which determine the speaker's understanding of its general Use regardless of his special employments of it. Neglect of this distinction and the concommitant conflation of Meaning with use (disregarding the difference between Use and use) accounts for the metatheological sceptic's conviction that proving the non-cognitive uses of indicative 'G'-sentences is tantamount to proving their non-cognitive Meaning. The establishing of the distinction is alone sufficient to undo his conviction. But the point here would profit from illustration.

Consider the sentence 'Remember, Charlie, God is love' spoken to a religious person in the context of moral exhortation or advice. The contextual meaning or use of 'God is love' in suitable contexts may be the same as that of the imperative 'Love thy neighbour as thyself' or even the same as the conventional Meaning or Use of that command, the Meaning of which is to tell someone to behave in a certain manner rather than in some other manner. But the conventional Meaning or Use of 'God is love' could certainly never be *equated* with either the contextual meaning (use) or the conventional Meaning (Use) of 'Love thy neighbour as thyself'. For the Meaning of 'God is love' is that the property of love is to be predicated of the being designated by 'God', which has nothing to do with telling a person to behave in some stated fashion. From the fact, then, that 'God is love' and 'Love thy neighbour as thyself' can in certain contexts have the same meaning (use) it does not follow that they have the same Meaning (Use). And, to draw to a close the first of three general points addressed to the metatheological sceptic, the fact that indicative 'G'-sentences have non-cognitive uses in no way implies that they have non-cognitive Meaning.

The second general point that needs to be made clear to the metatheological sceptic who espouses a non-cognitive account of indicative 'G'-sentences is that sometimes these sentences are given their conventional cognitive Use (Meaning) rather than any non-cognitive use (meaning) in contexts the central thrust of which is clearly non-cognitive. Two biblical passages containing moral exhortation backed up by cognitive theological reasons will suffice to illustrate this point: 'Thus let us offer to

God acceptable worship, with reverence and awe; for our God is a consuming fire'[1] and 'Beloved, let us love one another; for love is of God, and he who loves is born of God and knows God. He who does not love does not know God; for God is love.'[2] The central thrust of both passages is hortatory, and they begin on that key-note with exhortations telling people to do something (to offer acceptable worship to God in the first case, to love one another in the second). Exhortations are non-cognitive linguistic instruments. The exhortations are followed by indicative 'G'-sentences or clauses, the use of which in their respective non-cognitive contexts is obviously co-incident with their conventional cognitive Use (Meaning). They function here as cognitive reasons for obeying the exhortations, though they could in other contexts be given a hortatory use (meaning). Not every time that indicative 'G'-sentences are used in non-cognitive contexts, therefore, is their use non-cognitive.

The third point for the exponent of a non-cognitive account is the most vital of the three. Not only is it the case that indicative 'G'-sentences can bear non-cognitive meanings (uses) in suitable contexts, and not only is it the case that in some non-cognitive contexts indicative 'G'-sentences bear only their cognitive Meanings (Uses), but it is also the case that whenever indicative 'G'-sentences bear non-cognitive meanings (uses) in non-cognitive contexts they bear their conventional cognitive Meanings (Uses) at the same time, and the former are functionally dependent upon the latter and could not be operative in the absence of the latter. This is only to say that the non-cognitive meanings of indicative 'G'-sentences (they have no non-cognitive Meaning, it must be remembered) are a function of their cognitive Meanings.

To illustrate this, the kerygma or preaching of the primitive Christian community was composed of a series of indicative 'G'-sentences (mostly) the Meaning (Use) of which was to narrate the mighty acts of God in history—a straightforwardly cognitive job. But the primary use to which the kerygma was put by the early church was non-cognitive—the function of converting men to Christ, of motivating them to a new life-

[1] Hebrews 12:28-29(RSV).
[2] I John 4:7-8 (RSV).

commitment. Presumably, there might have been other strategies available, other methods at hand for converting men to Christ than narrating to them the mighty acts of God. But these particular sentences could perform that particular *use* (conversion) only because they had the general *Use* (*Meaning*) that they had (narration) and because for some psychological reason narration can be a powerful instrument of conversion.

Our exploration of the non-cognitive *uses* of indicative 'G'-sentences has yielded no substantiation for the metatheological sceptic's claim that these same sentences have non-cognitive *Meanings* only. On the contrary, the entire investigation has shown that as far as *Meaning* (*Use*) is concerned, for indicative 'G'-sentences it is solidly cognitive.

3. DEMAND FOR A RULING ON 'COGNITIVELY SIGNIFICANT'

The pilot question intrudes itself once again: 'Are "G"-sentences as understood by classical Christian theism cognitively significant? Are they used to make G-statements?' This question was initially asked in order to guide us in the exploration of the meaning of 'G'-sentences. Now the question manifests itself in a new light, not as a request for information about the meaning of 'G'-sentences, but as a request for a decision whether or not to enforce the rules for the use of 'cognitively significant' in the special case of 'G'-sentences. In other words, the question at this stage is not so much about 'G'-sentences as about 'cognitively significant'. It is not a request for the meaning of the expression 'cognitively significant', for we are clear enough on that. Nor is it a request for information about the extension or range of application of 'cognitively significant' as it presently exists, for we are clear enough about that too. It is instead a demand for a ruling: Should the extension of 'cognitively significant' be changed so as to exclude indicative 'G'-sentences, or should its present extension be enforced so as to continue to include indicative 'G'-sentences? Should we enforce the ruling already in practice for the extension of 'cognitively significant', or should we make a new ruling?

The line of reasoning sustained throughout this study argues

R

for the enforcement of the presently existing ruling. The logical affinities of 'G'-sentences are decidedly with empirical propositions and other sorts of indisputably cognitive discourse. The metatheological sceptic, on the other hand, still impressed with the ephemeral differences between G-statements and empirical statements and with the superficial likenesses between the *uses* of some indicative 'G'-sentences and some kinds of non-cognitive discourse, might continue to propagate his challenge and vote for changing the rules for the use of 'cognitively significant' so as to exclude 'G'-sentences. If that were the case, he should be admonished on three scores.

First, he must be told that unless he can advance very compelling arguments in favour of changing the rules which determine the bounds of 'cognitively significant' (rules which are well entrenched and well backed), the course of wisdom is to bow before existing practice. It is difficult indeed to imagine what reasons he could advance on behalf of changing these rules. G-statements satisfy his checkability criterion, indicative 'G'-sentences make sense in cognitive frames and have no non-cognitive *M*eaning (*U*se), etc. The case for enforcing the existing rules for the extension of 'cognitively significant' with respect to 'G'-sentences is deficient in no critical requirement.

Secondly, he must face the fact that his position is now manifestly paradoxical, because the logical affinities of 'G'-sentences have been shown to lie with cognitive discourse. The metatheological sceptic's paradox (latent until now) has served to illuminate the differences between 'G'-sentences and the sentences used in making empirical propositions, and the similarities between the former and non-cognitive utterances—a valuable service not to be minimized. It has served also to break the spell of 'cognitively significant', so that we no longer need regard it as some sort of mystical watchword. For the *M*eaning of 'G'-sentences will remain constant regardless of whether we apply 'cognitively significant' to them or withhold it from them. And this is not to say that no importance attaches to the application of that metalinguistic epithet to 'G'-sentences, or else there would be no point in arguing so vigorously for its application. But the paradox is false despite these valuable services and, its work accomplished and its lessons learned, should be discarded.[1] It should be discarded, because if it is allowed to remain unchallenged an unreproved, it is liable to overshadow its good works with evil and blind us to the great similarities between 'G'-sentences and the sentences used in making empirical propositions as well as to the great differences between the former and specimens of non-cognitive discourse. The potential mischief inherent in the metatheological sceptic's paradox (i.e., the paradox that 'G'-sentences are never cognitively significant) argues for its dismissal.

And lastly, the metatheological sceptic must be warned against withdrawing into linguisitic solipsism, from which only a hollow victory is to be gained. Annoyed by the insistence throughout this study that his arguments consistently depend upon departures from ordinary language, existing linguistic rules, and meanings well entrenched in practice, the metatheological sceptic might choose to over-rule ordinary language and set up his own linguistic kingdom of rules in which he arrogates for himself the last word. Then what he says about the non-cognitivity of religious language is bound to hold, but only for his private realm. His results are not to be read back into the common sense world where not his meanings but the meanings of ordinary speech hold. The metatheological sceptic can have his victory, it would seem, but only at the price of losing semantical contact with the very people with whom he wants to dialogue.

The present writer is prepared, therefore, to stand behind an affirmative answer to the question 'Are "G"-sentences as understood by classical Christian theism cognitively significant in the requisite G-statement making use we have been investigating?', aware of both the implications and the limitations of that answer. This ground gained, there remains the task of working out some of the other philosophical puzzles which surround the word 'God' in classical Christian theism and of extending the whole project to other systems of theological understanding. Perhaps the present study suggests some guidelines for that continuing task. It is my personal conviction that modern

---

[1] John Wisdom, who in general seems to favour perpetuating the dialectical tension between philosophical paradoxes and the platitudes they oppose, agrees with this conclusion in the case of the metatheological sceptic's paradox. See *Paradox and Discovery*, pp. 53-56.

metatheology has recently entered into a more positive and constructive era from which should issue through the growing rapprochement between philosophers and theologians rich dividends in terms of increased comprehension of the whole complex field of religious conceptualization, discourse, and logic.

BIBLIOGRAPHY

BOOKS

Ayer, Alfred Jules. *Language, Truth and Logic.* Second Edition. New York: Dover Publications, n.d. (Second edition first published in 1946: London, Victor Gollancz.)
——————. *The Problem of Knowledge.* Harmondsworth, Middlesex: Penguin Books, 1956.
Ayer, A. J., *et al. The Revolution in Philosophy.* London: Macmillan Co., 1956.
Baillie, John. *The Sense of the Presence of God.* New York: Charles Scribner's Sons, 1962.
Bendall, Kent, and Ferré, Frederick. *Exploring the Logic of Faith: A Dialogue on the Relation of Modern Philosophy to Christian Faith.* New York: Association Press, 1962.
Blackstone, William T. *The Problem of Religious Knowledge: The Impact of Contemporary Philosophical Analysis on the Question of Religious Knowledge.* Englewood Cliffs: Prentice-Hall, 1963.
Bochenski, Joseph M. *The Logic of Religion.* New York: New York University Press, 1965.
Braaten, Carl E. and Harrisville, Roy A. (eds. and trs.). *The Historical Jesus and the Kerygmatic Christ: Essays on the New Quest of the Historical Jesus.* New York and Nashville: Abingdon, 1964.
Braaten, Carl E. and Harrisville, Roy A. (eds. and trs.). *Kerygma and History: A Symposium on the Theology of Rudolf Bultmann.* New York and Nashville: Abingdon, 1962.
Braithwaite, R. B. *An Empiricist's View of the Nature of Religious Belief.* Cambridge: Cambridge University Press, 1955.
Bultmann, Rudolf, *et al. Kerygma and Myth: A Theological Debate.* Edited by Hans Werner Bartsch, and revised edition of this translation by Reginald H. Fuller. New York: Harper & Brothers, 1961.
——————. *Essays Philosophical and Theological.* Translated by James C. G. Greig from the German *Glauben und Verstehen: Gesammelte Aufsätze,* II. London: SCM Press, 1955.
——————. *Jesus Christ and Mythology.* New York: Charles Scribner's Sons, 1958.
——————. *Theology of the New Testament.* Translated by Kendrick Grobel. 2 vols. New York: Charles Scribner's Sons, 1951.

R*

Burke, Kenneth. *The Philosophy of Literary Form: Studies in Symbolic Action*. Revised Edition, Abridged by the Author. New York: Vintage Books, 1957.

———. *The Rhetoric of Religion: Studies in Logology*. Boston: Beacon Press, 1961.

Charlesworth, Maxwell J. *Philosophy and Linguistic Analysis*. Pittsburg: Duquesne University Press, 1959.

Christian, William A. *Meaning and Truth in Religion*. Princeton: Princeton University Press, 1964.

Copi, Irving M. *Introduction to Logic*. Second Edition. New York: Macmillan Co., 1961.

Copleston, Frederick. *Contemporary Philosophy: Studies of Logical Positivism and Existentialism*. London: Burns & Oates, 1956.

Cullmann, Oscar. *Heil als Geschichte*. Tübingen: J. C. B. Mohr (Paul Siebeck), 1965.

Dilley, Frank B. *Metaphysics and Religious Language*. New York and London: Columbia University Press, 1964.

Downing, F. Gerald. *Has Christianity a Revelation?* London: SCM Press, 1964.

Eaton, Ralph M. *General Logic: An Introductory Survey*. New York: Charles Scribner's Sons, 1931.

Ebeling, Gerhard. *Word and Faith*. Translated by James W. Leitch from the German *Wort und Glaube*. Philadelphia: Fortress Press, 1963.

Feigl, Herbert and Sellars, Wilfred (eds.). *Readings in Philosophical Analysis*. New York: Appleton-Century-Crofts, 1949.

Ferré, Frederick. *Basic Modern Philosophy of Religion*. New York: Charles Scribner's Sons, 1967.

———. *Language, Logic and God*. New York: Harper & Brothers, 1961.

Filson, Floyd V. *Jesus Christ the Risen Lord*. New York: Abingdon Press, 1956.

Findlay, J. N. *Language, Mind and Value*. London: Allen & Unwin, 1963.

Flew, Antony. *God and Philosophy*. London: Hutchinson and Co., 1966.

Flew, Antony (ed.). *Essays in Conceptual Analysis*. London: Macmillan Co., 1956.

——— (ed.). *Logic and Language*. First Series. Oxford: Basil Blackwell, 1951.

——— (ed.). *Logic and Language*. Second Series. Oxford: Basil Blackwell, 1953.

Flew, Antony, and MacIntyre, Alasdair (eds.). *New Essays in Philosophical Theology*. New York: Macmillan Co., 1955.

Hare, R. M. *The Language of Morals*. Oxford: Clarendon Press, 1952.

Hartshorne, Charles. *The Logic of Perfection and Other Essays in Neo-classical Metaphysics*. La Salle: Open Court Publishing Co., 1962.

Hartshorne, Charles and Reese, William L. *Philosophers Speak of God*. Chicago and London: University of Chicago Press, 1953.

Harvey, Van A. *A Handbook of Theological Terms*. New York: Macmillan Co., 1964.

——————————. *The Historian and the Believer: The Morality of Historical Knowledge and Christian Belief*. New York: Macmillan Co., 1966.

Hepburn, Ronald W. *Christianity and Paradox: Critical Studies in Twentieth-Century Theology*. London: Watts, 1958.

Hick, John. *Faith and Knowledge: A Modern Introduction to the Problem of Religious Knowledge*. Ithaca: Cornell University Press, 1957.

——————————. *Philosophy of Religion*. Englewood Cliffs: Prentice-Hall, 1963.

Hick, John (ed.). *The Existence of God*. New York: Macmillan Co., 1964.

—————————— (ed.). *Faith and the Philosophers*. London: Macmillan Co., 1964.

High, Dallas M. *Language, Persons, and Belief: Studies in Wittgenstein's 'Philosophical Investigations' and Religious Uses of Language*. London: Oxford University Press, 1967.

Hook, Sidney (ed.). *Religious Experience and Truth: A Symposium*. New York: New York University Press, 1961.

Hordern, William. *Speaking of God: The Nature and Purpose of Theological Language*. New York and London: Macmillan Co., 1964.

Hutchison, John A. *Language and Faith: Studies in Sign, Symbol, and Meaning*. Philadelphia: Westminster Press, 1963.

Lazerowitz, Morris. *The Structure of Metaphysics*. London: Routledge & Kegan Paul, 1955.

Lewis, H. D. (ed.). *Contemporary British Philosophy*. Third Series. London: Allen & Unwin, 1956.

——————————. *Our Experience of God*. London: Allen & Unwin, 1959.

Linsky, Leonard (ed.). *Semantics and the Philosophy of Language*. Urbana: University of Illinois Press, 1952.

MacIntyre, Alasdair (ed.). *Metaphysical Beliefs: Three Essays*. London: SCM Press, 1957.

Macquarrie, John. *An Existentialist Theology: A Comparison of Heidegger and Bultmann.* London: SCM Press, 1955.

Martin, C. B. *Religious Belief.* Ithaca: Cornell University Press, 1959.

Mascall, E. L. *Words and Images: A Study in Theological Discourse.* New York: Ronald Press Co., 1957.

McPherson, Thomas. *The Philosophy of Religion.* London: D. Van Nostrand Co., 1965.

Miles, T. R. *Religion and the Scientific Outlook.* London: Allen & Unwin, 1959.

Mitchell, Basil (ed.). *Faith and Logic: Oxford Essays in Philosophical Theology.* London: Allen & Unwin, 1957.

Moore, G. E. *Philosophical Papers.* New York: Collier Books, 1962. (First published in 1959: London, Allen & Unwin.)

——————. *Philosophical Studies.* Paterson, New Jersey: Littlefield, Adams & Co., 1959. (First published in 1922: London, Routledge & Kegan Paul.)

Morris, Charles. *Signs, Language and Behaviour.* New York: George Braziller, 1955. (First published in 1946: New York, Prentice-Hall.)

Munz, Peter. *Problems of Religious Knowledge.* London: SCM Press, 1959.

Niebuhr, Richard R. *Resurrection and Historical Reason: A Study of Theological Method.* New York: Charles Scribner's Sons, 1957.

Ogden, C. K., and Richards, I. A. *The Meaning of Meaning: A Study of the Influence of Language Upon Thought and of the Science of Symbolism.* Eighth Edition. New York: Harcourt, Brace & Co., n.d. (First published in 1923: London, Routledge & Kegan Paul.)

Ogden, Schubert M. *Christ Without Myth: A Study Based on the Theology of Rudolf Bultmann.* London: Collins, 1962.

——————. *The Reality of God and Other Essays.* New York: Harper and Row, 1966.

Pannenberg, Wolfhart, *et al. Offenbarung als Geschichte.* Göttingen: Vandenhoeck and Ruprecht, 1961.

Paton, H. J. *The Modern Predicament: A Study in the Philosophy of Religion.* London: Allen & Unwin, 1955.

Phillips, D. Z. *The Concept of Prayer.* London: Routledge and Kegan Paul, 1965.

Pitcher, George (ed.). *Truth.* Englewood Cliffs: Prentice-Hall, 1964.

Plantinga, Alvin (ed.). *The Ontological Argument from St Anselm to Contemporary Philosophers.* Garden City: Doubleday and Co., 1965.

Pole, David. *The Later Philosophy of Wittenstein: A Short Introduction with an Epilogue on John Wisdom.* London: Athlone Press, 1958.

Popper, Karl R. *The Logic of Scientific Discovery.* English Edition, translated by the author with the assistance of Dr Julius Freed and Lan Freed. London: Hutchinson & Co., 1959. (First published in 1935 as *Logic der Forschung:* Vienna, J. Springer.)

Ramsey, Ian T. *Christian Discourse: Some Logical Explorations.* London: Oxford University Press, 1965.

—————————. *Miracles: An Exercise in Logical Mapwork.* Oxford: Clarendon Press, 1952.

—————————. *Religious Language: An Empirical Placing of Theological Phrases.* London: SCM Press, 1967.

Randall, John H., Jr. *The Role of Knowledge in Western Religion.* Boston: Starr King Press, 1958.

Rice, Philip B. *On the Knowledge of Good and Evil.* New York: Random House, 1955.

Robinson, James M. *A New Quest of the Historical Jesus.* Naperville: Alec R. Allenson, 1959.

Robinson, James M. and Cobb, John B. (eds.). *The New Hermeneutic.* New York: Harper and Row, 1964.

Schleiermacher, Friederich. *The Christian Faith.* 2 vols. English Translation of the Second German Edition edited by H. R. MacKintosh and J. S. Stewart. New York and Evanston: Harper and Row, 1963. (First published in 1928: Edinburgh, T. & T. Clark.)

Schmidt, Paul F. *Religious Knowledge.* Glencoe: The Free Press, 1961.

Smart, Ninian. *Reasons and Faiths: An Investigation of Religious Discourse, Christian and Non-Christian.* London: Routledge & Kegan Paul, 1958.

Strawson, P. F. *Introduction to Logical Theory.* London: Methuen & Co., 1952.

Taylor, Richard. *Metaphysics.* Englewood Cliffs: Prentice-Hall, 1963.

Tennant, F. R. *Philosophical Theology.* 2 vols. Cambridge: Cambridge University Press, 1928 and 1930.

Tillich, Paul. *Systematic Theology.* 3 vols. Chicago: University of Chicago Press, 1951, 1957 and 1963.

Toulmin, Stephen E. *An Examination of the Place of Reason in Ethics.* Cambridge: Cambridge University Press, 1950.

—————————. *The Uses of Argument.* Cambridge: Cambridge University Press, 1958.

Urmson, J. O. *Philosophical Analysis: Its Development Between the Wars.* Oxford: Clarendon Press, 1956.

van Buren, Paul M. *The Secular Meaning of the Gospel: Based on an Analysis of Its Language.* London: SCM Press, 1963.

Warnock, G. J. *English Philosophy Since 1900.* London: Oxford University Press, 1958.

Westermann, Claus (ed.). *Essays on Old Testament Hermenutics.* English Translation edited by James Luther Mays. Richmond: John Knox Press, 1963.

White, Morton (ed.). *Academic Freedom, Logic, and Religion.* 2 vols. Philadelphia: University of Pennsylvania Press, 1953.

Wiener, Philip P. *Leibniz: Selections.* New York: Charles Scribner's Sons, 1951.

Wilson, John. *Language and Christian Belief.* London: Macmillan Co., 1958.

————————. *Philosophy and Religion: The Logic of Religious Belief.* London: Oxford University Press, 1961.

Wisdom, John. *Other Minds.* Oxford: Basil Blackwell, 1952.

————————. *Paradox and Discovery.* Oxford: Basil Blackwell, 1965.

————————. *Philosophy and Psycho-Analysis.* Oxford: Basil Blackwell, 1953.

Wittgenstein, Ludwig. *The Blue and Brown Books.* Oxford: Basil Blackwell, 1958.

————————. *Lectures and Conversations on Aesthetics, Psychology and Religious Belief.* Edited by Cyril Barrett. Oxford: Basil Blackwell, 1966.

————————. *Philsophical Investigations.* Second Edition. Translated by G. E. M. Anscombe. Oxford: Basil Blackwell, 1958.

————————. *Tractatus Logico-Philosophicus.* Translated by C. K. Ogden. London: Routledge & Kegan Paul, 1922.

Zuurdeeg, Willem F. *An Analytical Philosophy of Religion.* New York: Abingdon Press, 1958.

PERIODICALS

Aldrich, Virgil C., *et al.* 'The Sense of Dogmatic Religious Expression', *Journal of Philosophy*, LI (1954): 145-172.

Berlin, I. 'Empirical Propositions and Hypothetical Statements', *Mind*, N.S. LIX (1950): 289-312.

Brown, Patterson. 'St Thomas' Doctrine of Necessary Being', *Philosophical Review*, LXXIII (1964): 76-90.

Bultmann, Rudolf. 'Welchen Sinn hat es, von Gott zu reden?', *Theologische Blätter*, IV (1925): 129-135. Translated by Franklin H. Littell as 'What Sense Is There to Speak of God?', *The Christian Scholar*, XLIII (1960): 213-222.

Cameron, J. M. 'R. F. Holland on "Religious Discourse and Theological Discourse"', *Australasian Journal of Philosophy*, XXXIV (1956): 203-207.

Copleston, Frederick C. 'The Philosophical Relevance of Religious Experience', *Philosophy*, XXXI (1956): 229-243.

Coval, S. 'Worship, Superlatives and Concept Confusion', *Mind*, N.S. LXVIII (1959): 218-222.

Cox, David. 'The Significance of Christianity', *Mind*, N.S. LIX (1950): 209-218.

Demos, Raphael. 'The Meaningfulness of Religious Language', *Philosophy and Phenomenological Research*, XVIII (1957): 96-106.

Duff-Forbes, D. R. 'Reply to Professor Flew', *Australasian Journal of Philosophy*, XL (1962): 324-327.

——————. 'Theology and Falsification Again', *Australasian Journal of Philosophy*, XXXIX (1961): 143-154.

Ewing, A. C. 'Awareness of God', *Philosophy*, XL (1965): 1-17.

——————. 'Pseudo-Solutions', *Proceedings of the Aristotelian Society*, N.S. LVII (1956-57): 31-52.

——————. 'Religious Assertions in the Light of Contemporary Philosophy', *Philosophy*, XXXII (1957): 206-218.

——————. 'Two "Proofs" of God's Existence', *Religious Studies*, I (1965): 29-45.

Ferré, Frederick. 'Mapping the Logic of Models in Science and Theology', *The Christian Scholar*, XLVI (1963): 9-39.

Findlay, John. 'The Logic of Mysticism', *Religious Studies*, II (1967): 145-162.

Fitch, Frederic B. 'On God and Immortality', *Philosophy and Phenomenological Research*, VIII (1948): 688-693.

Flew, Antony. 'Falsification and Hypothesis in Theology', *Australasian Journal of Philosophy*, XL (1962): 318-323.

——————. 'Reflections on "The Reality of God" ', *Journal of Religion*, XLVIII (1968): 150-161.

Franklin, R. L. 'Necessary Being', *Australasian Journal of Philosophy*, XXXV (1957): 97-110.

Gibson, A. Boyce. 'Empirical Evidence and Religious Faith', *Journal of Religion*, XXXVI (1956): 24-35.

——————. 'Modern Philosophers Consider Religion', *Australasian Journal of Philosophy*, XXXV (1957): 170-185.

Glasgow, W. D. 'Knowledge of God', *Philosophy*, XXXII (1957): 229-240.

Hepburn, Ronald W. 'From World to God', *Mind*, N.S. LXXII (1963): 40-50.

Hick, John. 'God as Necessary Being', *Journal of Philosophy*, LVII (1960). 725-734.

——————. 'The Idea of Necessary Being', *The Princeton Seminary Bulletin*, LIV (1960): 11-21.

Hick, John. 'Theology and Verification', *Theology Today*, XVII (1960): 12-31.

Holland, R. F. 'Modern Philosophers Consider Religion: A Reply', *Australasian Journal of Philosophy*, XXXVI (1958): 208-209.

——————. 'Religious Discourse and Theological Discourse', *Australasian Journal of Philosophy*, XXXIV (1956): 147-163.

Horsburgh, H. J. N. 'The Claims of Religious Experience', *Australasian Journal of Philosophy*, XXXV (1957): 186-200.

——————. 'Professor Braithwaite and Billy Brown', *Australasian Journal of Philosophy*, XXXVI (1958): 201-207.

Hudson, H. 'Is God an Entity?', *Australasian Journal of Philosophy*, XLII (1964): 35-45.

Hutchings, P. AE. 'Discussion: Necessary Being', *Australasian Journal of Philosophy*, XXXV (1957): 201-206.

——————. 'Necessary Being and Some Types of Tautology', *Philosophy*. XXXIX (1964): 1-17.

Lewis, H. D. 'The Cognitive Factor in Religious Experience', *Proceedings of the Aristotelian Society*, Supplementary Volume XXIX (1955): 59-84. (Volume title: *Problems in Psychotherapy and Jurisprudence.*)

——————. 'Contemporary Empiricism and the Philosophy of Religion', *Philosophy*, XXXII (1957): 193-205.

——————. 'Philosophical Surveys X: The Philosophy of Religion, 1945-1952', *Philosophical Quarterly*, IV (1954): 166-181, 262-274.

Matthews, Gareth B. 'Theology and Natural Theology', *Journal of Philosophy*, LXI (1964): 99-108.

McPherson, Thomas. 'The Existence of God', *Mind*, N.S. LIX (1950): 545-550.

Miles, T. R. 'A Note on Existence', *Mind*, N.S. LX (1951): 399-402.

Nidditch, Peter. 'A Defense of Ayer's Verifiability Principle Against Church's Criticism', *Mind*, N.S. LXX (1961): 88-89.

Nielsen, Kai. 'Can Faith Validate God-Talk?', *Theology Today*, XX (1963): 158-173.

——————. 'On Fixing the Reference Range of "God" ', *Religious Studies*, II (1966): 13-36.

——————. 'On Talk About God', *Journal of Philosophy*, LV (1958): 888-890.

——————. 'Wittgensteinian Fideism', *Philosophy*, XLII (1967): 191-209.

Ogden, Schubert M. 'God and Philosophy: A Discussion with Antony Flew', *Journal of Religion*, XLVIII (1968): 161-181.

Passmore, John A. 'Christianity and Positivism', *Australasian Journal of Philosophy*, XXXV (1957): 125-136.

Penelhum, Terence. 'Divine Necessity', *Mind*, N.S. LXIX (1960): 175-186.

Phillips, D. Z. 'Philosophy, Theology, and the Reality of God', *Philosophical Quarterly*, XIII (1963): 344-350.

Ramsey, Ian T. 'Contemporary Empiricism: Its Development and Theological Implications', *The Christian Scholar*, XLIII (1960): 174-184.

Ruja, Harry. 'The Present Status of the Verifiability Criterion', *Philosophy and Phenomenological Research*, XXII (1961): 216-222.

Schmidt, Paul F. 'Is There Religious Knowledge?', *Journal of Philosophy*, LV (1958): 529-538.

Smart, J. J. C. 'Philosophy and Religion', *Australasian Journal of Philosophy*, XXXVI (1958): 56-58.

Smart, R. N. 'Being and the Bible', *Review of Metaphysics*, IX (1956): 589-607.

Smith, Huston. 'Do Drugs Have Religious Import?', *Journal of Philosophy*, LXI (1964): 517-530.

Trethowan, Illyd. 'In Defense of Theism—A Reply to Kai Nielsen', *Religious Studies*, II (1966): 37-48.

Tyson, Ruel. 'Philosophical Analysis and Religious Language: A Selected Bibliography', *The Christian Scholar*, XLIII (1960): 245-250.

Wainwright, W. J. 'Religious Statements and the World', *Religious Studies*, II (1966): 49-60.

Weiss, Paul. 'Religious Experience', *Review of Metaphysics*, XVII (1963): 3-17.

Weitz, Morris. 'Oxford Philosophy', *Philosophical Review*, LXII (1953): 187-233.

Whitely, C. H. 'The Cognitive Factor in Religious Experience', *Proceedings of the Aristotelian Society*, Supplementary Volume XXIX (1955): 85-92. (Volume title: *Problems in Psychotherapy and Jurisprudence.*)

Wisdom, John. 'Gods', *Proceedings of the Aristotelian Society*, XLV (1944-45): 185-206.

Wisdom, J. O. 'Metamorphoses of the Verifiability Theory of Meaning', *Mind*, N.S. LXXII (1963): 335-347.

Yourgrau, Wolfgang and Works, Chandler. 'A New, Formalized Version of the Verifiability Principle', *Ratio*, X (1968): 54-63.

INDEX

(a) Index of Names

Matthews, G. B., 77 n., 268
Mavrodes, G. I., 11, 182 n.
Mays, J. L., 150 n., 266
Miles, T. R., 22 n., 24 n., 30 n., 107 n.,
    111 n., 211 n., 251, 253 n., 264, 268
Mill, J. S., 157 n.
Mitchell, B., 19 n., 20 n., 22 n., 77 n.
    100 n., 253 n., 264
Moore, G. E., 19, 20 n., 52 n., 264
Morris, C., 253 n., 264
Moses, 215 n.
Mothershead, J. L., 11
Munz, P., 19 n., 22 n., 24 n., 30 n.,
    39 n., 251, 264

Nidditch, P., 66 n., 268
Niebuhr, R. R., 175 n., 177 n., 264
Nielsen, K., 77 n., 107 n., 253 n., 268
Nowell-Smith, P., 77 n., 211 n.

Ogden, C. K., 20 n., 24 n., 253 n., 264,
    266
Ogden, S. M., 42 n., 44 n., 77 n., 93 n.,
    145 n., 170 n., 264
Otis, B., 11
Otto, R., 20 n., 222

Pannenberg, W., 150 n., 264
Panthera, 173 n.
Passmore, J. A., 21 n., 88 n., 111 n.,
    269
Paton, H. J., 22 n., 25 n., 264
Paul, St, 175
Pears, D. F., 20 n.
Penelhum, T., 161 n., 269
Peter, St, 175 n.
Philip II, k., 151
Phillips, D. Z., 22 n., 108 n., 264, 269
Pitcher, G., 33 n., 264
Plantinga, A., 161 n., 264
Pole, D., 35 n., 264
Popper, K., 88 n., 193 n., 265
Price, H. H., 210 n.

Rainier, A. C. A., 161 n.
Ramsey, I. T., 22 n., 166 n., 211 n.,
    215 n., 265, 269
Randall, J. H. (Jr), 253 n., 265

Reese, W. L., 93 n., 263
Rice, P. B., 31 n., 265
Richard I, k., 151
Richards, I. A., 24 n., 253 n., 264
Robinson, J. A. T., 112
Robinson, J. M., 41 n., 170 n., 265
Ruja, H., 66 n., 127 n., 269
Russell, B., 19
Ryle, G., 20

Saladin, 161
Schleiermacher, F., 43, 109, 145 n.,
    170, 265
Schmidt, P. F., 22 n., 24 n., 124 n.
    252 n., 253 n., 265, 269
Sellars, W., 31 n., 262
Smart, J. J. C., 111 n., 161 n., 211 n.,
    269
Smart, N., 22 n., 39 n., 107 n., 124 n.,
    265, 269
Smith, H., 210 n., 269
Socrates, 222
Stephen, St, 175 n.
Stewart, J. S., 145 n., 265
Strawson, P. F., 29 n., 48 n., 52 n.,
    53 n., 113 n., 116 n., 180 n., 189 n.,
    194 n., 231 n., 254 n., 265

Taylor, R., 211 n., 265
Tennant, F. R., 15, 265
Thomas Aquinas, St, 111 n., 225
Tillich, P., 42, 43, 109, 111, 111 n.,
    112, 145 n., 170–1, 171 n., 177 n.,
    265
Toulmin, S. E., 47 n., 161 n., 204 n.,
    253 n., 265
Toynbee, A. J., 148 n.
Trethowan, I., 77 n., 107 n., 269
Tyson, R., 21 n., 269

Urmson, J. O., 15 n., 66 n., 265

Vienna Circle, 19, 21

Wainwright, W. J., 124 n., 269
Waismann, F., 33 n., 35 n., 64 n.,
    66 n., 184 n., 185 n., 192 n., 193 n.
Warnock, G. J., 15 n., 35 n., 265

INDEX

(b) Index of Subjects